D1116259

# FROM ANTIQUARIAN
# TO ARCHAEOLOGIST

# FROM ANTIQUARIAN TO ARCHAEOLOGIST

*The History and Philosophy of Archaeology*

Tim Murray

First published in Great Britain in 2014 by
PEN & SWORD ARCHAEOLOGY
*an imprint of*
Pen and Sword Books Ltd
47 Church Street
Barnsley
South Yorkshire S70 2AS

ISBN 978 1 78346 352 7

Printed and bound in England
by CPI Group (UK) Ltd, Croydon, CR0 4YY

Typeset in Times New Roman by
CHIC GRAPHICS

*Pen & Sword Books Ltd incorporates the imprints of*
Pen & Sword Archaeology, Atlas, Aviation, Battleground, Discovery,
Family History, History, Maritime, Military, Naval, Politics, Railways,
Select, Social History, Transport, True Crime, and Claymore Press,
Frontline Books, Leo Cooper, Praetorian Press, Remember When,
Seaforth Publishing and Wharncliffe.

*For a complete list of Pen and Sword titles please contact*
Pen and Sword Books Limited
47 Church Street, Barnsley, South Yorkshire, S70 2AS, England
E-mail: enquiries@pen-and-sword.co.uk
Website: www.pen-and-sword.co.uk

# Contents

# Details of first publication

I very gratefully acknowledge the publishers who have graciously permitted the reprinting of these papers and book chapters. I also gratefully acknowledge the Bromley Museum and the State Library of Victoria for permission to republish the images in Chapter 14.

Chapter 2: First published in V. Pinsky and A. Wylie (eds.) *Critical Directions in Contemporary Archaeology*, pp. 55-67. Cambridge University Press. (1990)

Chapter 3: First published in *Antiquity* 66:730-743. (1992)

Chapter 4: First published in *World Archaeology* 25(2):175-186. (1993)

Chapter 5: First published in *Archaeological Dialogues* 3:55-69. (1996)

Chapter 6: First published in T. Murray (ed.) *Archaeologists: A Biographical Encyclopaedia*, pp. 869-883. ABC-CLIO: Santa Barbara. (1999)

Chapter 7: First published in A. Gustafsson and H. Karlsson (eds) *Glyfer och arkeologiske rum – en vänbok til Jarl Nordbladh*, pp. 501-515. University of Göteborg, Sweden. (1999)

Chapter 8: First published in R. Corbey and W. Roebroeks (eds) *Studying Human Origins: Disciplinary History and Epistemology*, pp. 29-44. Amsterdam: University of Amsterdam Press. (2001)

Chapter 9: First published in *Antiquity* 76:234-238. (2002)

Chapter 10: First published in Leonid Vishnyatsky (ed.) *The Archaeologist: Detective and Thinker*, pp. 204-215. St Petersburg University Press. (2004)

Chapter 11: First published in *Bulletin of the History of Archaeology* 15(2):26-37. (2005)

Chapter 12: First published in *Bulletin of the History of Archaeology* 17(2):14-22. (2007)

Chapter 13: First published in N. Schlanger and Jarl Nordbladh (eds) *Archives, Ancestors, Practices – Archaeology in the Light of its History*, pp. 59-71. Berghahn Books: New York and Oxford. (2008)

Chapter 14: First published in *Antiquity* 83: 488-499. (2009)

Chapter 15: First published in J. Carman, C. McDavid and R. Skeates (eds) *Oxford Handbook of Public Archaeology*, pp. 135-152. Oxford University Press. (2012)

# Acknowledgements

It is hardly surprising that after 37 years of teaching and research in this field I have a great many people to thank and to acknowledge for assistance and advice on matters great and small. However, limitations of space prevent me from acknowledging all but those who have made the most significant contributions as colleagues and mentors, and those who have helped this book to happen.

First, to the two people who taught me most about the history and philosophy of science, the late Ian Langham, and the murky world of 19th century race theory, the late Bob Dreher. Then to colleagues who have done so much to take the history of archaeology from boutique accessory to mainstream research, particularly the late Bruce Trigger, Alain Schnapp, Chris Evans and the late Doug Givens (the founder of the *Bulletin of the History of Archaeology*). Finally to colleagues who have shaped my life as an archaeologist, especially Jim Allen, Roland Fletcher, Geoff Bailey and Norman Yoffee. Clearly, none of these people should be held responsible for the consequences of all that support, guidance and stimulation!

The arduous task of scanning was undertaken by Jo Muscat and Jane Schleiger from the Faculty of Humanities and Social Sciences, and Susan Bridekirk did sterling work on editing the resultant manuscripts for consistency and accuracy. This book would not exist without them.

Much of the research for these publications was the product of funding received from the Australian Research Council, and I also gratefully acknowledge the support of La Trobe University, Melbourne, Australia.

Finally many thanks to my family who have had to put up with frequent absences and much distraction for so many years. Dedicating this book to them is a small token of the debt I owe.

*Chapter 1*

# Explorations in the historiography of archaeology: a personal account

The papers and book chapters collected here were published between 1990 and 2012, but the themes they explore all grew out research and writing that took place between 1976 and 1987 for three dissertations, all submitted to the University of Sydney.

The first dissertation, *Aspects of Polygenism in the Works of Robert Knox and James Hunt* (1976), explored the space between historiography and the histories of anthropology and archaeology that had been recently charted by John Burrow (1966) and George Stocking (1968, 1971). My focus was on the history of race theory in Europe as it came to be expressed within the formal structures of disciplines as they were emerging from Natural Philosophy in the nineteenth century. Chapters 2, 3, 7 and 11 report developed versions of this research.

The second dissertation, *Patterns in Prehistory: Gordon Childe Reconsidered* (1978), traced the influence of race theory in nineteenth and twentieth century prehistoric archaeology through the work of Australian archaeologist Vere Gordon Childe. Of course I was hardly the only person interested in Childe, as witnessed by the flood of monographs and papers that have since appeared (see eg Gathercole *et al.* 1995; Green 1981; McNairn 1981; Trigger 1980), but my specific concern was to investigate the role of the concept of culture (particularly its ethnic connotations) in Childe's treatment of the prehistory of what he called European Civilization. Chapter 5 presents a later application of this research to a broader question of the nature of archaeological theory in understanding the 'identity' of Europe.

Shortly after completing these undergraduate dissertations I began work on my doctoral dissertation *Remembrances of Things Present: Appeals to Authority in the History and Philosophy of Archaeology* (1987). Its thesis was straightforward and the approach (and areas of focus) I developed has been the foundation of Chapters 2, 4, 8, 9, 13 and 14, and has also played a significant role in my use of the history of archaeology to explore the broad question of the nature of time in archaeology.

In that dissertation I observed that over the past thirty years virtually every aspect of archaeology – from its nature as a discipline to its relationship with society – has been the subject of inquiry, debate and change. Not only has there been a vast increase in the amount of archaeology being done and the number of archaeologists doing it, but the development of new techniques of dating and analysis has also helped to broaden and deepen the scope of the discipline itself. New methodological links have been forged with the human, earth, and life sciences, with practitioners ranging far in search of approaches that could help them expand their understanding of the meaning and significance of the archaeological record.

It was also clear that not all of these changes have met with universal approval. Over the past three decades archaeology has become more disputatious than ever before, as practitioners have openly debated conceptual and epistemological issues lying at the core of the discipline itself. Indeed, much at the outset of the 'new' archaeology (particularly in the 1970s up to the mid 1980s) which was considered to be stable and unproblematic, such as the goals of archaeology, or even the nature of the archaeological record itself, are now openly questioned. Archaeology (particularly in its connections to contexts of practice such as heritage, especially indigenous heritage) continues to exhibit such internal dissension that we are entitled to question whether there are any disciplinary 'cultural norms' left, and whether there are bedrock goals and understandings among practitioners that can survive such disputation.

The core argument of *Remembrances of Things Present* was that such changes provide an opportunity to re-examine the nature, meaning, and value of archaeological knowledge, especially to question the relationship between past and present, and the nature of archaeology as a distinct discipline. I was also keen to point out that this investigation into disciplinary fundamentals could be both time consuming and potentially destabilizing, as what had been considered to be natural knowledge about the process of archaeology would come under severe scrutiny.

In that dissertation I adopted what was then a pretty standard history, philosophy and sociology of science approach to primarily prehistoric archaeology, so that I could get a clearer picture of the determinants of the production, dissemination and reception of archaeological knowledge within specific societies (primarily, but not exclusively, European) and at specific times. I have continued this approach ever since, but it has been adapted to incorporate developments within history, philosophy and sociology of science, and expanded to apply to the rapidly growing areas of historical archaeology and the archaeology of the contemporary past and, perhaps more controversially, the very diverse social contexts of archaeological practice (see eg Lucas 2007; Murray Chapter 15 of this book). The primary point of continuity has been to use the history of archaeology as a 'possibility space' within which to evaluate the performance of contemporary archaeological method and theory (to drill down into the methodological rhetoric of contemporary archaeology), and to canvas the existence of other ways of thinking about the project of archaeology as it has evolved.

Each of the works republished in this book follow an intertwined set of themes that continue to underwrite all aspects of my archaeology, whether it be the archaeology of cities, transnational archaeologies of the nineteenth and twentieth centuries, the archaeology of indigenous and settler conflicts, or inquiries into the constitution of archaeological epistemologies and ontologies (especially an understanding of archaeological time). The fundamental theme concerns arguments about the importance of a historical perspective on archaeological knowledge claims in order to establish that current theoretical and methodological orthodoxies have histories, and that archaeological knowledge is contingent. Establishing the historical and cultural contingencies of archaeological knowledge is not just about avoiding the consequences of Whig history, or as George Stocking would have it, of 'presentism'. Exploring the reality of contingency also acts to undermine the assumption (either conscious or unconscious) that our current aspirations, questions, methods and theories are not natural or *sui generis* – they have histories and they also have within them the seeds of alternatives not currently explored.

A related theme concerns the interplay between practices and perspectives that archaeologists hold in common, and those which act to diversify and differentiate archaeology from other disciplines engaged in the business of researching and understanding human history. At root this is an inquiry into the existence of archaeology as a distinct discipline. At a time when researchers are beginning to break down disciplinary silos through the development of multidisciplinary programs tackling complex problems through a more effective articulation of past and present, we need to be very clear about the importance of distinctive types of data, method and theory so that these are not compromised within a multidisciplinary research context. I have noted many times previously the tendency, right across the history of our discipline, for that distinctiveness to be lost in an attempt to make data meaningful in conventional terms used by humanities and social sciences (see especially Chapter 8 of this book). This is a fundamental reason why building archaeological theory is of the first importance.

These have been some of the stimuli to *my* development as a historian of archaeology. Over that same period the history of archaeology has developed into a rich and rewarding field of inquiry for many other reasons than its potential contribution to the rehabilitation of archaeological theory. It should come as no surprise, as Christopher Evans and I observed in the introduction to our reader *Histories of Archaeology* (2008), that histories of archaeology are being written to serve many purposes, some complex and many others quite straightforward. This diversity of goals is matched by a diversity of approach and treatment. Over the past thirty years practitioners have explored perspectives that focus on the internal (through biographies and institutional histories) and external workings of archaeology (stressing the importance of social, political and cultural contexts of its practice). Historians of archaeology have also sometimes sought to significantly refashion our understandings of disciplinary history, most memorably in Alain Schnapp's elegant and passionate defence of the importance of antiquarianism (1996). Indeed, my experience of editing the five volumes of the *Encyclopedia of the History of Archaeology* (ABC-Clio 1999-2001) drove home an understanding of both unity and diversity in archaeological practice, but its greatest message (for me at least) was what Glyn Daniel referred to as 'backward looking curiosity' (1976) that carries benefits both for an enhanced understanding of past times, but also of the means by which we reach that understanding.

## The future of the historiography of archaeology?

I have focused on the role of the historiography of archaeology in the building and assessment of archaeological theory, as well as simply being an end in itself. The history of archaeology is littered with larger-than-life characters doing extraordinary things in even more extraordinary places and there is no sign of a slackening of public interest in the likes of Aurel Stein or Stevens and Catherwood. Its also true that archaeologists regularly turn to the history of their discipline to fight contemporary battles about disciplinary approach or purpose. The same applies to others who, willingly or unwillingly, have been directly affected by what archaeologists have done (and in some cases continue to do). This is especially the case for indigenous peoples who can turn to the history of archaeology in search of an understanding of how their present conditions came to pass – an understanding that frequently proves a very useful resource in creating much more culturally sustainable and viable futures. All of these are well and truly in the picture for the future for the history of archaeology, but I want to advocate for an additional reason for undertaking research and teaching in this field.

If there is one thing we have learnt from several decades of the philosophy of science it is that we need to pay close attention to the ways in which scientists persuade each other and members of the general public of the value of arguments or bodies of theories and perspectives that underpin everyday practice (called 'normal science' by Thomas Kuhn). It is this social and cultural context within which the plausibility of statements is negotiated that lies at the heart of each discipline, and it is crucial to remember that each discipline essentially goes about this process in quite different ways. In the early days of the philosophy of archaeology (really an application of logical positivism to the discipline) practitioners such as Lewis Binford genuinely believed that determinate rules of scientific method could be applied to archaeology and that this would ensure that archaeology became 'scientific'. Several decades later we know that this is not the case, but we are still grappling with our responsibility as archaeologists to fashion a truer account of archaeological epistemology and archaeological ontology. The history of archaeology, specifically the detailed analysis of how arguments are made, justified and accepted in the discipline, has a truly vital role in this most important phase in the coming of age of archaeology.

## References

BURROW, J.W. 1966. *Evolution and Society*. Cambridge: Cambridge University Press.

DANIEL, G. 1976. *Cambridge and the Backward-looking Curiosity: an Inaugural Lecture*. Cambridge: Cambridge University Press.

GATHERCOLE, P., IRVING, T. and G. MELLEUISH (eds) 1995. *Childe and Australia*. St Lucia, Qld: University of Queensland Press.

GREEN, S. 1981. *Prehistorian. A Biography of V. Gordon Childe*. Bradford-on-Avon: Moonraker Press.

LUCAS, G. 2007. Visions of archaeology: An Interview with Tim Murray. *Archaeological Dialogues* 14(2): 155-177.

McNAIRN, B. 1980. *The Method and Theory of V. Gordon Childe*. Edinburgh: Edinburgh University Press.

MURRAY, T. 1995. Gordon Childe, archaeological records, and rethinking the archaeologist's project. In P. Gathercole, T. Irving and G. Melleuish (eds) *Childe and Australia*, pp. 199-211. St Lucia, Qld: University of Queensland Press.

MURRAY, T. (ed.) 1999-2001. *Encyclopedia of Archaeology*, 5 Vols. Santa Barbara: ABC-CLIO Press.

MURRAY, T. and C. EVANS 2008b. The historiography of archaeology – an editorial introduction, pp. 1-12, in T. Murray and C. Evans (eds). *Histories of Archaeology*. Oxford: Oxford University Press.

SCHNAPP, A. 1996. *The Discovery of the Past: the Origins of Archaeology*. London: British Museum Press.

STOCKING, G.W. 1968. *Race, Culture and Evolution: Essays in the History of Anthropology*. New York: Free Press.

—1971. What's in a name? The origins of the Royal Anthropological Institute (1837-71). *Man* (ns) 6: 369-390.

— 1987. *Victorian Anthropology*. New York: Free Press.

— 1989 *Romantic Motives: Essays on Anthropological Sensibility*. Madison, Wisc.: University of Wisconsin Press.

— 1991. *Colonial Situations: Essays on the Contextualization of Ethnographic Knowledge*. Madison, Wisc.: University of Wisconsin Press.

TRIGGER, B. 1980. *Gordon Childe. Revolutions in Archaeology*. London: Thames and Hudson.

*Chapter 2*

# The history, philosophy and sociology of archaeology: the case of the *Ancient Monuments Protection Act* (1882)

## Introduction

At the conclusion of his last speech as President of the Royal Anthropological Institute (RAIGBI) in 1872, Sir John Lubbock announced his intention to try to introduce legislation that would protect the ancient monuments of Great Britain. He was optimistic about his chances for success:

> *As there seems to be a general wish throughout the country to take some adequate steps for the preservation of these ancient monuments and graves of our forefathers, I am not without hope that the Bill may meet with favorable reception* (1872: 442).[1]

It transpired that the Ancient Monuments Protection Bill (AMPB) was to sorely try Lubbock's patience and sap his optimism, because the *Ancient Monuments Protection Act* (AMPA) was not to receive Royal assent until 1882, ten years after Lubbock's resignation from the presidency of the RAIGBI.

The long battle to get the first AMPA onto the statute books had entailed a great many compromises concerning the machinery of protection and the degree of state interference in the property rights of landed citizens. The most important of these compromises was made in 1881, when Lubbock changed his parliamentary tactics. After years of obstruction in the Commons, Lubbock abandoned his Private Member's Bill and carried a resolution through the House that forced the Gladstone Liberal government to introduce a public Bill of its own. This Bill became the basis of the first AMPA, and it

---

1. The primary source for this chapter is Hansard's Parliamentary Debates for the years 1873-82. The major debates concerning the AMPB took place on: I5 April 1874; I4 April 1875; 7 March1877; a Parliamentary Select Committee report published 9 July1877; 19 February 1878; House of Lords 11 March 1880; Lubbock's Resolution in the House of Commons March 11, 1881; 11 August 1882. References to these debates and other relevant materials take the form of the Member concerned, the context, and date and page number.

was a pale reflection of Lubbock's own proposed measure, even exempting the monuments of Ireland from protection until the *Ancient Monuments Protection (Ireland) Act* 1892. In the second reading debate of the government's Bill (11 August 1882) Lubbock observed:

> *As regards the present Bill, while it was, no doubt, a step in the right direction, especially in providing for the appointment of an Inspector, he could not hope that it would prove altogether effectual. It was natural that he should prefer the Bill that had been before the House in previous Sessions... He relied on the Government to introduce a stronger Bill hereafter, if the present measure failed to secure its object* (1882: 1,600).

There is general agreement among historians of archaeology, and of preservationism, that the first AMPA 'was in no way a great Act' (Hudson 1981: 56). Thompson has described it 'as "permissive" and may perhaps be regarded more as a declaration of intent rather than a serious legislative measure' (1977: 61), an opinion largely supported by Hudson (1981: 58). This viewpoint does not do the Act sufficient justice.

Notwithstanding its obvious shortcomings, it is clear from the debates around both Lubbock's and the government's versions of the AMPB that no stronger measure could have been passed at that time. In fact, it is a tribute to Lubbock's persistence, his tireless advocacy of the scientific status of prehistoric archaeology, and the widespread acceptance that archaeological remains could be used to write the prehistory of Britain, that there was an Act at all.

Perhaps it is because the first AMPA was so restricted in its provisions and such a disappointment to its promoters that no detailed account of its history has ever been attempted, despite the fact that it 'was important as being the first occasion on which the State had admitted any responsibility for national monuments or attempted a schedule of outstanding monuments' (Hudson 1981: 56).[2] Indeed, the best available general history of archaeology (Daniel 1975) does not even mention it, either in connection with Lubbock's important contributions to the foundation of prehistoric archaeology, or the reasons for increased public interest in prehistory from 1840 to 1880 (Daniel

---

2. Saunders (1983) presents a brief assessment of the first AMPA as an introduction to a more comprehensive survey of British ancient monuments legislation. At the time of writing, I was unaware of C. Chippindale's (1983) 'The making of the first *Ancient Monuments Act*, 1882, and its administration under General Pitt-Rivers', in the *Journal of the British Archaeological Association* 86: 1-55.

1975: 111-121, and chapter 4). More specific or problem-oriented studies, such as the history of the Society of Antiquaries of London (SAL) (Evans 1956) and of Scotland (SAS) (Bell 1981), the social history of archaeology (Hudson 1981), and the biography of Pitt-Rivers, the first Inspector appointed under the AMPA (Thompson 1977), offer only a cursory treatment. Even Lubbock's biographer, Hutchinson (1914), devotes less than a few pages to it. The same applies to Hunter's interesting and important attempt to place the Act within a more general account of the rise of the preservationist movement in Britain (1981), and to Rantlett's discussion of late Victorian environmental preservation societies (1983). The best general account of the first AMPA, within the context of European and American preservation legislation, is also one of the oldest (Brown 1905).[3]

The purpose of this essay is to provide a fuller account of the history of the first AMPA as a basis for the pursuit of two specific goals, rather than to reconstruct a largely neglected episode in the history of British archaeology. The first of these goals is to argue for a more sociological account of archaeological epistemology by applying the methods and orientations of recent work in the history, philosophy, and sociology of science to the history of archaeology. The second is to use the debates surrounding the passage of the first AMPA to support the hypothesis that the exigencies of preservation have been an important context for the building of archaeological theory, and for the legitimation of claims to knowledge about the archaeological past since the widespread acceptance of the scientific status of prehistoric archaeology in the second half of the nineteenth century. The difficult birth of the first AMPA and its inherent defects make it a suitable vehicle for the pursuit of both goals.

Although the history of the first AMPA is used to support more general objectives, my account is not presentist in orientation or purpose (see Stocking 1968: 2-12). The socio-political context of that history, as far as it can be reconstructed through the actions and utterances of the participants in the debates around the first AMPA, is of critical importance to the characterisation of the sociological dimensions of nineteenth century archaeological epistemology. While this case study emphasises the close links between epistemology and the ideology of preservationism in the second half of the nineteenth century, I argue that a similar association existed in Britain and elsewhere both before, and after, that period.

---

3. An earlier comprehensive survey of ancient monuments legislation not reviewed in this chapter is David Murray (1896) *An Archaeological Survey of the United Kingdom. The Preservation and Protection of Our Ancient Monuments*, Glasgow. This is cited in Saunders (1983: 14).

Three specific issues arising from the discussion of the debates surrounding the first AMPA provide a focus for my defence of a more general position, that a philosophy of archaeology, which is devoid of historical or sociological content, is no coherent philosophy at all. While I shall endeavour to move beyond programmatic statements about the sociological dimensions of archaeological epistemology, I cannot claim to do much more than indicate the potential of detailed studies of this kind for the development of a broader base for the discussion of either philosophical or historical issues within archaeology.

The first of these issues is the critical importance of race, ethnicity, and nationalism in the assessment of the plausibility of claims to knowledge of the prehistoric past during the nineteenth century. The second is the existence of explicit discussion of the nature of scientific methodology in archaeology, primarily based on an inductive account of scientific knowledge. The third is the importance of institutions such as the British Museum (BM), the British Association for the Advancement of Science (BAAS), the SAL, the Royal Archaeological Institute (RAI), the British Archaeological Association (BAA), and the Royal Anthropological Institute of Great Britain and Ireland (RAIGBI), both as lobby groups and as the professional guardians of scientific standards in British archaeology during the period under review.

Needless to say, a complete discussion of each of these issues is well beyond the scope of this chapter. More extended discussion is presented elsewhere (Murray 1987).

## Why write the history of archaeology?

No one could deny that there has been a great deal written on the history of archaeology – even a partial bibliography would run for pages. Much of this writing has been devoted to particular theories, methods, discoveries, and the lives of 'great' archaeologists. While these are obviously important in establishing some of the dimensions of archaeology, they alone do not produce satisfying accounts of the production of knowledge about the archaeological past. Although historians of archaeology have become much more sensitive to the demands of context (see Fahnestock 1984; Trigger 1980a), there remain precious few analyses of the institutional structures of the discipline (but see Dyson 1985; Evans 1949, 1950, 1956; Griffin 1985b; Meltzer 1983a, 1985; Thompson 1943; Yellen and Green 1985), or of other sociological aspects of the production of archaeological knowledge (see Gero 1985; Gero et al. 1983; Haag 1985; Kristiansen 1981).

The result of these shortcomings is that much of the history of archaeology reads as a kind of travel journal, an account of the slow journey out of the darkness of subjectivity and speculation towards objectivity, rationality, and science. In such histories the nature of archaeological knowledge transcends social and historical context, and the determinants of archaeological knowledge are themselves treated as ahistorical and acultural. Consequently, only on rare occasions are we presented with the detailed analysis of the taken-for-granteds of the history of archaeological practice, such as institutional structures, relations with governments and the general public, organising concepts and categories, and archaeology's relationships with its cognate disciplines. These shortcomings are now much less prominent in the histories of such sciences as physics, chemistry, biology, geology, palaeontology, and psychology, which have attracted considerable attention from exponents of the history, philosophy, and sociology of science.[4]

The persistence of non-contextual histories of archaeology demands a remedy because such histories are based on what must now be seen as an untenable assumption: that of the temporal and cultural universality of the scientific method. Apart from raising the obvious problems of teleology and presentism, such accounts can actually contribute to a widespread perception of the history of archaeology as a trivial or marginal pursuit, certainly of secondary importance to the collection of data or the proposition of methodological rules for the discipline. The history of archaeology has so far played only a minor role in our search for an understanding of the nature of archaeological knowledge in particular, and of scientific knowledge in general.

Significantly, since the establishment of the three-age system, many archaeologists have accepted that scientific knowledge is the most rational and reliable form of knowledge, and that the scientific method (best seen in the practice of the natural sciences and codified by philosophers) is the true path to science itself. Perceptions of the nature of scientific knowledge have changed since then, and archaeologists, to a greater or lesser extent, have attempted to keep pace with them. However, through all of this change and accommodation the tension between what archaeologists have desired to know of the past, and what they have considered possible to know, has been constrained by their understanding of the nature of scientific knowledge itself. Even in the post-Kuhnian era the dominant perceptions of the nature of scientific knowledge held by archaeologists come from the analysis of the experiences of other sciences, thereby perpetuating the view that scientific knowledge is a universal kind of knowledge, existing independently of the histories of many individual sciences.

---

4. Shapin (1982) lists many of the more important examples, but Latour and Woolgar (1979), Mackenzie (1981), Pickering (1981), and Yeo (1979, 1981) are further thoroughly worked examples of the approach in these specific fields.

Like most human sciences, archaeology faces the problem of convincing self-definition, a problem which extends to the establishment and justification of appropriate and defensible concepts, categories, and methodology (see Clarke 1972, 1973; Outhwaite 1983: 1- 4). It has long been argued that the history of disciplines at least allows us a broader context in which to pursue a solution to this problem, and I argue that the history of archaeology is not, in principle, an exception to this argument. Clearly the changes wrought to accounts of the nature and history of scientific knowledge by the investigations of Feyerabend (1975), Hanson (1958), Koyre (1956), Kuhn (1970, 1977), Lakatos (1978), Merton (1970), Toulmin (1961), and their successors, whom I shall discuss below, allow us every expectation that similar studies in the history of archaeology will at least call into question current dogmas about the nature of archaeological metaphysics and epistemology.

Stocking (1968) and Hymes (1963) also contend that the history of disciplines can provide a matrix for the evaluation of prior theories 'to the end of separating that which stands accomplished from that which is definitely surpassed' (Rupp-Eisenreich 1981: 15). The evaluation of this prior theory is an essential facet of critical self-reflection on the nature of archaeology as a discipline.

History has two further aspects to commend it. The first is the notion that it creates some distance between the past and our present preoccupations, allowing at least the prospect of a different perspective on what we currently do, or aspire to achieve. Clearly we have to be careful about the degree of independence we expect, but there appear to be some limited justifications for this notion. The second is that historical analysis allows us to at least perceive that the concepts and categories we take for granted are not in fact *sui generis*, and that they often need demystification before we can understand their influence on our thinking.

Daniel, the doyen of historians of archaeology, has claimed two great benefits for the history of archaeology. The first is that it can help us guard against the 'repetition of past errors' (1981a: 10). The second is more closely connected to the notions of distance and the understanding of the history of concepts and categories: 'By studying how we have learnt about our own past, we may expose, if not answer, some vital issues about the name and nature of man himself' (Daniel 1981a: 13). Kristiansen's excellent summary of changes in the context of Danish archaeology over the last 170 years adds a further dimension to Daniel's last point:

*It follows from this that the importance of archaeological history extends far beyond the teaching of students about the scientific*

*development of the discipline, and must be placed in a wider social*
*context, owing to the simple fact that the evidence of the cultural*
*sciences contributes to the formation of the conceptual framework of*
*Man from which the decisions of tomorrow are taken. The study of*
*archaeological history should therefore be part of a constant and*
*conscious concern with the place and the utilization of our science in*
*society* (Kristiansen 1981: 37).

I have already mentioned the existence of pressing philosophical reasons for an emphasis on the historical and sociological dimensions of the nature of scientific knowledge in general, and of archaeological knowledge in particular. I cannot here give a full account of these reasons and the shifts in philosophical approach they have caused, nor attempt to resolve the very real disputes between these new approaches. Useful though conflicting discussions of these issues, including the pressing problem of epistemological relativism, can be found in Agassi (1963), Barnes (1974, 1977), Bloor (1976), Hesse (1980), Mulkay (1979), Shapin (1982), and the references presented with them.[5]

My purpose here is to state the causes of a change in philosophical tack that have given a new significance not only to the historiography but also to the sociology of scientific knowledge. The most important symptom of change has been the shift from logical to historical and sociological models of scientific epistemology. All participants in this critical project are agreed that the assumptions that powered the logical empiricist justification of science have been seriously threatened by work in the history of science, and the philosophy of science itself. These assumptions are: naive realism, the possibility of a universal presuppositionless scientific language, and the correspondence theory of truth. Embedded in these assumptions is the notion that the natural sciences are different in kind from the social sciences.

For convenience of exposition these assumptions can be restated as four separate areas of concern: the uniformity of nature, the distinction between fact and theory, the role of observation in science, and the assessment of

---

5. There is a vast literature in the history, philosophy, and sociology of science, stemming as much from internal disagreements over orientations and goals, as from the rich and varied storehouse of information being tapped. Edge (1983) has outlined some of the schools of thought, as have Bourdieu (1975), Brannigan (1981), Collins and Pinch (1982), Freudenthal (1979), Gilbert and Mulkay (1982, 1984), Knorr-Cetina (1981), Knorr-Cetina and Mulkay (1983), and Schuster (1984). Berman (1972), Jacob (1975), Mulligan and Mulligan (1981), Shapin and Barnes (1977), and Wood (1980) are examples of the analysis of scientific institutions.

knowledge claims. In all four areas, what previously seemed to be strong justifications for the assumptions mentioned above have been demonstrated to be the result of contingent circumstances related to the traditions of scientific practice. It now appears that scientific representations are not simply determined by the nature of reality.

It is this recent recognition that justifies the reorientation of the sociology of knowledge away from a sole concentration on the social sciences. In so doing, our understanding of the nature of scientific explanation is changed towards an historical and sociological analysis of the production of scientific knowledge in general. The primary impact of this reorientation is that a greater concern with the mechanics of conviction and plausibility in the assessment of claims to knowledge has now been justified. In other words, an understanding of the production and legitimation of knowledge strongly reinforces the value of the sociology of knowledge.

Historians and sociologists of science have sought the mechanics of the legitimation of knowledge claims in the institutional structures of the sciences (government policies, scientific societies, etc.), the background cognitive presuppositions of scientists that determine, to some extent, the plausibility of knowledge claims, and the influence of prevailing epistemologies at any point in time.

Archaeology has rarely figured in these studies, primarily because historians of the discipline (following the lead of the majority of the practitioners of archaeology) have continued to conceptualise science and archaeology in positivist terms. Positivist approaches have allowed scientists to treat the history of science and the philosophy of science as two mutually exclusive fields of inquiry. This has resulted in a similar pattern of relationship between the history and the philosophy of archaeology.

Despite the fact that over the last twenty years there has been an exponential increase in the amount of research devoted to explicating philosophical issues in archaeology (see Salmon 1982b; Wylie 1982c, 1985a – and the references presented with them), in all but a few cases, discussions of these issues have been divorced from historical cases or sociological interpretation. My brief discussion of the history of the first AMPA is informed by the different perspectives sketched above, and is offered as an example of the value of the history and sociology of archaeology as an approach to understanding the production of archaeological knowledge.

## The background to the *Ancient Monuments Protection Bill*

I mentioned that part of my task is to demonstrate the importance of preservation as a context of archaeological theory building and legitimation. To this end, I advance the following hypothesis, which while it can be only partially sustained in the present context, is nonetheless useful as an orientation-point for discussion of the history of the first AMPA.

My hypothesis is that preservationism is an important stimulus to the development of theory and method in prehistoric archaeology. The need to produce rational justifications for efforts to protect from destruction the material remains of past human action, be they structural remains, monuments, or portable artefacts and their stratigraphic contexts, is recognised both by professional archaeologists as well as by interested members of the general public.

For the archaeologist this is a matter of protecting the database of the discipline. For the layperson it is a matter of preserving similar (but not necessarily identical) physical phenomena for their historical and cultural, as well as their scientific values. Historically, the needs of these two broadly defined interest groups have necessitated a close and binding relationship.

Archaeologists, as members of society and the practitioners of a discipline, also share common social values and preoccupations. In the case of the history of the first AMPA, these values and preoccupations extended from a belief in progress through to the notion that racial and ethnic differences could both be identified and explained through the analysis of prehistoric material culture, and that knowledge of these differences was considered to be important for an understanding of the past as well as the present. In this example, archaeologists sought to make the meaning of the material remains manifest through a concept of culture, which had already been developed in philology, ethnology, and geography. The plausibility of the archaeologist's claims to knowledge of the prehistoric past, stemming from the concept of culture was guaranteed by the authority culture had as a vehicle for the interpretation of the present.

In the case of the first AMPA, the plausibility of archaeological methodology was also critical to the preservationist cause because any appeal by preservationists to the value of an historical perspective on the present, hence to the historical potential of material things from prehistoric times, could only convince when that potential was established and justified beyond a mere love or respect for the past. Archaeological knowledge, and the ancient monuments which were its subject, had to have recognised social utility before preservation could be assured. Thus, the problem for Lubbock and other promoters of the AMPB was to demonstrate two facts: first, that prehistory could be written from the monuments, and second, that this prehistory was useful and important. Although Lubbock was a tireless advocate of a generalising archaeology that was part of the generalising discipline of ethnology, he was also prepared to see the value of particularist national prehistories of the kind written by Worsaae. Lubbock sought to blend the two styles of writing prehistory in his own work, as had Nilsson and Wilson.

The provision of a convincing basis for writing prehistory from archaeological data has been a major challenge for archaeologists and preservationists since the nineteenth century, because the nature of what will convince has also changed. In simple terms, the first AMPA could not have succeeded without the demonstration of the historical potential of archaeological data that had flowed from the work of Thomsen, Worsaae, Lubbock, and others, and prehistoric archaeology did not develop independently of the socio-political context of preservationism, nationalism and racial theoretics.

There is an additional aspect of plausibility that extends from archaeological methodology. This centres on the notion of reliability. Although I concentrate here on the epistemology of nineteenth-century archaeology, I claim that appeals to dominant understandings of appropriate scientific epistemology are also continually made throughout the histories of archaeology and preservationism for the purpose of justifying the plausibility of knowledge claims.

I have briefly discussed the plausibility of the theories, which guided the observation statements of prehistoric archaeologists during the mid-to-late nineteenth century, but the explicit advocacy of the inductive method for archaeological methodology was also critical for the plausibility of archaeological knowledge claims. By the late 1870s it was widely accepted that prehistoric archaeology had become a science, and that it had achieved this status both through field discoveries and the adherence to induction.

Despite the fact that the methodological rhetoric of the advocates of prehistoric archaeology emphasised induction (see Dawkins 1880; Lubbock 1865, 1868; Pouchet 1864), it is now clear that these researchers constantly violated their own methodological principles. Theories of human nature and interpretations of the meaning of human history, themselves so underdeveloped that there were no indisputable empirical data that could be appealed to for their justification, presupposed the inductions of the archaeologists and antiquarians. Yet these researchers were to pay no penalty for their violation. More importantly, it was rare indeed for this difference between rhetoric and performance even to be noted, far less discussed. The plausibility of the observation statements made by practitioners of prehistoric archaeology during this period, despite the very real conflicts between them, was guaranteed by the existence of plausible theories, which were analytically prior to induction itself. Again, despite the fact that there was considerable conflict over human nature and the meaning of human history, the basket of opposing theories proved resistant to analysis. Adherence to any of the multitude of positions was justified, despite a constant barrage of scientific rhetoric, only on religious or ideological grounds. The data of prehistoric archaeology were freely enlisted in these conflicts, providing at least part of a justification for their scientific significance.[6]

Obviously, there has been a longer history of concern for the preservation of classical monuments than for prehistoric remains. Brown (1905) and others have indicated several examples of government policy and the activities of antiquarian societies that helped define the background of the preservationist movements of the nineteenth century – such as the appointment of Raphael as controller of the remains of ancient art in Rome by Pope Leo X; Winkelmann's work at Herculaneum and Pompeii; Stuart and Revett's work on ancient Athens; the influence of *The Gentleman's Magazine*, the Society of Dilettanti (SD), and the Society of Antiquaries of London. It is important to remember that in areas of Europe that had not been occupied by the Romans, an interest in the preservation of national monuments of other kinds was also of long standing (see, for example, the edicts of Gustavus Adolphus and Charles XI of Sweden). The history of preservation in Scandinavia leading to the establishment of the Danish Royal Commission in 1807 demonstrates the early association of prehistoric ancient monuments with national identities and aspirations in that part of Europe (see Brown 1905; Klindt-Jensen 1975; Kristiansen 1981).

By the middle of the nineteenth century, preservation had become a European-wide phenomenon and was reflected in government policies and the agitation of interest groups formed as antiquarian societies (see also Sklenár 1983). This framework of government policy and popular interest, while originally established for the preservation of classical and medieval remains, was eventually adapted to incorporate prehistoric remains once the values accorded them by the Danes and Swedes were recognised in the rest of Europe after 1840.

The rise of the preservationist movement in Europe has been linked to romantic nationalism and historicism. Both Hunter (1981) and Kristiansen (1981) have also seen that these same forces extended beyond the traditional heartland of antiquarianism – the aristocracy and the wealthy bourgeoisie –

---

6. These issues are more fully discussed in Murray (1987), especially in chapter 4. An example of one of the rare debates about the validity of ideas of progress and the use of the comparative method is that between Lubbock and the Duke of Argyll (see Gillespie 1977). The theoretical conflicts between practitioners of prehistoric archaeology were predominantly centred around adherence to either ethnology or anthropology, whether human beings had a single or multiple origin, and the degree to which human nature was shaped by natural or cultural forces. These conflicts are discussed in Burrow (1966), Stocking (1968, 1971), and Weber (1974).

to a wider popular base, and were instrumental in the development of prehistoric archaeology during the nineteenth century. Kristiansen (1981: 20-21) has also argued that agrarian reform, and the changed system of agricultural land-use that resulted from it, was the 'most important' cause of the development of archaeology during this period. There is no doubt that a change in farming practice exposed many more prehistoric remains, in contemporary parlance bringing them 'under threat', but the increase in the amount of data is only one aspect of the development of archaeology. A framework for the ascription of popular meanings and values to this new data is another, more important, factor.

The search for national or ethnic identity that seized Europe during this period was informed by archaeology, and in turn influenced archaeology's sense of problem and its categorical and conceptual structure. The significance of prehistoric remains was enhanced by archaeological discoveries, as well as by a wider socially and ideologically bounded grid of meanings and values. Indeed, archaeology and preservation were intimately connected in Worsaae's mind, and his clear demonstration of the practical value of archaeological data was not fortuitous:

*It was not my plan to write a book merely for the archaeologist, but more particularly for the general reader. I endeavoured to prove the use and importance of archaeological researches, by shewing how the early history of our country could be read through the monuments, and I wanted in that way to excite a more general interest for the preservation of our national remains* (Worsaae 1849: iv).

The same depth of connection was also argued for archaeology and nationalism:

*A nation which respects itself and its independence cannot possibly rest satisfied with the consideration of its present situation alone. It must of necessity direct its attention to bygone times... For it is not until these facts are thoroughly understood, that the people acquire a clear perception of their own character, that they are in a situation to defend their independence with energy, and to labour with success at the progressive development, and thus to promote the honour and well-being of their country* (Worsaae 1849: 1).

Worsaae's views had considerable impact on the institutions of British archaeology, predisposed as they were to the preservationist cause. Not only did they enter the SAL (Evans 1956: 280-281), but they were also the cause of rising dissatisfaction within the Antiquaries over the lack of concern manifested in the preservation of British national antiquities (Evans 1956: 272-276). This was a contributing factor in the formation of a breakaway society, the BAA, and led to further splits within the Association itself (Evans 1949, 1950).

Worsaae's and Nilsson's claims concerning the historical value of prehistoric archaeology were further enhanced by the revelation of high human antiquity and the building-up of evidence which was taken to support claims for cultural and social evolution in the prehistoric past (see Daniel 1975; Grayson 1983). The synthesis of this new evidence presented by Lubbock in *Pre-historic Times* (1865) and *The Origin of Civilization and the Primitive Condition of Man* (1870), and in the work of Tylor and others, made the new knowledge part of the public domain. Indeed, in his new translation of Nilsson's *Primitive Inhabitants of Scandinavia* (1868), Lubbock could not restrain himself from comparing the enlightened management of archaeological remains in Scandinavia with the unthinking attitude prevailing in Britain:

> *In conclusion, I would venture to suggest that the Government should be urged to appoint a Royal Conservator of National Antiquities ... We are apt to blame the Eastern peasants who use the grand old monuments of Egypt or Assyria as mere stone-quarries, but we forget that even in our own country, Avebury, the most magnificent of Druidicial remains, was almost destroyed for the profit of a few pounds; while recently the Jockey Club has mutilated the remaining portion of the Devil's Dyke on Newmarket Heath, in order to make a bank for the exclusion of scouts at trial races. In this case also, the saving, if any, must have been very small; and I am sure that no society of English gentlemen would have sanctioned such a proceeding, if they had given the subject a moment's consideration* (Lubbock 1868: xli-xlii).

Hudson, through citations from *The Antiquarian* (1981: 53-4), has emphasised the importance of local archaeological and antiquarian societies as pressure groups for preservation, while Thompson provides evidence of concern among metropolitan societies such as the Ethnological Society of London (ESL), and international bodies such as the International Congress on Prehistoric Archaeology (ICPA), (1977: 58-9). Finally, the expansion of popular antiquarian periodicals such as *Notes and Queries* provided an effective means of disseminating the preservationist message.

While the discovery of this new evidence did much to advance the cause of prehistoric archaeology and of preservation, the other forces of romantic nationalism and historicism were also important in shaping the meanings and values of the prehistoric remains. Nipperdey has usefully defined romantic nationalism as being 'first of all a particular kind of nationalism moulded by romanticism, namely a cultural nationalism. Its central characteristics are a) the nationalizing of culture and b) the founding of the nation on the basis of a common culture' (1983: 1). Culture was shaped by the nation and both were the expressions of the spirit of the nation (*Volksgeist*). The central tenet was the uniqueness of nations and this was revealed through the analysis of language, history, and material culture. The Scandinavian countries, among others, were directly affected by this new movement because 'romantic nationalism is above all a nationalism of peoples who do not enjoy independence' (Nipperdey 1983: 8). The archaeology of Thomsen, Worsaae, and Nilsson was the direct product of these influences (see Aarnes 1983; Kristiansen 1981; Kuhn 1983).

Great Britain, with subject peoples of its own and a long history of invasions and migrations, was also directly affected by the new movement. Hunter (1981), Prince (1981), and the essays in Fawcett (1976) chart the influence of historicism and romanticism, through commentators such as Ruskin, Arnold, and Morris, on the architectural and monumental preservationist movements (e.g., the Society for the Preservation of Ancient Buildings (SPAB) and the Society for the Preservation of Ancient Monuments (SPAM)). Again and again in the debates on the AMPB, Lubbock and others would appeal to the popular strength of these movements. Importantly, the opponents of the Bill never rejected the importance of preservation either.[7]

Yet Lubbock's archaeology, with its emphasis on social evolution, and the notions of psychic unity that were essential to both his and Nilsson's, and to a lesser extent Worsaae's, use of ethnographic analogy, set up a tension between historicism and universalism in archaeology that exists to this day. While these archaeologists used ethnographic analogy to establish culturally meaningful interpretations of the prehistoric remains, they did so in a way that was directly opposed to the principles of historicism. Romantic nationalism stressed the historicism of 'the singular, the particular, the individual' (Nipperdey 1983: 3), not the universalism of psychic unity and the comparative method. Not all archaeologists shared Lubbock's belief in progress, but there was an implicit understanding among them that without comparison and generalisation, the prehistoric archaeological record would

---

7. Lubbock's was not the first attempt to introduce ancient monuments legislation in Britain. Saunders (1983: 11, see note 4) mentions that in 1841 a Parliamentary Select Committee on National Monuments and Works of Art advanced arguments for the introduction of effective preservation measures. These came to nothing.

remain mute and of little use for the definition of cultures or ethnic groups. The paradox therefore appears to be that while historicism provided one of the contexts of meaning and value for the prehistoric remains, the empiricist approach of Lubbock and others, with its emphasis on demonstration by induction, provided another, opposed, context.

Historicism and romantic nationalism were also closely linked to racial theoretics, as the identity of *Volksgeist* was considered to have an obvious racial component. The truly daunting task of configuring the relationships between archaeology and racial theoretics is well beyond the scope of this essay. The least painful introduction to this murky pond can be found in a combination of Bolt (1971), Curtis (1968), Field (1977), Horsman (1976) and the references presented with them. The crucial link between racial theoretics, and the rise of ethnology and anthropology, has already been sketched by Burrow (1966), Stocking (1968, 1971), and Weber (1974), among others. In the discussion of the AMPB I shall indicate several examples of racist rhetoric, which were used to argue against the preservation of ancient British and Celtic remains. Furthermore, it is well to remember that running alongside the debates over the AMPB was an even more contentious issue – that of Irish Home Rule. It was to prove the downfall of both Liberal and Tory governments on more than one occasion.

Lubbock therefore drafted the AMPB against a rising tide of preservationism and strong early indications of the historical potential of prehistoric remains. Indeed, we have seen in Worsaae's work and in Lubbock's own *Pre-Historic Times* (1865: 55) that archaeology, nationalism, and preservationism were closely linked. Although there had been a long tradition of collection and preservation of classical and post-Roman antiquities in England that was reflected in the history of the SAL and the Dilettanti, among others, strong popular concern about the fate of the 'unwritten records of the country' was the result of the foundation of prehistoric archaeology in the period between 1830 and 1865.

### Lubbock and the *Ancient Monuments Protection Act*

The broad outlines of the history of the AMPB are easily drawn. First introduced to the Commons as a Private Member's Bill on 7 February 1873, it was reintroduced (not counting the government's public Bill which replaced it) eight times, passing the second reading six times, a Select Committee once, a Committee of the Whole House twice, a third reading once, and a first and second reading in the House of Lords. During this period, Lubbock lost his Maidstone seat in the general election of 1879, and was out of Parliament until he was returned as Member for the University of London in

1880. On 11 March 1881, Lubbock pushed a resolution through the House that forced Gladstone's Liberal government to take charge of the protection of ancient monuments. This resolution eventually bore fruit, under the authority of Gladstone's First Commissioner of Works, Mr Shaw Lefevre, in the government's own AMPB which eventually received Royal assent on 18 August 1882.

I have mentioned that modern commentators (even Lubbock himself) have considered the first AMPA to be permissive, because of the exclusion of any form of compulsion. I have also mentioned that Irish monuments were excluded from the Act. Another revealing compromise was the fact that the government retained control over the listing and assessment of the ancient monuments. In Lubbock's original draft there was to be an independent Board of Commissioners, but this was changed in Committee to the Trustees of the BM and was finally dropped entirely from the government's measure, to be replaced by a government-appointed Inspector.

My object here is to explain why those compromises had to be made. I will do this outlining the provisions of Lubbock's AMPB, the numerous objections to it, and the arguments used by Lubbock and his supporters to answer these objections. I also explain why a protection measure of any kind took so long to reach the statute books by sketching the kinds of obstructive tactics employed by opponents of the Bill.

An important facet of the history of the first AMPA was the exclusion of antiquarian and scientific societies from the administration of the Act, despite strong lobbying within Parliament. I will argue that the reasons for their exclusion are tied both to the government's desire to control the operation of the Act, and to the view held by some influential parliamentarians that the Act would be better administered by those who were not overcome by sentimental attachment to the remains. In other words, these parliamentarians were concerned to limit the public power of the antiquarians and archaeologists by arguing that their associations and societies were unfit.

There was another dimension to this proposal, which had more to do with a centralisation of control over monuments preservation. In the government's Act the antiquities of Scotland were administered by the Inspector rather than by the SAS (see Stevenson 1981). The aspirations of the Scots antiquaries to control their own national history were not accepted by the government in Westminster.

Lubbock's role in the parliamentary career of the AMPB is crucial; indeed, to all intents and purposes, it was his Bill. I have mentioned that his writings had helped reveal the significance of prehistoric remains, but it was Lubbock's position within Victorian science and society that gave his efforts in Parliament real weight.

Lubbock's scientific credentials were impeccable. Hutchinson's biography (1914) and the collection of vignettes edited by Grant Duff (1934), including Keith's contribution (pp. 13-34) give the bare facts about what was in any terms a remarkable scientific and political career. Not only was Lubbock the confidant and equal partner of many of the preeminent Victorian scientists, but he was also a member, fellow, or office-bearer of the core scientific societies of the time – such as the BAAS and the Royal Society (RS). An example of how well connected Lubbock was is his membership of the X Club. The other members were George Busk, Edward Frankland, T. A. Hirst, Joseph Hooker, Herbert Spencer, John Tyndall, W. Spottiswoode, and T. H. Huxley. From this group were drawn six presidents of the BAAS and three presidents of the RS.

Lubbock was not just drawn in to the power structures of Victorian science – he was a foundation of them. Yet this accounts for only part of his prestige. As a Baronet, Liberal parliamentarian, and influential banker, Lubbock had access to influential people such as Gladstone. Here was no impractical preservationist sworn to oppose progress and utility – just the reverse. The fact that he was a co-founder of a company that introduced Edison's system of electric light to Britain in 1882 is a case in point. Lubbock's personal credibility as an archaeologist was to be constantly raised by opponents of the Bill, and strenuously defended by the Bill's supporters.

The best summary of the provisions of the AMPB and its justifications is provided by Lubbock's 'On the preservation of our ancient national monuments' (1879), originally published in *Nineteenth Century* in 1877: 'The principle of our bill is, that if the owner of one of these ancient monuments wishes to destroy it, he should be required, before doing so, to give the nation the option of purchase at a fair price' (1877: 162).

A Board of Commissioners was to be charged with the protection of the monuments. This Board was to consist of the Enclosure Commissioners, the Master of the Rolls, the President of the SAL, the President of the SAS, the President of the Royal Irish Academy (RIA), the Keeper of the British Antiquities at the BM, and seven nominated Commissioners. Among the seven originally suggested were the Duke of Devonshire, the Duke of Argyll, Lord Talbot de Malahide, Colonel Lane Fox, John Evans, and John Stuart.

The schedule of the bill was a list 'of some of the best preserved and most typical examples of the various classes of monuments, approved, as regards England and Wales, by the Society of Antiquaries; as regards Ireland, by the Royal Irish Academy; and as regards Scotland, by the Society of Antiquaries of Scotland' (Lubbock 1877: 162). An important residual power of the Commissioners was their ability to apply the Act to any British, Celtic,

Roman or Saxon remains that were threatened. The owner's title was only at risk when a monument was to be destroyed.

For the purposes of exposition, the justifications for the measure are divided between those used in the initial reading of the Bill, and those, which were developed to respond to the numerous objections that quickly flowed from it. The justifications were as follows: monuments were rapidly being destroyed; they were not destroyed for utilitarian reasons; the schedule to the Bill had been drawn up by the greatest authorities; the British people and government had protested the destruction of antiquities overseas and had spent large sums acquiring antiquities from Egypt, Assyria, Cyprus, Greece and other places; the argument of rapid destruction was supported by the fact that petitions expressing this view and supporting the Bill had come from every archaeological society in Great Britain and Ireland; the Irish Church Act established the principle of government intervention for the purposes of preservation; almost every other European country had legislation of this kind; and lastly, the ancient monuments were the unwritten history of the country and part of the national patrimony. Needless to say, these initial justifications did not convince the majority of Members.

Predictably, the most popular objections to the Bill (usually from the Tories and Whig Liberals) were that it was an attack on the rights of private property. This was raised continuously, even in connection with the government's more permissive measure. Bentick set the tone of this objection in the second reading debate of 15 April 1874, by opposing 'the practice of spoilation by legislation' (p. 579). He went on to argue that it 'was easy to show that the measure would be a distinct invasion of the rights of property... Putting that into plain English, it meant legalizing a burglary by daylight' (p. 580).

Other opponents who first emphasised that 'of course they all accepted the principle that the ancient monuments in the kingdom should be preserved' (Sir George Jenkinson: 15 April 1974: pp. 582-3), went on to suggest that the monuments were already well-protected by the private landowners. If they were not protected by interest and reverence then the monuments in question clearly were not important enough. Importance in this sense related to aesthetic principles or historical associations. Allied to this objection was the continual criticism over the fact that the AMPB was a Private Member's Bill. The position here was that if private rights were to be eroded then this should be the result of a public Bill.

The argument that really significant national monuments were already being preserved became the most popular objection after the issue of private rights, and in the course of the Bill's history it attracted much more attention among parliamentarians. On no single occasion was there an objection to preservation *per se*; rather, the issue was what was to be preserved and how.

Mr Walter's speech of 15 April 1874 first broached the issue by asking whether the monuments listed in the schedule really were national monuments.

There were several important implications to emerge from this question: were the people who drew up the schedule competent? Were these the monuments of the nation or of racial groups within the nation? Were there to be an almost unlimited number of these monuments attached to the schedule over time? Why did the Bill seek protection for pagan monuments only? Speaking of the Old Kitchen at Glastonbury, Walter made his position clear: 'which was the better worth preserving – such a building as that, or some one of the innumerable barrows on the Salisbury Plain' (p. 584). Or 'Which was the more worthy of protection of the State – the house in which Shakespeare lived, or some ancient barrow which few people cared about' (pp. 584-5). The antiquarian and archaeologist as self-interested nincompoops was a favourite target during discussion of these issues. The first direct attack on their credibility (and, incidentally, that of Lubbock himself) came from Sir Edmund Antrobus on 15 April 1874:

*Some of the ancient barrows, through having been first rifled by antiquarians, have been carted away and levelled by farmers... For himself, he believed it was the antiquarians who had done the most mischief in England: and if ancient monuments were to be placed in their hands they would do still more* (pp. 588-9).

This was followed by some even more stinging attacks by Sir Charles Legard (14 April 1875: p. 884), Lord Francis Hervey: 'Antiquaries were bad men of business' (14 April 1875: p. 886), and again, on 7 March 1877. Sir George Bowyer even managed to raise the caricature of the antiquary provided by Scott:

*He did not expect the Commissioners would mistake an old limekiln for the remains of a Roman or Saxon castle; but they all recollected how Mr Oldbuck, in The Antiquary, was undeceived by Edie Ochiltree in regard to his purchase of the Roman camp, when the old bedesman said, 'Pretorian here - Pretorian there - I mind the biggin' of it'* (7 March 1877: p. 1,545).

The purpose of such remarks is clear: by attacking the authors of the schedule and the students of the monuments as being either easily gulled or unreasonably self-interested, the schedule would lose its authority as a worthwhile list and classification of types of important national monuments.

However, not all opponents of the Bill attacked the great antiquarian societies, although we have seen them lose their position on the Board of Commissioners, first to the BM and later to the Commissioner for Works. Some argued that it was preferable that the societies protected the monuments on a voluntary basis, at the behest of the government, but without the presence of legislation. Both sides combated this suggestion.

The national nature of the ancient monuments also had a clear racial dimension. While many opponents confined themselves to the temporal or cultural limitations of the schedule, or to the view that most of the monuments were not very interesting despite what Lubbock and others had said about them, others pursued a racial line of argument that devalued prehistoric archaeology and its monumental database. Lord Francis Hervey's speech of 14 April 1875, provides the best example:

*It was said that there were Celtic monuments which ought to be preserved. England was once inhabited by barbarians - he would not call them our ancestors, but our predecessors - who stained themselves blue, ran about naked, and practised absurd, perhaps obscene, rites under the mistletoe. They had no arts, no literature; and when they found time hanging heavily on their hands, they set about piling up great barrows, and rings of stones. Were these the monuments that the hon. Baronet was about to preserve?* (p. 886).

On 7 March 1877, he went on to say that he:

*Could sympathize with anybody who desired to preserve monuments of antiquity and of great historical interest which were connected with some page in our history, some famous battle, some striking deed. All that was perfectly intelligible and reasonable. What he did not understand was that Englishmen should be called upon to exhibit enthusiasm for the monuments of that barbarous and uncivilized race which our forefathers took the trouble to expel from our country... He did not quarrel with his Irish Friends for wishing to preserve their round towers and mounds- what he objected to was their preserving ours - the relics of the ancient Britons - which were destitute of all art and of everything that was noble or that entitled them to preservation* (pp. 1,530-1).

Many supporters of the Bill were also keen to have the measure extended to later periods, but it was a move, which Lubbock and the government rejected. The primary justification for this limitation was economy. Ancient field monuments required protection because they could not be housed in museums. They also required little in the way of maintenance. Finally, unlike the model legislation in Denmark, Holland, or France, these more recent monuments would be more effectively dealt with by separate legislation. The irony of the situation is well expressed by Thompson: 'It was indeed an extraordinary situation that in a Christian country only the pagan monuments should be protected, on the grounds of economy' (1977: 6o).

Notwithstanding Lubbock's frequent recourse to the factor of expense, there is another explanation, mentioned only once by him, that reflects the essential differences between the ancient and medieval monuments. The care of medieval monuments involved 'aesthetic questions, with reference to which there are great differences of opinion' (1879: 165). No such disagreements had attended the compilation of the schedule, and it seems a strong possibility that Lubbock wished to avoid the extra threat to the success of the bill that would have resulted from the inclusion of later monuments.

Lubbock and his supporters responded to the objection that their existing owners properly cared for the relics by presenting long lists of destroyed monuments – the history of Caesar's Camp at Wimbledon was used as a case in point (see, for example, Shaw Lefevre: 19 February 1878: pp. 1,987-8). They also continually raised the issue of government support for the purchase of antiquities, or the funding of overseas expeditions and its lack of support for the antiquities of the homegrown variety. Osborne Morgan was forthright about this inconsistency:

*As to the objection that the Bill would saddle the public with some small expenses, the House had freely voted sums of money for observing the Transit of Venus, and for an Expedition to the North Pole; and he would urge that liberality of that kind should like charity begin at home* (14 April 1875: p. 894).

And, on the same day, Sir Henry Peek compared the fate of Caesar's Camp and the government support of the BM:

*The other day he saw a gentleman with a vase from Cyprus in his hand, which had been sold to the British Museum for 50 pounds. The acquisition of such curiosities was very desirable; but that a country like this, which had spent its money by hundreds and thousands in increasing the treasures of the British Museum, should allow such interesting national monuments as Caesar's Camp to be destroyed, he considered a great shame* (p. 907).

However, these arguments did not address the crucial issues of private property and the validity of the schedule. On the question of rights to private property, Lubbock and his supporters found that they could do little more than attempt to get the House to accept the principle that the defence of the national patrimony was sufficient reason for restricting the owner's rights to destroy. The associated factor of compulsion was never accepted by Parliament, even though the House and the government eventually accepted the principle that the state was responsible for the ancient monuments. The only previous occasions where government compelled property owners to give up title was for the defence of the realm – typified by the Defense Act and the Fortification Act.

The House was clearly not persuaded by Lubbock's attempts to convince them that a situation of National emergency existed with regard to the national patrimony. Indeed, opponents of the Bill such as Earl Percy were of the opinion that the antiquarian and archaeological societies were not the proper bodies for assessing the actual condition of the monuments. Although his motion for a parliamentary Select Committee on the issue was blocked (see 25 May 1880: p. 479), the government eventually structured the terms of its Inspector's appointment around Percy's suggestion.

Fortunately, they had more success defending the schedule and the value of prehistoric remains. Two tactics were employed here: the first was an appeal to the knowledge that had been derived from prehistoric archaeology, and the second an argument that the remains were part of the national rather than the racial patrimony. Lubbock defended archaeology with vigour:

*We are told that these remains have taught us nothing. To a great extent, no doubt, we have still their lessons to learn. It is, however, scarcely true that they have taught us nothing; on the contrary, they have thrown a flood of light on the history of the Past: and perhaps no branch of science had made more progress of late years than has Prehistoric Archaeology* (1879: p. 168).

Beresford Hope, in response to Lord Francis Hervey's sally about blue-painted Britons, expressed his belief in the potential of the discipline and its database:

*The word 'prehistoric' had become a misnomer. We were going backward and backward into history - not centuries merely, but thousands and thousands of years - and problems of infinite importance to the antiquary, the historian and the religionist - whatever his religion might be - were being solved by the inductions of an ever increasing array of specimens. We were bound to support the development of those studies...* (14 April 1875: p. 889).

Establishing the importance of the studies was one thing, but convincing Parliament that the prehistoric remains had significance as part of the national patrimony was another. The supporters of the Bill used two diametrically opposed arguments for preservation. On the one hand, because so little was known about these monuments, they were not protected because their significance was not apparent. On the other, because some people knew what they were, they were also under threat. A variation of this argument had been used by Antrobus and others as an attack on the antiquaries: because they presented a threat to the owner's enjoyment of private property, many owners would destroy their monuments rather than have their use of them restricted in any way. Despite this, the most plausible arguments for the monuments as part of the national heritage appealed to the fact that the public perceived them to be what they were, and that the science of prehistoric archaeology needed these monuments to solve the vital issue of the racial history of England. In essence, both made equal appeal to race, and it was a tactic that was to have meaning well into the next century.

Brown (1905: pp. 3-4) put the first line of argument clearly, and it is close to a paraphrase of Ferguson's speech of 14 April 1875:

*Whatever may be the future in other respects of Great Britain in relation to the Empire at large, it must always remain the soil in which are rooted all the traditional memories of race. In the tangible evidences of a storied past, this island possesses what is necessarily wanting to our colonies and to the off-shoots from those colonies... The feelings thus kindled help us keep alive throughout the Empire the sense of the unity of the stock... These streets and houses, as well as the more conspicuous monuments of which they are the setting, are imperial assets, and on economic, almost on political grounds, the duty of safeguarding them might well be recognized even by the least artistic and least antiquarian of the population* (p. 906).

Beresford Hope expressed the value of the science of prehistory to the writing of the racial history of England on 7 March 1877, when he rebuked Lord Francis Hervey for a narrow understanding of the significance of the monuments:

*To him they were, without a shadow of doubt, 'ancient rubbish'. In the course of his studies - cultured as they knew him to be - he had never come across a theory of a discovery which had led him to realize that their date and the ethnology of those who raised them were questions as interesting as they were difficult. He himself (B.H.) had a literary roving general acquaintance with the science of pre-historic Research, but this acquaintance was enough to make him appreciate that the testing of all these matters, which his noble friend so easily took for granted, was an irresistible argument for keeping intact that evidence on which the investigation must proceed* (p. 1,533).

Grant Duff also made the reflexive relationship between the development of prehistory, and the significance of the prehistoric monuments, clear on the same day. For him, the significance of the remains was the end product of the success of prehistoric archaeology, and it was only because the discipline was new and unusual that the issue of the national significance of the monuments needed to be debated at all (p. 1,536).

The history of the AMPB is also an object lesson in parliamentary tactics. Any explanation of the delay in getting consent for the Act must incorporate a discussion of the chicanery and obstruction practised both by the supporters and opponents of the Bill. I have outlined the principles of the Bill, the objectives to them, and the responses to those objections, and have concluded that the issue of private property and questions over the administration of the Act were the primary causes of delay. Although I have emphasised the attacks on antiquarians and archaeologists, and the racial aspects of the debate, it is clear that these were used as arguments in support of resistance to government interference in private rights, and government control over the administration of the Act.

The position of the AMPB as a Private Member's Bill is crucial here. On more than one occasion, Lubbock attempted to force the government of the day to accept responsibility for the monuments through the vote on the second reading of the Bill. Although he lost on 15 April 1874, Lubbock's intentions were clear:

*He had no wish to commit the House to the details of the Bill, but was anxious that by reading the Bill a second time the House should express its opinion that it was the national duty to take steps to preserve the ancient monuments of the country* (p. 595).

On another occasion (17 June 1875), he had come close to getting the government to introduce a Bill of its own (pp. 90-1), but was to be disappointed by a 'parliamentary promise'. Lubbock and his supporters clearly recognised that over an issue such as the invasion or limitation of private rights, a Private Member's Bill would stand little chance of success. Accordingly, when he finally achieved his object by passing a Resolution: 'That, in the opinion of this House, it is desirable that Her Majesty's Government should take steps to provide for the protection of the Ancient Monuments' (11 March 1881: p. 867), a portion of his argument was devoted to the difficulties of Private Member's Bills and the obstruction that the AMPB had experienced (p. 868).

That Lubbock succeeded with his resolution may be seen as a defeat for the prospect of an effective measure, but it should also be considered as a victory for the principle Lubbock had been fighting to establish. By 1881 he had managed to convince enough Members of the importance of some kind of legislation that the preceding means of obstruction and delay could be rendered harmless. Thompson, in particular, has explained the long delay as being partially Lubbock's fault: 'Had he been able to devise some formula by which the owner retained the title but was restricted as to use (like modern scheduling) he might have been able to take the wind out of the sails of the opposition' (Thompson 1977: 60). This is highly unlikely, as scheduling would have been perceived as an invasion of private property to the extent that there was an entail on the title. In essence, Lubbock's Bill provided for compulsory purchase only in the case of destruction, which is in reality no more invasive than scheduling.

Hudson has provided two further reasons for the delay. He has maintained that prior to 1882 there was an insufficient body of archaeological knowledge and expertise to justify the expenditure of public funds, and no adequate theory on which action could have been based. While it is true that by 1882 the amount of data and the numbers of archaeologists had increased, the fact remains that adequate theory was present in Lubbock's own work and that of his colleagues, and adequate legislative and administrative models had been in place in Europe for decades prior to the passing of the first AMPA. What was missing in England was a sense of the significance of these remains to have percolated far enough through society to create a groundswell of public opinion favourable to the legislation. Kristiansen has argued that preservation in Denmark had the support of the monarchy and the government as an effective way of mobilising national feeling (Kristiansen 1981: 22-3). Yet this was hardly the case in Great Britain, where the Duchy of Cornwall was not covered by the AMPB because assent was withheld.

Hudson's second point, that it was the extension of the franchise that allowed the Act to be passed, therefore seems more convincing than his first (1981: 56). Rantlett (1983), in particular, has demonstrated that preservationism grew in popularity, especially with the middle classes, after the 1850s. This growing strength, represented in membership of SPAB and

SPAM, constituted a lobby group which politicians found increasingly difficult to ignore. Whether the rise of preservationism can be connected to the late-Victorian disenchantment with progress, or whether it owed its strength to a growing interest in English history and culture, the fact remains that an Act which did place some restrictions on the enjoyment of private property for the greater good of the national heritage was passed.

In this sense the history of the AMPB is a reaffirmation of the extent to which archaeology and society interpenetrate each other – the language, concepts, and categories of archaeology on the one hand, and the aspirations of the members of society on the other. The fact that the AMPA was passed at all is testimony to the successful foundation of prehistoric archaeology as a science with popularly intelligible meanings and values.

## Conclusions

Shortly after Royal assent had been given to the first AMPA, Lord Carnarvon, the President of the SAL, assessed the result of a battle which had first been joined nearly ten years before:

> *Gentlemen, I am sure you will agree with me that one of the first subjects on which I ought to congratulate both this Society and the archaeological world of England is the passing into law of the Bill for the Protection of Ancient Monuments to which successive Presidents of this Society have so often, during the last ten years, wished success from this place. Perhaps I ought to have said a Bill than the Bill, for we all know, and so knowing we all regret - no one more than Sir John Lubbock himself - in what a mutilated condition, shorn of many of its original provisions, crippled in its powers and limited in its scope that measure finally became the law of the land. For these untoward results we must thank the supineness of the public, the prejudices of Parliament and perhaps I may add the all absorbing pressure of Irish Measures* (Anniversary Address to the SAL, 1883, in Saunders 1983: 11).

It was an understandably harsh assessment. Notwithstanding the defeat of many of the provisions of Lubbock's original Bill, and the government's rejection of the great antiquarian societies and the BM, the first AMPA was a major success at a time when utility and the right of private property were the corner-stones of both Liberal and Tory ideology. While it was certainly true that the rights of private property had prevailed in this first major contest with preservationism, it is also true that Lubbock and his supporters had managed to establish a principle, which would consequently blossom into more worthwhile legislation. Significantly, archaeological data had provided the first major test case for the preservation movement. Subsequently, other aspects of the natural and cultural heritage of Britain would find their advocates and supporters. The British public would be less supine in future.

The long, tortured experience of the first AMPA has been used to illustrate the importance of the historical and sociological dimensions of archaeological practice. At a time when the generalisations of Lubbock and Tylor were beginning to be supplanted by culture historical archaeology, the requirements of preservation placed further supportive pressure for a more particularist archaeology. Further, notwithstanding the scientistic rhetoric of prehistoric knowledge being derived from 'strict inductions', the observation statements of prehistoric archaeology were clearly predicated by current social theory, and by notions about what a meaningful prehistory of Britain should incorporate and attempt to achieve.

In these debates, the methodology of prehistoric archaeology was never questioned, especially its ability to produce rationally defensible knowledge about a past previously felt to be accessible only through speculation and the 'tyranny of hypothesis'. It is important to remember that the validity of Lubbock's claims to scientific status for prehistoric archaeology was rarely even mentioned, and at no time was a full explication of that methodology ever called for, or volunteered.

Although some Members (Lord Francis Hervey in particular) queried whether such knowledge was worth having, their objections were motivated by fears of the erosion of rights to private property and the political implications of celebrating the pre-Anglo-Saxon past of England, not by a rejection of the process of knowledge production itself. While Members may have felt that the explanations of prehistoric archaeology appeared less plausible than those of history, Grant Duff could credibly explain this as being the result of novelty, rather than of any inherent weakness in the approach.

The debates around the first AMPA thus testify that in the few decades since its foundation by Thomsen, Worsaae, Nilsson, and Lubbock, prehistoric archaeology had successfully passed from the realms of speculation into mainstream nineteenth-century science. There is little doubt that this process was aided by classifications based on material culture and sociocultural inference, which were then legitimated by archaeological and ethnographic comparison, as well as by geological stratigraphy. The spectacular discoveries in Denmark and Switzerland, at Brixham Cave, and in the Somme Gravels, made appeals to the importance of the hitherto unimagined even easier to sustain.

However, these were not the only reasons for the plausibility of archaeological methodology. The debates also reveal popular attitudes to race and ethnicity, and to the strength of the links between race and material culture that provided a justification both for doing prehistoric archaeology, and for its methodology. These attitudes were not the product of prehistoric archaeology. Rather, they sprang from other disciplines such as philology and ethnology, that were themselves strongly influenced by less well-understood cultural forces finding expression in romantic nationalism. Those same forces provided much of the popular understanding of the significance of archaeological remains that Lubbock could appropriate for warranting his claims for the significance of the science of prehistoric archaeology itself.

Therefore, the history of the first AMPA also brings into focus the reflexive relationship between plausible scientific explanation and popular belief. It indicates the happy conjunction of Lubbock's goal of providing a universal prehistory with the more popular goal of using the archaeological data to write a racial history of the United Kingdom. Both goals, for the most part, were happily to coexist in prehistoric archaeology for the next fifty years, especially in the work of Montelius and Kossinna. The downfall of 'peaceful coexistence' at the hands of Childe, Gunther, and the Nazi race historians is the subject of another essay.

**References**

AARNES, S.A. 1983, Myths and heroes in nineteenth century nation building in Norway. In J. C. Eade (ed) *Romantic Nationalism in Europe*, pp. 101-113. Canberra: Humanities Research Centre, Monograph no 2.

AGASSI, J. 1963. Towards a historiography of science. *History and Theory*. Beiheft 2: 1-117.

BARNES, B. 1974. *Scientific Knowledge and Sociological Theory*. London: Routledge and Kegan Paul.

—1977. *Interests and the Growth of Knowledge*. London: Routledge and Kegan Paul.

BELL, A.S. 1981. *The Scottish Antiquarian Tradition*. London: John Donald.

BERMAN, M. 1972. The early years of the Royal Institution 1799-1810: a Re-evaluation. *Science Studies* 2: 201-240.

BLOOR, D.C. 1976. *Knowledge and Social Imagery*. London: Routledge and Kegan Paul.

BOLT, C. 1971. *Victorian Attitudes to Race*. London: Routledge and Kegan Paul.

BOURDIEU, P. 1975. The Specificity of the scientific field and the social conditions on the progress of reason. *Social Science Information* 14: 19-47.

BRANNIGAN, A. 1981. *The Social Basis of Scientific Discoveries*. Cambridge: Cambridge University Press.

BROWN, G.B. 1905. *The Care of Ancient Monuments*. Cambridge: Cambridge University Press.

BURROW, J. 1966. *Evolution and Society: a Study in Victorian Social Theory*. Cambridge: Cambridge University Press.

CLARKE, D.L. 1972. Review of Explanation in Archaeology: an Explicitly Scientific Approach, by P. Watson, S. LeBlanc and C. Redman. *Antiquity* 44: 237-239.

—1973. Archaeology: the loss of innocence. *Antiquity* 47: 6-18.

COLLINS, H.M. and T.J. and PINCH 1982. *Frames of Meaning: the Social Construction of Extraordinary Science*. London: Routledge and Kegan Paul.

CURTIS, L.P. Jr 1968. *Anglo-Saxons and Celts: a Study of Anti-Irish Prejudice in Victorian England.* Conference on British Studies at the University of Bridgeport, Conn. New York: New York University Press.

DANIEL, G. 1975. *A Hundred and Fifty Years of Archaeology.* London: Duckworth.

DAWKINS, W. Boyd. 1880. *Early Man and his Place in the Tertiary Period.* London: Macmillan.

DYSON, S.L. 1985. Two paths to the past: a comparative study of the last fifty years of *American Antiquity* and the *American Journal of Archaeology. American Antiquity* 50: 452-463.

EDGE, D. 1983. Is there too much sociology of science? *Isis* 74: 250-256.

EVANS, J. 1949. The Royal Archaeological Institute: a Retrospect. *The Archaeological Journal* 106: 1-11.

—1950. Archaeology in 1851. *The Archaeological Journal* 106: 1-8.

—1956. *A History of the Society of Antiquaries.* London: Society of Antiquaries.

FAHNESTOCK, P. J. 1984. History and theoretical development: the importance of a critical historiography of archaeology. *Archaeological Review from Cambridge* 3:7-18.

FAWCETT, J. (ed) 1976. *The Future of the Past: Attitudes to Conservation, 1174-1974.* London: Thames and Hudson for the Victorian Society.

FEYERABEND, P. 1975. *Against Method.* London: New Left Books.

FIELD, G.G. 1977. Nordic racism. *Journal of the History of Ideas* 38: 523-540.

FREUDENTHAl, G. 1979. How strange is Dr Bloor's 'Strong Programme'? *Studies in the History and Philosophy of Science* 10: 67-83.

GERO, J.M., LACY, D. and M.L. BLAKEY (eds) 1983. *The Socio-Politics of Archaeology.* Amherst, Mass: University of Mass. Anthropological Research Report series no 23.

GILBERT, G.N. and M. MULKAY 1982. Warranting scientific belief. *Social Studies of Science* 12: 383-408.

—1984. *Opening Pandora's Box: a Sociological Analysis of Scientists' Discourse.* Cambridge: Cambridge University Press.

GRANT DUFF, U. 1934. Later Years. In U. Grant Duff (ed) *The Life-Work of Lord Avebury (Sir John Lubbock) 1834-1913.* London: Watts and Co.

GRAYSON, D.K. 1983. *The Establishment of Human Antiquity.* New York: Academic Press.

GRIFFIN, J.B. 1985b. The formation of the Society for American Archaeology. *American Antiquity* 50: 261-271.

HAAG, W.C. 1985. Federal aid to archaeology in the Southeast, 1933-1942'. *American Antiquity* 50: 272-280.

HANSON, N.R. 1958. *Patterns of Discovery.* Cambridge: Cambridge University Press.

HESSE, M.B. 1980. *Revolutions and Reconstruction in the Philosophy of Science.* Brighton: Harvester Press.

HORSMAN, R. 1976. Origins of racial Anglo-Saxonism in Great Britain before 1850. *Journal of the History of Ideas* 37: 387-410.

HUDSON, K. 1981. *A Social History of Archaeology.* London: Macmillan.

HUNTER, M. 1981. The preconditions of preservation: a historical perspective. In D. Lowenthal and M. Binney (eds) *The Past Before Us: Why Do We Save It?* pp. 22-32. London: Temple Smith.

HUTCHINSON, H.G. 1914. *Life of Sir John Lubbock Lord Avebury.* 2 vols. London: Macmillan

HYMES, D. 1963. Notes toward a history of linguistic anthropology. *Anthropological Linguistics* 5: 59-105.

41

JACOB, J.R. 1975. Restoration, reformation and the origins of the Royal Society. *History of Science* 13: 155-176.

KLINDT-JENSEN, O. 1975. *A History of Scandinavian Archaeology*. London: Thames and Hudson.

KOYRE, A. 1956. The origins of modern science. *Diogenes* 16: 1-22.

KNORR-CETINA, K.D. 1981. *The Manufacture of Knowledge: an Essay on the Constructivist and Contextual Nature of Science*. Oxford: Pergamon.

KNORR-CETINA, K. and M. MULKAY (eds) 1983. *Science Observed: Contemporary Analytical Perspectives*. London: Sage.

KRISTIANSEN, K. 1981. A social history of Danish archaeology. In G. Daniel (ed) *Towards a History of Archaeology*, pp. 20-44. London: Thames and Hudson.

KUHN, T. 1970. *The Structure of Scientific Revolutions*. 2nd edn. Chicago: University of Chicago Press.

—1977. *The Essential Tension: Selected Studies in Scientific Tradition and Change*. Chicago: University of Chicago Press

LAKATOS, I. 1978. *The Methodology of Scientific Research Programmes*. Cambridge: Cambridge University Press.

LATOUR, B. and S. WOOLGAR 1979. *Laboratory Life: the Social Construction of Scientific Facts*. London: Sage.

LUBBOCK, J. 1865. *Pre-historic Times*. London: Williams and Norgate.

—1870. *The Origin of Civilization and the Primitive Condition of Man*. London: Longmans and Green.

—1879. On the preservation of our ancient national monuments. In *Addresses, Political and Educational*. London: Macmillan.

MACKENZIE, D.A. 1981. *Statistics in Britain, 1865-1930: the Social Construction of Scientific Knowledge*. Edinburgh: Edinburgh University Press.

MELTZER, D.J. 1983a. The antiquity of man and the development of North American Archaeology. In M. Schiffer (ed) *Advances in Archaeological Method and Theory*, pp. 1-51. Vol. 6. New York: Academic Press

—1985. North American archaeology and archaeologists, 1879-1934. *American Antiquity* 50: 249-260.

MERTON, R.K. 1970. *Science, Technology and Society in Seventeenth Century England*. New York: Howard Fertig.

MULKAY, M. 1979. *Science and Sociology of Knowledge*. London: Allen and Unwin.

MULLIGAN, L. and G. MULLIGAN 1981. Reconstructing restoration science: styles of leadership and social composition of early Royal Society. *Social Studies of Science* 11: 327-364.

MURRAY, T. 1987. Remembrances of things present: appeals to authority in the history and philosophy of archaeology. Unpublished PhD. Department of Anthropology: University of Sydney.

NILSSON, S. 1868. *The Primitive Inhabitants of Scandinavia*. J. Lubbock, trans. London: Longmans

NIPPERDEY, T. 1983. In search of identity: romantic nationalism, its intellectual, political and social background. In J. C.Eade (ed) *Romantic Nationalism in Europe*, pp.1-15. Canberra: Humanities Research Centre Monograph no 2.

OUTHWAITE, W. 1983. *Concept Formation in Social Science*. London: Routledge

PICKERING, A. 1981. The hunting of the Quark. *Isis* 72: 216-236.

POUCHET, G. 1864. *The Plurality of the Human Race*. London: Longmans for the Anthropological Society of London.

PRINCE, H. 1981. Revival, restoration, preservation: changing views about antique landscape features. In D. Lowenthal and M. Binney (eds) *The Past Before Us: Why Do We Save It?* pp. 33-50. London: Temple Smith.

RANTLETT, J. 1983. Checking nature's desecration: late Victorian environmental organization. *Victorian Studies* Winter: 197-222.

RUPP-EISENREICH, B. 1981. The history of anthropology in France. *History of Anthropology Newsletter* 8: 13-20.

SALMON, M.H. 1982b. *Philosophy and Archaeology*. New York: Academic Press.

SAUNDERS, A.D. 1983. A century of ancient monuments legislation, 1882-1982. *The Antiquaries Journal* 63: 11-33.

SCHUSTER, J.A. 1984. Methodologies as mythic structures: a preface to the future historiography of method. *Metascience* 1 / 2: 15-36.

SHAPIN, S. 1982. Phrenological knowledge and the social structure of early nineteenth century Edinburgh. *Annals of Science* 32: 219-243.

SHAPIN, S. and B. BARNES 1977. Science, nature and control: interpreting mechanics' institutes. *Social Studies Of Science* 7: 31-74.

SKLENAR, K. 1983. *Archaeology in Central Europe: the First 500 Years*. Leicester: Leicester University Press.

STEVENSON, R.B.K. 1981. The museum, its beginnings and its development. Part II: The National Museum to 1954. In A.S. Bell (ed) *The Scottish Antiquarian Tradition*, pp. 142-211. Edinburgh: John Donald.

STOCKING, G.W. Jnr 1968. On the limits of 'presentism' and 'historicism' in the historiography of the behavioural sciences. In G.W. Stocking (ed) *Race, Culture, and Evolution,* pp. 1-12. New York: the Free Press.

—1971. What's in a name? The origins of the Royal Anthropological Institute (1831-71). *Man* 6: 369-390.

THOMPSON, H. 1943. Address in commemoration of the centenary of the Royal Anthropological Institute. *The Archaeological Journal* 100: 1-15.

THOMPSON, M.W. 1977. *General Pitt-Rivers: Evolution and Archaeology in the Nineteenth Century.* Bradford-on-Avon: Moonraker Press.

TOULMIN, S. 1961. *Foresight and Understanding*. New York: Harper.

TRIGGER, B. 1980a. Archaeology and the image of the American Indian. *American Antiquity* 45: 662-676.

WEBER, G. 1974. Science and society in nineteenth century anthropology. *History of Science* 12: 260-283.

WORSAAE, J.J.A. 1849. *The Primeval Antiquities of Denmark translated, and applied to the illustration of similar remains in England*. W.J. Thomas trans. London: J.H. Parker.

WYLIE, A. 1982c. Positivism and the new archaeology. Unpublished PhD. SUNY at Binghampton.

—1985a. Between Philosophy and Archaeology. *American Antiquity* 50: 478-490.

YELLEN, J.E. and M.W. GREEN 1985. Archaeology and the National Science Foundation. *American Antiquity* 50: 332-341.

YEO, R. 1979. William Whewell, natural theology and the philosophy of science in mid-nineteenth century Britain. *Annals of Science* 36: 493-516.

—1981. Scientific method and the image of science. In R. MacLeod and P. Collins (eds) *The Parliament of Science: 1831-1981*, pp. 65-88. London: Science Reviews.

# Chapter 3

# The Tasmanians and the constitution of the 'Dawn of Humanity'

*But whom did this primitive race of Europe resemble most?*
*– the Australian, the most disgusting type of living savages!*
*Poor Adam! Poor Eve!* (Vogt 1864: 307).

In this paper I briefly (and quite superficially) discuss the place of the Tasmanians in the development of our understanding of early human history, and in the historiography of Australian prehistoric archaeology, both subjects deserving of much more intensive treatment than they will receive here (but see e.g. Mulvaney 1958; 1981; 1985; 1988; Smith 1960). Apart from noting that there seems to be an almost inexhaustible supply of quotable quotes about Aboriginal Tasmanians (and Australian Aboriginal people in general) – indeed, the better you know the byways of nineteenth century anthropological and archaeological literature, the richer the payoff – I will focus discussion on the fact that archaeologists (and anthropologists) have always been able to construct the Tasmanians to suit prevailing fashion.

There is no great difficulty in revealing and exemplifying this process of construction, and in demonstrating that the process did not stop with Sollas (1911), let alone with Lubbock (1865), Tylor (1865) or Vogt (1864). It is a much more difficult (and more rewarding) business to understand why this construction has happened, and why we need to reflect more deeply about its consequences.

One of the best ways of doing this is to consider the links between the cultural traditions of archaeology and ethnography. It is a commonplace that there is a deep and abiding relationship between archaeology and ethnography/socio-cultural anthropology. This relationship is one of the most important foundations of the disciplinary culture of archaeology, and through this culture, of the terms under which those constructions are generated and defended. It is also widely appreciated that archaeological data (no matter how detailed or complete) are not ethnographic data. It is therefore accepted practice that establishing the meaning of these data requires a process of translation into the conceptual and categorical language of the human sciences.

However, it has also frequently been noted that this process of translation does not always go smoothly, either because of an over-determination of empirical data by theory or a recognition that differences of scale and ontology between the archaeological and the anthropological cannot be overcome by existing conceptual vocabularies (see e.g. Bailey 1983; Binford 1981; Murray 1987: chapter 8; Murray and Walker 1988). Furthermore, sometimes archaeological data are so anomalous, so unexpected, that they have the potential to destabilize conventional disciplinary relationships and throw up the possibility that the conventions of contemporary social theory may not be the natural interpretative and explanatory structures which many archaeologists think them to be (see e.g. Murray 1997).

The best example of the discovery of archaeological data, which had the potential to profoundly disturb existing disciplinary relationships and theoretical conventions, is the acceptance of high human antiquity, after 1859, based on research at Brixham Cave and in the Somme Gravels. I have argued elsewhere that this potential was never realized (Murray 1987: chapter 4). Two linked explanations were offered for this, and for the fact that histories of archaeology (see e.g. Grayson 1983) always emphasize that the acceptance of high human antiquity was absolutely crucial for the successful foundation of prehistoric archaeology in the nineteenth century. As an aside, it is worth noting that the expertise displayed by the excavators, and the links between prehistoric archaeology and geology, played a vital part in the acceptance of the discoveries, but not necessarily in the establishment of their meaning.

First, alongside the process of construction in archaeology there operates a parallel process of 'normalization' where the conventional concepts and categories, which underwrite the interpretation of human action, defuse potentially disturbing archaeological data. Secondly, there is a strong disincentive to emphasize what amount to ontological differences between archaeology and disciplines such as history and anthropology, because there are no conceptual or methodological structures, which allow us to assign meaning to statements made outside the conventions of human science. Indeed, these conventions have been established largely through the practice of history, anthropology and sociology.

The most obvious consequence of the normalization of the discoveries at Brixham Cave and on the Somme was the denial of history to Tasmanian Aboriginal people, and through them to other peoples whose cultures were (and to some extent still are) taken to exemplify the various stages of human sociocultural evolution. But there were significant tensions arising from the appropriation and denial of 'savage history' because it was also quite clear that the Tasmanian Aboriginal people must have had a history, be it of drift voyaging from Melanesia, forced emigration from continental Australia due to depredations of 'more advanced' Aboriginal groups or simply of slow decline in population and cultural strength as a result of isolation.

What allowed the denial to occur, and for the most part to go unremarked, was the greater need to support linear theories of social and cultural evolution by extending their coverage to the dawn of humanity. A radical break between historic and prehistoric pasts would plunge human history back into the void of unintelligibility (see e.g. Lubbock 1865; Morgan 1877; Tylor 1865). Another reason, which played an equally important role in the building of Australian archaeology, was the view that, notwithstanding some evidence of 'degeneration', the Tasmanians really had no history because they had remained unchanged throughout aeons. Thus their history counted for little because it was not a history of civilization, or as Manning Clark put it in the first volume of his epic *History of Australia* (1962: 4), 'of the way of life of these... peoples before the coming of European civilization, little need, or indeed can, be said'.

Beneath this discussion of normalization and the denial of history lie the relationship between metropolitan (or imperial) science and the science of the colonies. I cannot explore this relationship in any detail here, although there is a large literature which discusses the role of science in building post-colonial cultures, and further characterizes the development of national identities of former British colonies (see e.g. Eddy and Schreuder 1988; MacLeod 1988b; Mulvaney 1988). In the present paper I will demonstrate that this relationship has changed over the last century, to the extent that Australian archaeologists are now somewhat less prepared to ignore high levels of spatio-temporal cultural variability within the archaeological record of the country in favour of normal, conventional, metropolitan images of 'gatherer-hunter-fisher-foragers' (see e.g. Cosgrove *et al.* 1990).

There is an additional lesson we can learn from the experience of the Tasmanians, and it has to do with the power of archaeological data to transform archaeological research agendas. Such transformations help us understand more about normalization, because they give us a standpoint from which to critique its products. Since 1981, but especially since 1987, a series of dramatic discoveries have been made among the karst caves of southern Tasmania. These have revealed evidence of a long history of occupation for a region, which was thought to be uninhabited at contact (and therefore uninhabited during the whole human history of the region). The significance of the discovery rests on the fact that for over 20,000 years a social system flourished, only to be extinguished by changing ecological conditions in the area nearly 10,000 years before Europeans arrived in Tasmania. Thus there currently appears to be no direct culture-historical link between the Tasmanians of the nineteenth century and those of 11,000 years ago that lived in this area.

Such discoveries provide a spur to a critique of construction and normalization, but they also raise powerful questions, such as what kind of history can be written for societies where there is no linear pathway of 'progress' from simple to complex, and where the causes of change within the archaeological record are rarely simply specified and observed. Moreover, what is to be the role of ethnographic analogy (particularly of the direct historical kind) in building an understanding of such societies? Would theories of statics and dynamics derived from actualistic studies of contemporary societies ever escape from problems of over-determination when applied to archaeological records, which seem to be palimpsests of chaos rather than a linear succession of synchronic events? (see Murray 1997).

These are difficult, foundational matters which encompass discussion about the nature and purpose of the archaeologist's project, the role of cognitive plausibility in adjudicating knowledge claims and, of course, the possibilities of a critically self-reflective archaeology. But these issues are abstracted from my primary purpose, which is simply to highlight some of the broader implications of a move to historicize the Tasmanians and to understand the nature of variability in prehistoric Australia.

## Construction and normalization in action

*To confine our studies to mere antiquities is like reading by candle-light at noonday; but to reject the aid of archaeology in the progress of science, and especially of ethnological science, is to extinguish the lamp of the student when most dependent on its borrowed rays... We are no longer permitted to discuss merely the diversities of existing races. It seems as if the whole comprehensive question of man's origin must be re-opened, and determined afresh in its relations to modern science* (Wilson 1862: vii).

The recursive relationship between the discourse of metropolitan archaeology and anthropology (particularly during their formative years) and the discourse of Australian prehistory is founded on the processes of construction and normalization. Prior to the discoveries at Brixham Cave and the Somme, and clearly antecedent to the publication of Lubbock's (1865) and Tylor's (1865) great works of synthesis, the Tasmanians and the Australians had been seen as the essence of 'natural man'. Of course, they had their rivals in this. Nilsson was particularly fond of the 'Esquimaux' (1868), and Daniel Wilson (1862) based his account of prehistoric archaeology on the ethnography of the American 'Indians', but in the league of savagery only the Hottentots, and occasionally the Fuegians, were seen as rivals.

It is well known that interpretative fashions changed during the late eighteenth and early nineteenth centuries. First came the image of noble savagery portrayed in Rousseau's *Of the Social Contract* (1762), which was typified by the art and ethnographic observations of Cook's great voyages to Australia, and in Labillardiere's (1800) account of Tasmanian life. Then, after the turn of the century, as Hobbes replaced Rousseau, contacts with Tasmanian Aboriginal people were reported in an entirely different way. Where first there was nobility and beauty, there was now disgust and ugliness (see e.g. Peron 1809). The reasons for this change in vision are complex, but have received considerable scholarly attention (see e.g. Smith 1960). Manning Clark summarized the complexity in straightforward fashion (1962: 4):

> *For all writings on the aborigines both on the mainland and in Tasmania, have mirrored the civilization of their authors, of those driven by the hope of salvation or the fear of damnation, as well as those in pursuit of some secular millennium, or the advancement of knowledge.*

These changes in fashion kept pace with a developing confidence in the value of generalizations about human beings in a savage state. Links between technology and subsistence strategies were forged into more inclusive statements about the nature of savage culture and social institutions. Thus it became possible to infer social and cultural attributes from observations of technology and subsistence, and *vice versa*. These inferences were used in a systematic way in Lubbock's *Prehistoric Times* (1865) and Tylor's *Researches into the Early History of Mankind* (1865); indeed the whole rationale of these synthetic works was that present savagery was a reliable guide to the early history of Europeans, and their collective account of the identities of the 'men of the Cave and of the Drift' (Brixham and the Somme) was a case in point.

The acceptance of the coexistence of human beings and extinct fauna which flowed from the discoveries at Brixham Cave and in the Somme raised two questions in 1859: what kind of human being made the stone tools, and how long ago did this happen? Lubbock, among others, followed standard ethnological practice by providing a solution to the former question based on comparative ethnography, and a standard of empirical practice by substituting the methods of geology for an appeal to 'untrustworthy tradition':

> *Although, then, traditions and myths are of great importance, and indirectly throw much light on the condition of man in ancient times, we must not expect to learn much directly from them... Deprived,*

*therefore as regards this period, of any assistance from history, but relieved at the same time from the embarrassing interference of tradition, the archaeologist is free to follow the methods which have been so successfully pursued in geology the rude stone and bone implements of bygone ages being to the one what the remains of extinct animals are to the other. The analogy may be pursued even further than this... in the same manner, if we wish clearly to understand the antiquities of Europe, we must compare them with rude implements still, or until lately, used by the savage races in other parts of the world. In fact the Van Diemaner and the South American are to the antiquary what the opossum and the sloth are to the geologist* (Lubbock 1865: 336-7).*

Much has been written on the role of ethnographic analogy in archaeology, and this particular passage of Lubbock's has been more widely cited than almost any other. More than enough has also been written about the role of the assumption of the psychic unity of mankind in the work of both Lubbock (1865; 1882; and Tylor 1865; 1870; see especially Harris 1968). In the present context it is important to note two things. First, both Lubbock and Tylor needed a 'human face for the Palaeolithic', because the standards of proof and interpretation established by ethnology and anthropology required such an image. Palaeolithic man would be only the most ghostly of shadows without the Van Diemaner, and both Lubbock's and Tylor's (and, of course, Morgan's) systems demanded more than that. The doctrine of psychic unity and the intellectualistic concept of culture provided the archaeologist (or antiquary) with a basis for rationally reconstructing the customs, institutions and technologies of contemporary savages as well those of primeval man.

Secondly, neither Lubbock nor Tylor could argue that the Van Diemaners were 'frozen moments' from the Palaeolithic. Indeed, the intellectualistic concept of culture they shared dictated that this could not be so:

*The civilization, moreover, of the Stone Age differs not only in degree, but also in kind, varying according to climate, vegetation, food, etc., from which it become evident - at least to all those who believe in the unity of the human race, that the present habits of savage races are not to be regarded as representing exactly those which characterized the first men, but as depending also on external conditions, influenced indeed to a certain extent by national character, which, however, is after all the result of external conditions which have acted on external generations* (Lubbock 1865: 549).

Tylor was in complete agreement:

*But if we may judge that the present condition of savage tribes is the complex result of not only a long but an eventful history, in which the development of culture may have been more or less interfered with by degeneration caused by war, disease, oppression, and other mishaps, it does not seem likely that any tribe known to modern observers should be anything like a fair representative of primary conditions... Still, positive evidence that anything lower than the known state of savages is scarce in the extreme* (1865: 379-80).

This was all well and good. However, even taking into account the claims that there were no direct analogies between current savages and the humans of the Palaeolithic, and that to some extent Palaeolithic society could be theoretically reconstructed on the basis of psychic unity and the reconstruction of conditions of existence, the practical result was that the Van Diemaners and the South Americans did become the fossil representatives of the Palaeolithic, precisely because they were the meaningful (reliable) image of the terms in which the prehistoric past was to be known. By providing an interpretable image of Palaeolithic humanity, evolutionary archaeology and anthropology not only effectively denied a history to contemporary savages, but also made an understanding of the Palaeolithic effectively synchronous with the present. The vast time-scale, which was supposed to characterize the acceptance of a high human antiquity effectively, disappeared for the very reason that it could not be articulated by any of the ethnological or anthropological theories available at the time.

I have mentioned the process of normalization whereby potentially disturbing data are defused through a process of reinterpretation or reformulation. Berry (1968) among others has discussed this issue with respect to the impact of Darwinian biology in its association with uniformitarian geology. However, despite the work of Grayson (1983) and Stocking (1968), we still lack a vantage point on the operations of this process of normalization in prehistoric archaeology. Out of all of the numerous references to 'vast', 'unimaginable' antiquity – 'a period we cannot sum up in years', it is the transformation of the stone tools of Brixham and the Somme from posing a problem of interpretation to being interpreted as being made by people similar to Tasmanian Aborigines that most clearly demonstrates normalization in action.

This normalization took less than five years to bear fruit in the synthetic prehistories of Lubbock and Tylor. Consider John Phillips' address to the Geological Society of London in 1860. After remarking that the conversion of geological time into historical time required numbers 'so large as to elude the grasp of memory or imagination' (1860: liv), Phillips pondered the meaning of the rude stone implements from the Somme. What manner of human made tools that were 'inferior to that which we recognize even amongst the rudest tribes of Mankind' (1860: liii). He was not slow to perceive the implications of this difference. The people who made those tools were in the:

*possession of a rude kind of art and a low degree of intelligence. If we must ascribe these flint implements (which seem inferior even to the specimens of Australian art) to the agency of the children of Adam, geological time, marked by the extinct mammalia, seems to be at last joined, though not clearly, to the human periods but not with any known data of properly historical time* (Phillips1860: liv).

The net result of normalization in this case was that the Tasmanians were drafted in to act as the model of inference, and that the self-evident stability of Tasmanian culture over what was assumed to be a long period of time (see also Etheridge 1890; Howitt 1898) meant that they were a society without a history. Their peculiarity was explained in other ahistorical ways, as being the product of a complex process, which included elements of stasis, regression and progress. This denial of history was itself a response to the daunting prospect of human action in the deep prehistoric past being unintelligible to contemporary observers armed with contemporary structures of knowing about human beings. Plausible models of inference were absolutely vital here, because the only way to preserve the universality of those structures was to demonstrate their general applicability to the explanation of other contemporary cultures, and then to argue that these contemporary societies could be ordered as modern representatives of prehistoric human socio-cultural types. This, when allied to the problem of quantifying the new time-scale, effectively squeezed it into a shorter, almost synchronic one, allowing for an easy relationship with ethnology and anthropology as the suppliers of substantive uniformitarian propositions.

Although a nearly a century was to elapse between the publication of *Prehistoric Times* and Jones' excavation at Rocky Cape and Sister's Beach, the general strategy employed by Lubbock and by Tylor to give meaning to the European Palaeolithic underwent few changes. It is worth noting that in the seven editions of *Prehistoric Times* published between 1865 and 1913 no substantive changes were made to the text about the Tasmanians, or even to the discussion of ethnographic analogy and living fossils. The only change of substance was the addition of an illustration of some Tasmanian fire sticks presented to Lubbock by George Augustus Robinson, which has a pleasing historical symmetry, if nothing else.

Things were different for E. B. Tylor who, by the last decade of the century, had begun to contemplate some changes to his earlier equation of the Tasmanians with the 'men of the Drift' (1865: 195), which had, after all been based on one stone tool brought to England by a Mr Thomas Dawson in 1860; it is now in the Somerset County Museum, see Figure 1). Beginning in 1893, after inspecting more Tasmanian stone tools sent over to Oxford in 1890, Tylor moved his Tasmanians even further back in time and hence in savagery (Tylor 1893; 1894; 1898; 1899; 1900), into what Sollas described as the 'raging vortex of the eolith controversy' (1911: 89). Although Sollas resisted the temptation to follow Tylor, Klaatsch (1908), and the other eolithomaniacs and to downgrade the Tasmanians even further, the bulk of observers, both in the metropolitan and in Australia were convinced that relegation was justified (see also Pulleine 1928). Thus, as the possibility of there being Tertiary stone tools began to be openly discussed by practitioners such as Rutot, Abbott and even Prestwich, the same need for a plausible model of inference arose, and the Tasmanians were drafted in again.

*Figure 1. The most significant stone tool in the history of Australian archaeology? Tylor's inspiration, now in the Somerset County Museum, Taunton.* Image courtesy of Somerset County Council Heritage Service.

Thus, despite Tylor's implication that this downgrading of the Tasmanians was the result of a rethink in those pathetically few scraps of information about them which had survived the holocaust of the 1820s and 1830s (see Ling Roth 1899), the real reason for it was that there was no-one else to fill in, due to the shortage of human bones found in association with the stones (a problem which had bedevilled Palaeolithic archaeology throughout the last half of the nineteenth century). Debate about the relative positions of the Neanderthals and us had not reached any firm conclusion by the end of the century. This uncertainty, and problems with *Homo erectus*, let alone 'Piltdown Man', made the ascription of simple technologies to other members of the human line a risky business indeed (see e.g. Spencer 1990).

The reaction of Australian archaeologists and anthropologists to the Tasmanians is somewhat more complex. It was early appreciated that the Tasmanians looked different to other Aboriginal people, and that their technology was simpler. For example, they had no spear-throwers and they did not grind stones to create an edge. Some observers argued that the Tasmanians were Melanesians (they were held to look more like that group than the others), which meant that some mechanism had to be found to get them there – either walking overland or drifting south on simple water-craft.

Given these assertions, and adding the detail that if they did get there by drifting then they must have degenerated in the sense that they lost the art of boat-building, observers from Captain Cook to Rhys Jones discussed every possible permutation of colonization and the effects of isolation (see Birdsell 1957; David 1923; Etheridge 1890; Howitt 1898; McCarthy 1958; Pulleine 1928; Tindale 1957). While there were some attempts at characterizing Aboriginal life in the Palaeolithic as being like the Tasmanian, most Australian observers were more interested in using the Tasmanians either as the marker fossil of first settlement of the continent, hence the initial phase of a long history of settlement and culture change (see especially Birdsell, McCarthy and Tindale), or simply as crucial evidence in the case for a high human antiquity in Australia (see especially Etheridge and Howitt).

Once again, because they were the lowest form of humanity, and because they had been out of the mainstream of continental prehistory since the Holocene, this history of change in the continent hardly applied to the Tasmanians. The 1960s brought fundamental challenges to all these arguments and justifications.

**Some consequences of construction and normalization:**

*What is known of the Tasmanians scarcely permits us to consider them superior to the Australians. It must, however, be admitted that these unfortunate islanders of Van Diemen's Land have not been so much attended to as the Australians. The English, so humane and patient as regards the latter, have committed upon the Tasmanian race, and that in the nineteenth century, execrable atrocities a hundred times less excusable than the hitherto unrivalled crimes of which the Spanish were guilty in the fifteenth century in the Antilles.*

*These atrocities have terminated in a regular extirpation caused, say the optimists, by the absolute unsociability of the Tasmanians. This is not, in our opinion, a mitigatory circumstance, but from all these facts it results evidently, that, of all human beings, the Tasmanians are, or rather were, with the Australians, nearest to the brutal condition* (Broca 1864: 45-6).

In 1963 the eminent anthropologist (and literary craftsman) W.E.H. Stanner made an impassioned plea to the Australian government to underwrite a wide-ranging research effort into the 'origins, history and character' of Australian Aboriginal people. Stanner deployed two strong arguments to support his case. One had been tried and tested since the first report of the Aborigines Protection Society (London) in 1838; the other argument was something new.

Stanner first made the conventional observation that the processes of colonization and assimilation had destroyed (and were still destroying) a great deal of valuable information about the origins and nature of humanity. Perhaps more to the point (given that Australia at this time still controlled Papua and New Guinea under a United Nations mandate) were the connections between knowledge about subject 'native' peoples, and the delivery of good colonial government. A more subtle, but clearly much more problematic, connection could be made between anthropology and the effective government of Australian Aboriginal people who were themselves the subject of assimilationist policies which were designed to destroy the very things Stanner was hoping to document. But all this is to mask a much more positive motive, which built on Stanner's (1963: xvii-xviii) belief that:

*there has been a revolution of public interest, and more precise methods of study are at hand, only a few years remain in which to bring together, as best we can, our new respect for the native Australians and the preservation for posterity - theirs and ours - of a true and competent record of their way of life.*

This appeal to a link between public interest and competent anthropology is supported by a bitter attack on the 'masquerade of preconception, fiction, and half-truth as demonstrated fact' (1963: xv), which made up for a much-needed empirical anthropology of Aboriginal Australia during the nineteenth century. In Stanner's view the cause of this incompetent record was the fact that the first rigorous studies of Aboriginal life did not occur until the 1890s, and therefore well after anthropology and its constituent sub-disciplines had taken shape. This, according to Stanner, allowed the historicist account of human social and cultural evolution fostered by Maine, Bachofen, Bastian, McLennan and Tylor to determine effectively the framework of inquiry into Aboriginal life. Significantly, this account has been recently echoed in a thoroughgoing re-analysis of the idea of primitivism in anthropology (Kuper 1988), and in Mulvaney's analysis of relations between metropolitan and colonial anthropology in the early years of the Australian and New Zealand Association for the Advancement of Science (1988).

In the course of an extended discussion of the genesis of the concept of totemism, Kuper (1988: 93) observed that, during the 1860s and 1870s, information about Australian Aborigines was seen to be central to the development of anthropological theory; the problem was that there was not much of it:

*Yet the information available on the Australian aborigines was very slight. There soon built up a considerable demand for information on Australia. Coupled with the lack of an indigenous tradition of ethnography this gave rise to a remarkable situation. The first serious students of Aboriginal society were in thrall to opinionated outsiders, who inspired, and often even arranged the finance for, their expeditions.*

Kuper was referring to Morgan's influence on Fison and Howitt, to Frazer's close links with Spencer and Gillen, and to the fact that behind Morgan and Frazer was E. B. Tylor, who had contact with both groups. But Stanner s argument that Aboriginal societies were intrinsically interesting in themselves, rather than as abstracted documents of general human history or testimonies to the variety of human social and cultural forms, required more than a recognition that Aboriginal society had been constructed for the benefit of others. He also needed to demonstrate the pernicious consequences of construction. Speaking of Tylor (and of his like) Stanner observed (1963: xv) that they:

*had also fostered the fallacy that primitive peoples, ancient and contemporary were directly comparable. Hence, even at the end of the century, it was still assumed that the native Australians were representative of the childhood of all humanity. Their ideas and customs, true or supposed, were used to illustrate and justify theories about primordial man's relations with nature, with his fellows, and with divinity, traced through an imagined course of universal development. Such facts as were known were used to vindicate historicist fabrications, not to illumine a way of life seen as having interest and importance in its own right.*

For Stanner this emphasis on the primordial, on the Aboriginal person as childlike, became part of the unexamined assumptions of scholars, the general public and of governments themselves. Baldwin Spencer, a former student of Tylor's and the pre-eminent academic authority on Australian Aboriginal people, acted as an adviser to the Australian Federal Government on the administration of Aboriginal welfare in the Northern Territory of Australia. His description of Aboriginal people as 'a very curious mixture; mentally, about the level of a child who has little control over his feelings... no sense of responsibility and, except in rare cases, no initiative' (Spencer 1913: 13-14 quoted in Mulvaney 1985: 74) fostered a destructive policy of paternalism that remained largely unchanged for nearly sixty years.

Stanner's mood of optimism in 1963 reflected a climate of change in the relationships between Aboriginal people and the rest of Australian society, which had begun in the late 1950s. There are many reasons why this happened, ranging from the recognition that Aboriginal people were not going to die out as the racial eugenicists had predicted (and that policy was going to have to be developed to cope with that fact), to increasingly confident and sophisticated movements for land-rights and self-determination among Aboriginal people themselves. Underlying these multiple causes was the fact that there was now a great deal more information about Aboriginal people, which was not cloaked with paternalistic attitudes about the fate of 'natural man', and which stood in stark contrast to the information made available to previous generations.

Stanner's optimism was justified by subsequent events. In the course of the 1960s and 1970s a great flood of research into Aboriginal archaeology, anthropology and history played a vital role in supporting Aboriginal moves for self-determination and in helping the Australian public find out more about the continent, its original inhabitants and the human costs of a shared history. Although Aboriginal people still have yet to gain a full measure of control over their lives, there has been a tremendous change in attitude, which will eventually make this possible. It is worth noting that these developments also began to change the relationships between metropolitan and Australian archaeology and anthropology, where the cultural context of practice began to shift from a data-mine for grand theory to one where practitioners sought to comprehend Aboriginal Australia for its own sake.

But other aspects of context were crucial too, particularly the application of radiometric chronologies to Australia and the great expansion in the population of archaeologists working in the country – many of whom were trained abroad. Thus it is probably fair to say that, although there was archaeology practised in Australia before Mulvaney's return from Cambridge, the intersection between the discourse of world prehistory and the discourse of Australian prehistory has greatly intensified over the last thirty years. Nowhere has the impact of that intersection been felt more keenly than in the reorientation of Tasmanian archaeology which began after 1981 (see also Bowdler 1979), but which has really gathered speed and strength since 1987, when Cosgrove began doctoral research in southern Tasmania (Cosgrove 1991) and Allen launched the Southern Forests Archaeology Project (see e.g. Allen *et al.* 1988).

## Recent developments in Tasmanian archaeology

The beginnings of an escape from the treadmill of over-interpretation, which had characterized previous accounts of Tasmanian Aboriginal life, came in 1963 when Rhys Jones excavated caves at Rocky Cape and at Sister's Beach in the northwest of the state. These sites, and the exploration of the large middens at West Point, established the reality of change in Tasmanian prehistory. More important, Jones' interpretation of the meaning of that change began a process of investigation (and much argument) which had the potential to alter radically our understanding of Australian prehistory.

The broad outlines of Jones' account of the cessation of fish eating at Rocky Cape are very well known and there is no need to rehearse them here (Jones 1971; 1977a; 1977b; 1978; vs H. Allen 1979; Bowdler 1980; Horton 1979; Lourandos 1977; Van Der Wal 1978). White and O'Connell, in the most thorough discussion of the issues (1982: 158-70) have queries about the quality of Jones' data, but these are minor in comparison to their reservations about matters of interpretation. They sensed that Jones' argument that Tasmania was the 'last refuge of a cultural system of immense antiquity and stability' (Jones 1971: 620) had a familiar Tylorian ring about it. The feeling that the archaeology of the 1960s had collided with the interpretative framework of the 1860s was compounded by an emphasis on the consequences of isolation. Kuper has also noted that, after Darwin, a clear link was seen between primitivism and isolation (1988: chapter 1).

In the Tasmanian case an already primitive culture was made more so by isolation, and the cessation of fish eating (with all the irrationality this implied) was seen as evidence of a society becoming irreversibly impoverished. Jones (1976: 620 quoted in White and O'Connell 1982:158) did not mince his words:

*Perhaps the culture, remote for thousands of years from any outside stimulus, was becoming simplified and losing some of its 'useful arts'? Perhaps in the very long run... 3000 people were not enough to support and maintain a culture even of the simplicity of that practised during Late Pleistocene Australia.*

In previous years, observers had argued that extinction was inevitable on a number of grounds, political, religious and 'ethnological'. Here, for the first time, was archaeological evidence not only of primitiveness, but also of the probability of degeneration brought on by isolation from continental Australia. Yet there is an inconsistency here, and it mirrors the uncertainty about the precise position of the Tasmanians on the scale of savagery, which had dogged Sollas, Howitt, Pulleine, David and the later Tylor.

On the one hand Jones could ask (1971: 630): 'Can we now look at the Tasmanians, not so much as the representatives of Palaeolithic man, but of late Pleistocene Australian man?', which implies that in the late Pleistocene all Aboriginal people would have been like the Tasmanians at contact. It also implies that the differences between the two populations such as ground-edge tools, and more complex technologies such as spear-throwers, were the result of Tasmania's exclusion from a wider continental culture (an aspect of which must have included contact with Southeast Asia, as the late arrival of the dingo testifies).

But this says nothing about degeneration, just a kind of stasis, and moves closer to the idea that had long been in play (see e.g. Oldfield 1865; Birdsell 1957; Tindale 1957) that the Tasmanians were a relict population who were either forced south by technologically more advanced invaders, or simply trapped by rising sea-levels and inadequate sailing-craft. Supporters of the eolith hypothesis such as Klaatsch (1908: 93-167) could be happy with the notion of stasis in human society, but not of degeneration, a process very much more difficult to historicize on the world scale. In effect Jones had it both ways, that they degenerated (because of isolation) and that they were static (because of isolation). Matters tended to rest there, with opposition to such claims being classed – sometimes even by the opponents, as being motivated by different perspectives on the possibilities of human beings (see especially White and O'Connell 1982: 170), rather than by a real inconsistency in argument as much derived from the traditions of metropolitan research into the Tasmanians as it was by colonial representations of them.

The first extended analysis of the unfolding possibilities of archaeological research into the Tasmanian Pleistocene came in 1979 with the publication of Bowdler's dissertation research on Hunter Island during the Pleistocene period. But all this paled into insignificance alongside the startling discovery, in 1981, by Jones and others, of the human occupation, during the Pleistocene period, of the frozen wastes of southern Tasmania. There has already been a great deal written about the meaning and significance of those discoveries, and the very brief and partisan sketch of it which I present here is based on the fact that sharp differences arise between the interested parties as soon as discussion moves beyond superficialities. Where Jones (see especially 1984; 1990) sees behavioural similarities with Franco-Cantabrian sites, and there being a low level of variability around a continent-wide model of human behaviour during the Pleistocene period in Australia (see also Kiernan *et al.* 1983), other researchers, particularly Cosgrove (1991: especially chapters 1 & 2) and Allen (1989) detect real regional variation in Australia and are greatly more circumspect about the value of superficial resemblances between northern and southern hemisphere systems.

The significance of the debate is that both groups seek to understand the nature of a system which has been extinct for over 10,000 years and for which there are no ethnographic parallels (even in Tasmania). But the sources of inspiration are dramatically different. On the one hand, Jones seeks understanding from Australian ethnography and European Upper Palaeolithic archaeology. On the other, Cosgrove and Allen find their inspiration in thinking through the structural properties of the data to hand, rather than from the traditions of metropolitan research. The difference represents a major departure in the traditions of Australian prehistoric archaeology, and perhaps demonstrates again that the Tasmanians have not lost their power to fascinate and to instruct.

**Concluding remarks**

*Aborigines wrote their history, maintaining that their ancestors were not immigrants, but were always here, and that white man's history was a catalogue of 'white lies'... Accounts of the past became part of the struggle for power in Australia. In an age of doubt about everything, even the past lost its authority* (Manning Clark 1987: 499).

If recent research in the forests of southern Tasmania challenges archaeologists to make sense of social systems which may well have been extinct for 10,000 years, and for which the archaeological evidence is enigmatic, the Tasmanian Aboriginal people face a different version of the same challenge. Where a growing number of archaeologists are persuaded by the likelihood of discontinuity and of there having been transformations in most areas of Tasmanian society over the course of 37,000 years, Aboriginal people see continuity and survival, which have a special significance for them, given the horrors of their colonial experience and the denial of their existence as Aboriginal people until the Franklin Dam decision of 1983 (see Schrire 1985). How are Aboriginal people to respond to a growing feeling among archaeologists, historians of Aboriginal Australia and anthropologists that Aboriginality needs to be historicized, and that for too long the diversity of prehistoric Australia has been masked by the teleology which necessitates that the goal of archaeology is to account for contact societies?

One strategy is to play the archaeologist's old game and to produce histories for Tasmania, which link deep past and the contact period into a kind of seamless web. While the evidence for these histories is slight (and deeply problematic), it is worth noting that many professional accounts of Tasmanian archaeology during the 1970s and 1980s have much in common with them. Perhaps the most interesting of these Aboriginal prehistories, that of the Lairmarenga people (Tasmanian Aboriginal Centre Inc. 1991), was written to give meaning to the Aboriginal heritage of the King River Valley in southern Tasmania, which was threatened by that great friend of archaeology, the Tasmanian Hydro-Electric Commission (HEC).

The last time the HEC was involved in a major difference of opinion about archaeological resources was in the celebrated Gordon-below-Franklin Rivers dispute which they waged between 1980 and 1983 against a loose alliance of conservation groups, Tasmanian Aboriginal people and archaeologists. The outcome was a victory for the forces of conservation, and a defeat for the Federal Liberal government in the general election of 1983. At that time there was much discussion of the similarities between the karst sites of southern Tasmania and the classic Upper Palaeolithic period sites of France and Spain (e.g. Hemisphere 1981; Kiernan *et al.*1983; Jones 1984: 56); indeed this was seen as a clear indication of the significance of the sites under threat and, by extension, an argument against inundation.

Schrire (1985) and Ryan (1985), among others (J. Allen 1983), have noted that the Gordon-below-Franklin Rivers dispute recast the relationships between Aboriginal people and archaeologists in Tasmania, a process that continues. It is also evident from the Aboriginal campaign to save the heritage of the King River that other, local, bases for the significance of archaeological sites can be now be established and defended. Not once in the Tasmanian Aboriginal Centre Inc.'s *The King River and the Lairmarenga: what Tasmania stands to lose* (1991) is there a mention of the Dordogne, of ice-age cultures of the northern hemisphere, of analogues between glacial refugia or even of the Mousterians (for a sharp contrast see Jones 1990). What we have instead is a story of Aboriginal life based on a pastiche of contact ethnography – none specifically from this area, and largely drawn from George Augustus Robinson's statements, explorer's notebooks and some fascinating and enigmatic preliminary data drawn from the reports of an archaeological consultant.

While there may be doubts about extrapolating very poor contact ethnographies back 37,000 years, there is no doubting that such stories do two important things. First, they clearly establish an Aboriginal interest in

Aboriginal heritage. Secondly, they emphasize that archaeologists are not the only ones who can make meanings about the prehistoric past. Yet accounts of this kind, which privilege the present, effectively trade continuity and easily accessible meanings for flexibility and dynamism. The fact that many archaeologists still cling to notions of continuity so that they might be able to provide conventional meanings for human action in the deep past, and thus establish one kind of relevance for prehistoric archaeology to the Australian community, indicates that the processes of construction and normalization are still going full swing for both archaeologists and Aboriginal people.

Another strategy is to recognize that while historicizing Aboriginal Australia might make Aboriginality a less stable category, it most certainly argues that prehistoric Aboriginal societies were dynamic and flexible and well and truly capable of change. In an important sense this restores a sense of balance to Aboriginal history, where, since the 1980s, historians have been piling up evidence for an active Aboriginal response to the experience of dispossession, and an equally active interaction with white communities on the Australian frontier (see especially Reynolds 1982, 1990). It also acts as a counterweight to the kind of judgements made by observers like Baldwin Spencer about the potential for Aboriginal people to change, and to take control of their lives. A dynamic Aboriginal history, which does not depend on the spurious progressivism of intensification to establish the reality of change and variation in Aboriginal society, may well provide the answer to Elkin's (1938: 20) dilemma about the fate of Aboriginal people which has been at the root of Aboriginal-white relations for much of this century:

*But on the whole, the question of their relative cultural position is pointless. They have evolved a working adaptation to their geographical and social environment, and in applying or even modifying their plan of economic, social and spiritual life, they show as much intelligence as does the average European with regard to the cultural adaptation of his own group. The problem is the extent to which the Aborigines are capable of working out a fresh adaptation to the changed conditions which have come upon them as a result of the settlement of their country by whites.*

It is tempting to conclude these reflections on the role of the Tasmanians as the eternal exemplar of 'brute savagery', and of the need to build an archaeology which might move us away from the need to have such simulacra, with an attack on the power of ethnographic analogy as a sanitizer of the archaeological imagination – somewhat akin to Beaudrillard's description of television in the media age (see Morris 1988: 163). However, the lesson of the Tasmanians in the 1990s is somewhat different from that taught by Lubbock, Tylor or Sollas (and their followers) since the mid nineteenth century.

We have seen that metropolitan anthropology and archaeology required the Tasmanians to be devoid of history, and their primitiveness was the cause of their deeply regretted, but equally inevitable, extirpation. We have also seen that Australian archaeologists have, until recent years, accepted notions of continuity and of linear progress over time as the best way to establish the meaning of the human history of the continent, rather than the much more difficult exploration of real change and variation occurring over the last 50,000 years. The needs of the metropolitan and of the colonialist have constructed an Australian archaeology which seems ill-placed to reshape the agenda of practice in Australia, by coming to grips with real variability in human behaviour during the Pleistocene period and the possibility that there are discontinuities in the prehistory of Aboriginal Australia. Furthermore, instead of recognizing variability and discontinuity as the basis of liberating insights into Aboriginal history and of Aboriginality generally, the traditions of archaeological research in Australia have trapped both archaeologists and Aboriginal people in the narrow confines of metropolitan research agendas played out in ethnographic simulacra of more complex and more variable archaeological pasts.

The lesson of the Tasmanians (and of the power of the archaeological record to transform archaeological research agendas) goes even further than this in that they give us the basis of a way forward. The difficulties faced by Australian archaeologists and by Aboriginal people in comprehending discontinuity and the idea that archaeological records are ontologically singular records of human action (see e.g. Murray 1987: chapter 7; Murray 1997; Murray and Walker 1988) are a microcosm of the situation, which obtains at the scale of world prehistory. In principle at least, it seems likely that reflections about the ways in which normalization has constructed the Tasmanians might do more than simply help us gain greater control over spurious cross-cultural generalizations. Indeed, they might well allow us the chance to denaturalize our approaches, and through this to reshape the agenda of the metropolitan in the last decade of this century, an overhaul which is long overdue.

I have based much of this discussion on Stanner's angry, but incisive, analysis of the history of anthropological research in Australia – a history written to justify the establishment of the Australian Institute of Aboriginal Studies in 1964 (see also Mulvaney 1986). In view of the arguments about the power of construction and normalization (and of cognitive plausibility) versus the power of the empirical and of the anomalous consequences of empirical research which have been presented here (see also Murray 1992), Stanner's belief in reasoned argument and clear links between the empirical and the theoretical still has much to commend it as a basis for defending all of us from the tyranny of hypothesis and the simple-minded rhetoric of empiricism (1963: xv):

> *If the full record of our empirical knowledge of the Aborigines could only be made available it might force a radical revision of many of the fundamental teachings about man and society.*

## Acknowledgements

I thank Jim Allen and Richard Cosgrove for much inspiration drawn from hard argument and from Allen (1989), Cosgrove (1991) and Cosgrove, Allen and Marshall (1990). However, they should not be held responsible for the result.

## References

ALLEN, H. 1979. Left out in the cold: why the Tasmanians stopped eating fish. *Artefact* 4: 1- 10.

ALLEN, J. 1983. Aborigines and archaeology in Tasmania. *Australian Archaeology* 16: 7-10.

—1989. When did humans first colonize Australia? *Search* 20: 149-54.

ALLEN, J., COSGROVE, R. and S. BROWN. 1988. New archaeological data from the Southern Forests region, Tasmania. *Australian Archaeology* 27: 75-88.

BAILEY, G.N. 1983. Concepts of time in Quaternary prehistory. *Annual Reviews in Anthropology* 12: 165-92.

BERRY, W.B.N. 1968. *Growth of a Prehistoric Timescale Based on Organic Evolution*. San Francisco Ca: Freeman.

BINFORD, L.R. 1981. Behavioral archaeology and the 'Pompeii premise'. *Journal of Anthropological Research* 37: 195- 208.

BIRDSELL, J. 1957. Some population problems involving Pleistocene man. *Cold Spring Harbour Symposium on Quantitative Biology* 22: 47-68.

BOWDLER, S. 1979. Hunter Hill, Hunter Island. Unpublished PhD. Australian National University, Canberra.

—1980. Fish and culture: a Tasmanian polemic. *Mankind* 12: 334-40.

BROCA, P. 1864. *On the Phenomena of Hybridity in the Genus Homo*. C. Carter Blake (ed). London: Kegan Paul, Trench, Trubner for the Anthropological Society of London.

CLARK, M. 1962. *A History of Australia 1: From Earliest Times to the Age of Macquarie*. Melbourne: Melbourne University Press.

—1987. *A History of Australia 6: 1916-1935. The old dead tree and the young tree green*. Melbourne: Melbourne University Press.

COSGROVE, R. 1989. Thirty thousand years of human colonization in Tasmania: new Pleistocene dates. *Science* 243: 1703-5.

—1991. The illusion of riches: issues of scale, resolution and explanation of Pleistocene human behaviour. Unpublished PhD. Department of Archaeology, La Trobe University.

COSGROVE, R., ALLEN, J. and B. MARSHALL 1990. Palaeoecology and Pleistocene human occupation in south central Tasmania. *Antiquity* 64: 59-78.

DAVID, T.W.E. 1923. Geological evidence for the antiquity of man in the Commonwealth with special reference to the Tasmanian Aborigines. *Papers and Proceedings of the Royal Society of Tasmania*: 109-50.

EDDY, J. and D. SCHREUDER. 1988. *The Rise of Colonial Nationalism*. Sydney: Allen & Unwin.

ELKIN, A. 1938. *The Australian Aborigines: how to understand them*. Sydney: Angus & Robertson.

ETHERIDGE, R. 1890. Has Man a geological history in Australia? *Proceedings of the Linnean Society of New South Wales* 15: 259-66.

GRAYSON, D. 1983. *The Establishment of Human Antiquity*. New York (NY): Academic Press.

HARRIS, M. 1968. *The Rise of Anthropological Theory*. New York (NY): Crowell.

Hemisphere. 1981. The extreme climatic place: interview with Rhys Jones. *Hemisphere* 26: 50-55.

HORTON, D. 1979. Tasmanian adaptation. *Mankind* 12: 28-34.

HOWITT, A.W. 1898. On the origin of the Aborigines of Tasmania and Australia. *Australasian Association for the Advancement of Science* 7: 723-59.

JONES, R. 1971. Rocky Cape and the problem of the Tasmanians. Unpublished PhD. University of Sydney.

—1977a. The Tasmanian paradox. In R.V.S. Wright (ed) *Stone Tools as Cultural Markers: Change, Evolution and Complexity*, pp.189-204. Canberra: Australian Institute of Aboriginal Studies.

—1977b. Man as an element of a continental fauna: the case of the sundering of the Bassian Bridge. In J. Allen, J. Golson and R. Jones (eds) *Sunda and Sahul: Prehistoric Studies in Southeast Asia, Melanesia and Australia,* pp. 317-86 Canberra: Australian National University.

—1978. Why did the Tasmanians stop eating fish? In R. Gould (ed) *Explorations in Ethnoarchaeology*, pp. 11-48. Albuquerque: University of New Mexico Press.

—1984. Hunters and history: a case study from Western Tasmania. In C. Schrire (ed) *Past and Present in Hunter Gatherer Studies*, pp. 27- 65. London: Academic Press.

—1990. From Kakadu to Kutikina: the southern continent at 18,000 years ago. In O. Soffer and C. Gamble (eds) *The World at 18,000 BP 2: Low Latitudes*, pp. 264-95. London: Unwin Hyman.

KIERNAN, K., JONES, R. and D. RANSON 1983. New evidence from Fraser Cave for glacial age man in Southwest Tasmania. *Nature* 301: 28-32.

KLAATSCH, H. 1908. *The Skull of the Australian Aboriginal*. Sydney: New South Wales Lunacy Department, Pathological Laboratory Reports 1 (3).

KUPER, A. 1988. *The Invention of Primitive Society: Transformations of an Illusion*. London: Routledge.

LABILLIARDIERE, M. 1800. *Voyage in Search of La Perouse 1791-1794*. London.

LOURANDOS, H. 1977. Aboriginal spatial organization and population: southwestern Victoria reconsidered. *Archaeology and Physical Anthropology in Oceania* 12: 202-25.

LUBBOCK, J. 1865. *Prehistoric Times*. London: Williams & Norgate.

—1882. *The Origin of Civilization and the Primitive Condition of Man*. 4th edn. London: Longmans Green.

McCARTHY, F. 1958. Culture succession in southeastern Australia. *Mankind* 5: 177-90.

MACLEOD, R. 1988a. *The Commonwealth of Science*. Melbourne: Oxford University Press.

—1988b. From Imperial to National Science. In R. MacLeod (ed) *The Commonwealth of Science*, pp. 40-72. Melbourne: Oxford University Press.

MORGAN, L.H. 1877. *Ancient Society.* New York.

MORRIS, M. 1988. Panorama: the live, the dead and the living. In P. Foss (ed) *Island in the Stream: Myths of Place in Australian Culture*, pp. 160-87. Sydney: Pluto Press.

MULVANEY, D.J. 1958. The Australian Aborigines 1606-1929: Opinion and Fieldwork, Parts I and II. *Historical Studies Australia and New Zealand* 8:131-51 & 297-314.

—1981. Gum leaves on the Golden Bough: Australia's Palaeolithic survivals discovered. In J.D. Evans and C. Renfrew (eds) *Antiquity and Man*, pp. 52-64. London: Thames & Hudson.

—1985. The Darwinian perspective. In I. Donaldson and T. Donaldson (eds) *Seeing the First Australians*, pp. 68-75. Sydney: Allen & Unwin.

—1986. 'A sense of making history ': Australian Aboriginal Studies, 1961-1986. *Australian Aboriginal Studies* 2: 48-56.

—1988. Australasian anthropology and ANZAAS. 'Strictly scientific and critical'. In R. MacLeod (ed) pp. 196-221. *The Commonwealth of Science*. Melbourne: Oxford University Press.

MURRAY, T. 1987. Remembrances of Things Present: appeals to authority in the history and philosophy of archaeology. Unpublished PhD. University of Sydney.

—1997. Dynamic modelling and new social theory of the mid-to-long term. In S. Van Der Leeuw and J. McGlade (eds) *Time, Process, and Structured Transformation*. London: Routledge.

—1992. Aboriginal (pre)history and Australian archaeology: the discourse of Australian prehistoric archaeology. In B. Attwood and J. Arnold (eds) *Power, Knowledge, and the Aborigines*. Melbourne: La Trobe University Press. Special Issue of the Journal of Australian Studies.

MURRAY, T. and M. J. WALKER. 1988. 'Like WHAT?' A practical question of analogical inference and archaeological meaningfulness. *Journal of Anthropological Archaeology* 7: 248-87.

NILSSON, S. 1868. *The Primitive Inhabitants of Scandinavia*. Longmans: London.

OLDFIELD, A. 1865. On the Aborigines of Australia. *Transactions of the Ethnological Society of London* 3: 215- 99.

PERON, M.F. 1809. *A Voyage of Discovery to the Southern Hemisphere*. London.

PETERSON, N. 1990. 'Studying man and man's nature': the history of the institutionalisation of Aboriginal anthropology. *Australian Aboriginal Studies* 1990 (2): 3- 19.

PULLEINE, R. 1928. The Tasmanians and their stone culture. *Australian Association for the Advancement of Science* 19: 294- 314.

REYNOLDS, H. 1982. *The Other Side of the Frontier*. Ringwood: Penguin.

—1990. *With the White People*. Ringwood: Penguin.

ROTH, H. LING. 1899. *The Aborigines of Tasmania*. Halifax.

RYAN, L. 1981. *The Aboriginal Tasmanians*. St Lucia, Qld: University of Queensland Press.

—1985. Extinction theorists and Tasmanian Aborigines. In C. Schrire and R. Gordon (eds) *The Future of Former Foragers in Australia and Southern Africa*, pp. 47-54. Cambridge, MA: Cultural Survival Inc.

SCHRIRE, C. 1985. Aborigines and environmental politics. In C. Schrire and R. Gordon (eds) *The Future of Former Foragers in Australia and Southern Africa*, pp. 83-92. Cambridge, MA: Cultural Survival Inc.

SCHRIRE, C. and R. GORDON (eds) 1985. *The Future of Former Foragers in Australia and Southern Africa*. Cambridge, MA: Cultural Survival Inc.

SMITH, B. 1960. *European Vision and the South Pacific 1768-1850*. Oxford: Clarendon Press.

SOLLAS, W.J. 1911. *Ancient Hunters and Their Modern Representatives*. London: Macmillan.

SPENCER, F. 1990. *Piltdown: a Scientific Forgery*. Oxford: Oxford University Press.

STANNER, W.E.H. 1963. Introduction. In W.E.H. Stanner and H. Shiels (eds) *Australian Aboriginal Studies*: xii-xviii. Melbourne: Oxford University Press.

TASMANIAN ABORIGINAL CENTRE INC. 1991. *The King River and the Lairmarenga: What Tasmania Stands to Lose*. Hobart: TAC Inc.

TINDALE, N. 1957. Culture succession in South Eastern Australia from Late Pleistocene to the Present. *Records of the Australian Museum* 13: 1-49.

TYLOR, E. B. 1865. *Researches Into the Early History of Man*. London: John Murray.

—1870. *Primitive Culture*. London: John Murray.

—1893. On the Tasmanians as representatives of Palaeolithic man. *Journal of the Royal Anthropological Institute* 23: 141-52.

—1894. On the occurrence of ground stone implements of Australian type in Tasmania. *Journal of the Royal Anthropological Institute* 24: 335-40.

—1898. On the survival of Palaeolithic conditions in Australia and Tasmania. *Journal of the Royal Anthropological Institute* 28: 199.

—1900. On the Stone Age in Tasmania, as related to the history of civilization. *Journal of the Royal Anthropological Institute* 30: 33-4.

VAN DER WAL, R. 1978. Adaptive technology in southwest Tasmania. *Australian Archaeology* 8: 107-26.

VOGT, K. 1864. *Lectures on Man*. J. Hunt (ed). London: Kegan Paul, Trench, Trubner for the Anthropological Society of London.

WHITE, J.P. and J.F. O'CONNELL. 1982. *A Prehistory of Australia, New Guinea and Sahul*. Sydney: Academic Press.

WILSON, D. 1862. *Prehistoric Man*. London: Macmillan.

## Chapter 4

# Archaeology, ideology and the threat of the past: Sir Henry Rider Haggard and the acquisition of time

### Introduction

*The human race can no more be expected to testify to its own origins than a child can be tendered as witness to its own birth* (Huxley 1893: 73).

During the nineteenth century perceptions of time (and space) in Western societies changed dramatically. Some of the forces for change, particularly those associated with industrialization, and complex processes of production (see e.g. Thompson 1967), as well as with transportation and communication technologies, regularized time and squeezed space. The telephone, the wireless telegraph, the bicycle, the motorcar, and the steam ship all helped to foster an environment where material progress seemed unstoppable and human nature infinitely perfectible (see e.g. Kern 1983; Pick 1989). Time became standardized and global. Although uniform time (that derived from clocks) had existed prior to the nineteenth century, global time was the net result of the industrial and communications revolutions, as railways spanned whole continents, and ships sailed the oceans of the world at 'breakneck' speed. Thus the measurement of time had to cope with changing contexts of temporality itself.

Other forces for change, especially those deriving from geology, palaeontology, biology, archaeology, and from physics, also profoundly disturbed traditional contexts of temporality. During the course of the nineteenth century scientists began to debate the age of the earth (and the extent of human antiquity) in units of time, which had, hitherto literally, been unimaginable, and for many practitioners they remained that way (see e .g. Phillips 1960). In an important sense nineteenth-century society encountered an abyss of *terrestrial* time, a precursor of the abyss of *cosmological* time, which began to take shape after the publication of Einstein's special theory of relativity early in the next century. Given this focus on terrestrial time, the social and cultural significance of such discussions was enhanced by the fact that they were closely linked to an understanding of both natural and human history, of the origins of life on earth and of its subsequent career. In this sense during the late nineteenth century physics and geology, but especially biology and archaeology, essentially recreated the context within which ageless debates about human nature and human morality would take place (see e.g. Bagehot 1881; Burrow 1966; Dean 1985; Huxley 1894; Paradis and Postlewait 1985).

The significance of these changes was widely understood by those living through them, and stimulated one of the great passions of Victorian society – a contemplation of the antinomies between progress and degeneration, of perfectibility and original sin, of the particulars of history and the great generalizations about the course of human history. Yet these antinomies reflected a more encompassing uncertainty which stemmed from the sheer scale of terrestrial history, and the yawning gulf which seemed to separate a richly-textured *knowable* present and a shady, insubstantial and potentially *unintelligible* prehistoric past. The origins of humanity, because they were not recorded in texts, and because so much of human history was now claimed to be the product of random forces of mutation and selection, seemed unrecoverable (see also Beer 1989: 14). Consequently, the drive for knowledge of self seemed stalled by entropy and by the *structural properties* of the data of human prehistory.

This widespread obsession with comprehending origins and succession found expression in the pre-eminently popular Victorian disciplines of history (see e.g. Bann 1984; Burrow 1983; White 1973), archaeology, anthropology, biology, and geology. It also had a profound impact on literature, particularly through changing conceptions of the structure of narrative, and of the relationship between nature and culture in fostering a credible treatment of their motivation of characters within a narrative. Gillian Beer has cogently argued for 'connections between the ordinary act of ceasing to remember and deep anxieties about the extent of oblivion, the remoteness and unreclaimableness of origins, in Victorian creativity' (1989: 12).

Given that both the novelist and the prehistorian needed to tell a story of origins and outcomes which linked 'events' and motivations in a meaningful way, intuitively it seems proper that the form and content of fictional narratives of human prehistory (which might be found in the late nineteenth-century 'science fictions' of Jules Verne and Rider Haggard) should resemble those found in scientific prehistories produced during the same period. What is perhaps of greater interest is the extent to which prehistorians were themselves influenced by the constructions of the novelists (see also Evans 1989). This influence was expressed in two ways. First, through the structure of narrative itself. Here the large novels and complex plots, favoured by artists such as Dickens and Trollope, allowed the novelist to situate characters in more complex contemporary and historical contexts.

Second, a cultural context was created in which meanings were given (by novelists and poets as well as by prehistorians) to a potentially unintelligible past. These meanings became popular, almost natural, knowledge and gave expression to cultural presuppositions, which were rarely, if ever, subjected to explicit scrutiny. This recursive relationship, where the plausibility of knowledge claims made by prehistorians was enhanced by their appeal to culturally acceptable knowledge, was further enhanced because both the artist and the scientist were deeply involved in both the production of that knowledge, and in the management of its consumption. There are many significant implications flowing from the symbiotic relationship, not the least of which is the fact that there are grounds for a claim that the relationships between science and 'science fiction' were (and are) very much more complex and ambiguous than a simple linear relationship of influence and exemplification.

## Goal and rationale

This paper examines what can happen when first practitioners, and subsequently members of the general public, have to find a way of comprehending information about the human past, which has the potential to throw normative structures into disarray. Although it is intrinsically interesting to explore the social and cultural ramifications of archaeological knowledge during the nineteenth century, and such explorations are clearly vital if we are to comprehend the contexts of archaeological practice during that time, there is an additional justification for this return to the issue of high human antiquity (see e.g. Murray 1987 (especially chapter 4); 1992; 1993).

I have previously observed that during the nineteenth century the theoretical challenge posed by 'deep time' was avoided because prehistorians (and others) found a plausible way of humanizing prehistory in the same terms as the historical past and the ethnographic present. In the following section I will briefly restate this argument and conclude that intelligibility was retained by literally *creating* a prehistoric past which was broken up into a series of ethnographic presents, linked vertically by small-scale processes such as diffusion and migration to explain demonstrable change. Two important questions are raised by this highly successful act of creation.

First, how did prehistoric archaeology move from the possibility of oblivion and unintelligibility towards the status of a pre-eminently popular science? I have also previously observed that during this time practitioners accomplished the trick of systematically violating their own methodological principles (they said they were following the truth path of inductivism when there was a very large measure of the *a priori* in their statements) without any loss of scientific credibility (Murray 1989). It seems obvious enough that the cultural plausibility of the statements being made by prehistorians, as well as the fact that oblivion could never be allowed to suffice for history in the age of progress, were vital elements of the process, which led to the successful foundation of a science of prehistoric archaeology during the late nineteenth century. My reading of Haggard sustains this view by outlining an example of how science and art supported each other in combating the threat of the past.

The second question arising from this successful defusing of the threat of unintelligibility is whether twentieth-century archaeology would have handled the problem any better. Although millions of years have since been added to the evolutionary history of human beings, and a very great deal more is now known about the high levels of variability detectable even in the 'low intensity' societies of the Palaeolithic, the prospect of oblivion, of unintelligibility, has rarely been raised since the 1860s. While there has been much argument about the form of interpretation, and about what one should do with ambiguity and polyvocality, the idea that the prehistoric past poses a threat to the universality of the structures through which we interpret contemporary experience (social theory as well as the very identity of 'human behaviour') has received very little support (but see e.g. Dunnell 1982). Even a somewhat softer argument, such as the claim that contemporary social theory should be better grounded in archaeological phenomena, and that the act of grounding will lead to a change in the precepts of that theory, fares badly beside the appeal of the circularity of material culture 'theory', or the notion that our problems will be solved by finer scales of resolution.

Perhaps more important, with the possible exception of the 'Pompeii premise' debate which was brought to a premature close in the late 1980s, there has been little overt discussion of the implications of radiometric chronologies or of the perception of the archaeological record as a distinctive order of reality (established as much by the units of time which characterize its phenomena, as by an understanding of palimpsest and site formation processes). I have also previously remarked that all of these developments have created a crisis of intelligibility no less serious than that posed by the original acceptance of a high human antiquity nearly 130 years ago (Murray 1992; 1993).

Yet this crisis of interpretation hardly exists for the proponents (and adherents) of either processual or postprocessual archaeology, where debates rage about agency and structure, about text or present practice, about the political implications of 'heritage', or indeed about the need to widen the frame of interpretation still further to include the legitimate interests of the oppressed. In this sense the crisis of intelligibility is a conflict between different images of the prehistoric past and our need to find a process through which we might work to come to defensible choices between such images. This context forms the background to the second general observation of this paper which is that the cultural traditions of prehistoric archaeology (formed out of the resolution of the first threat of oblivion) have remained essentially unaltered after 130 years.

## The problem for the prehistorian: humanizing the past

It is often stated in histories of archaeology that the discovery of high human antiquity was fundamentally important for the recognition of prehistoric archaeology as a science. A year or so around 1860 is considered to be the date when prehistoric archaeology gave long time depth to the human sciences. Uniformitarian geology had passed its greatest test because in this instance it directly impinged on human self-perception. But how much time were we dealing with? What kinds of people made the stone implements recovered from the Somme, Brixham, and Gray's Inn Road? Thus finding high antiquity was one thing: quantifying it and finding a way of understanding the human behaviour involved was quite another.

One major problem was the fact that the ancient stones did not co-occur with the bones of fossil humans. Indeed, for the rest of the nineteenth century (certainly until the widespread acceptance of *Homo Erectus),* getting the archaeology onto a biological timescale was an act of faith rather than anything more concrete. Added to this was the fact that Lord Kelvin's application of his second law of thermodynamics to geology allowed the absolute quantification of geological time – the only problem was that at 100 million years it seemed way too short to allow for a gradualist reading of evolution, particularly that of human beings.

Another problem was the prospect of an unintelligible human past. George Stocking (1968: 105-106) put the situation clearly:

> *Tylor's central anthropological problem, in simplest terms, was to fill the gap between Brixham Cave and European Civilization without introducing the hand of God – that is to show that human culture was, or might have been, the result of natural evolutionary development.*

There is more to it than this, because the gap had to be explained (and exemplified) in human terms. Social evolutionary theory had explanatory power because of the notion of ethnographically known primitive societies functioning as fossil survivals. It was therefore imperative that the gap be filled with ethnographic analogy, an eternal ethnographic present. Timescale therefore lost its punch, and its ability to threaten the theoretical hegemony of the concepts and categories used to interpret the prehistoric past as well as the present was lost. These concepts and categories were to remain safe and resilient, because it was literally inconceivable that the past could be understood in any other way.

Obviously this generalized kind of evolutionary framework suffered constant subdivision in the course of the nineteenth century. The high degree of what was thought to be contemporaneous variation also found reference in the present. This was the notional link between race, language and culture. Differing rates of change and variation were explained by notions such as diffusion and migration, the effects of environmental context, and the psychologies of the presumed ethnic groups involved.

These progressively smaller subdivisions required a kind of interpretation that accorded with anthropological theory and present political experience. What happened though was that what had been a vast timescale was squeezed into a smaller ethnographic scale. While part of the explanation for this lies in the unquantified nature of time, all time being relative, the other part lies in the domain of what was culturally possible for the Victorians. The prospect of there being human behaviour without modern referents raised the possibility of an unintelligible past rather than a past that required a different kind of social theory to explain it. As it turned out we had to wait for the advent of radiometric dating in the second half of the twentieth century to get a quantifiable picture of elapsed time. By that stage, the interpretative theories of the discipline were already locked into place, and they had proved incredibly difficult to shift.

## A literary response: Sir Henry Rider Haggard

Rider Haggard, perhaps because his work has not been included in the canon of established nineteenth-century fiction, has not been well served by his biographers. Wendy Katz's *Rider Haggard and the Fiction of Empire. A Critical Study of British Imperial Fiction* (1987) sees the major novels as propaganda, consciously crafted to shape the ideology of what Jan Morris once called the *Pax Britannica* of the late nineteenth century. Haggard, for Katz, was a racist (his special targets being Blacks and Jews), a crypto-fascist, and a sexist.

This focus on the ideology of imperialism is not shared by D. S. Higgins (1981) in *Rider Haggard: The Great Storyteller.* Higgins certainly sees the context of imperialism (it would be difficult to miss it), but seeks to locate Haggard's motivation in his messy personal life. Haggard had a horrendous father, he was thought to be stupid, his great love married someone else and he nursed her during the final stages of tertiary syphilis, he lost his only son, he was broke most of the time, and unsurprisingly, he felt himself to be grossly undervalued by his class. Higgins thus sees Haggard's fatalism and his emphasis on duty and the spiritual as being the result of repression, both sexual and social. Haggard kept a poem written for him by his mother on the occasion of his first trip to Africa on imperial service in 1875:

*That life is granted, not in Pleasure's round,*
*Or even Love's sweet dream, to lapse content: Duty*
*and Faith are words of solemn sound,*
*And to their echoes must thy soul be bent.*

While there might be some dispute about the nature of Haggard's muse, there is absolutely no doubting his popularity. He achieved prominence as an author in 1885 with the publication of *King Solomon's Mines*. His fame only grew when *She* appeared two years later in the same year as *Alan Quartermain*. By the time *Queen Sheba's Ring* was published in 1910 Haggard had settled into formula romance writing, notching up an incredible forty-two novels in this genre by 1925, the year of his death. Add to these were ten books on politics, agriculture, social reform, and the joys of gardening. Haggard wrote the novels for money, and the non-fiction material out of a sense of duty to the Salvation Army, the Royal Colonial Institute, and the British Government.

This very brief discussion of Haggard focuses only on his two greatest romances *She* and *Alan Quartermain* because they encapsulate much of Haggard's technique and preoccupation: death, time, archaeology, ethnology, human nature and the transience of civilizations. Only in a fraction of his romances, in my view his greatest ones, did Haggard choose settings either in the archaeological past, or in modern survivals of societies, which he thought had changed little for thousands of years. Others had more historical themes, such as *Montezuma's Daughter,* and *Eric Brighteyes,* his Icelandic Viking saga, or concentrated on particular geographic areas or modern tribes such as the Zulu. However, in all of these the welding of the past with the present, the appeal to moral and ethical universals, and the overwhelming power of Nature and Fate are aspects of his concern to destroy time by understanding the meaning behind its pattern and process.

Haggard was lionized by the literary establishment of his day not for the overtones of Empire and English manliness, but for his philosophical concerns and writing skills. R. L. Stevenson, Lang, Gosse, Kipling, William Morris, even D. H. Lawrence conceded that Haggard strove for a kind of moral understanding of the human condition that transcended fictional context. Wendy Katz might argue that at least Stevenson, Kipling and Lang were equally drawn by the need to propagandize the Empire, but this surely cannot apply to Gosse or Lawrence. There is more to him than his simply being a hack imperialist, just as there was to Stevenson and Kipling, but it is difficult to find amongst all the imperialist puff.

Haggard's Victorian sensitivity was counterbalanced by imperial pragmatism. At the core of his sensitivity was a strong belief in two things. First, the British Empire was doomed to fall, and second, its demise would be hastened by a diminution of its finest qualities at the hands of people from trade. The hard bit for Haggard was to persuade the rest of British society that although the Empire was doomed, it was their sacred duty to hold the lantern of civilization aloft, before passing it to the Americans. Imperialism, racism, ethnology and archaeology, when welded in a well-told yarn, could be a potent instrument of persuasion.

Haggard's romances were pure science fiction or science fantasy. My interest in Haggard stems from these science backgrounds for his fiction, and the way in which they were linked together to give credibility to the plot, to humanize a past that had suddenly become immensely deep and a present that was more varied than first thought, and above all, to increase the credibility of Rider's themes of Fate, Spirit, and Racial Destiny. Haggard, like the great archaeologists of the nineteenth century, assumed the strength of a relationship between the human, earth and life sciences that would explain the past and give it popular meaning and value. The course they charted, with its mix of culture histories warring with behavioural universals, still holds our attention today. In this way the past acquired a meaning that was cautionary and instructive, but not threatening. The singularity of archaeological phenomena was denied, because of their obvious importance to the defence of social and ideological values held in the present. Without the presence of these values, either (or both) the past or the present would become unintelligible. What would happen to the lessons of history that were so great a part in the imperial propaganda?

Haggard was vitally concerned with the ambiguity of the human place and purpose in a universe characterized by chance and change. Deeply influenced by evolutionism, archaeology and ethnology, but holding contradictory notions of the nature of time, Haggard used the span of history to critique his own society. Ideas of transience and decay were common during this period, their most beautiful expressions being Alfred Lord Tennyson's 'Locksley Hall Sixty Years After' and Matthew Arnold's 'Dover Beach', but they are also clearly there in Edward Bulwer Lytton's *A Coming Race* (1871), and in Samuel Butler's *Erewhon* (1872). None the less, it was Haggard who attempted to move beyond the subjective experience and produce proofs of these notions based on archaeological and ethnological evidence.

Haggard found no difficulty humanizing the immensity of time with characters and tribes drawn from another great Victorian discovery – the wide variety of cultures and societies. In this sense Haggard was the ultimate functionalist/evolutionist, because these ethnographically known peoples were pressed into fictional service literally to become the living fossils that Tylor, Lubbock, Pitt-Rivers and Sollas talked about. There was no question about the propriety of doing this; Victorian science justified it (see e.g. Stocking 1987). However, despite all this he was also a committed cultural relativist. He felt it important that the temporal insignificance of England could be best grasped through an understanding of different cultures. These were functioning societies with their own cultural logic, different but not inferior. England was not the sole repository of human virtue. For example in *Child of Storm* Alan Quartermain is made to say:

> *We white people think we know everything; for instance, we think we understand human nature. And we do, as human nature appears to us, with all its trappings and its accessories seen dimly through the glass of our own conventions, leaving out those aspects of it which we have forgotten or do not think to mention* (1913: first paragraph of the book).

Haggard was full of inconsistencies. On some occasions he defended the notion of the noble savage, comparing the forthright non-materialist ideology of Zulu society to the greed and conformity of his own. On other occasions he saw value in the present too, especially in science and Christianity as the great civilizing virtues which were joined by 'natural virtues', those of friendship, courage, loyalty and fair dealing, to underwrite the rise of all great civilizations. The dilution of these virtues (inevitable over the passage of time) was thought by Haggard to be the ultimate cause of collapse. In Haggard's view England was great because it had its best and brightest living outside, unable to stomach the moral lassitude and greed that he felt was on the rise at home. These were the English engaged in imperial service. None the less the seeds of collapse had been sown and the process of decline had already begun in England. Time in this reading of Haggard is morally cyclical. Antique civilizations thus formed more than a backdrop to his romances; they were a moral and ideological context to use for the enlightenment of Englishmen. Two quotes from *She,* when Ayesha is addressing Holly in the Tombs of Kor will make the point:

> *'Thou seest, 0 Holly', she said, 'this people founded the city, of which the ruins yet cumber the plain yonder, 4,000 years before this cave was finished. Yet when first mine eyes beheld it 2,000 years ago, it was even as it is now. Judge, therefore, how old must that city have been!*

*And now, follow thou me, and I will show thee after what fashion this*
*great people fell when the time came for it to fall ... ' (1887: 174-5).*
*I said 'it seems that the world is very old.' 'Old? Yes it is old indeed.*
*Time after time have nations, ay, rich and strong nations, learned in the*
*arts, been and passed away to be forgotten, so that no memory of them*
*remains. This is but one of several: for Time eat up the works of man...*
*Who knows what hath been on earth, or what shall be? There is no new*
*thing under the sun, as the wise Hebrew wrote long ago'(1887: 176).*

But time (both personal and cultural) was also linear. Death was the
inevitable end for both self and society. Haggard thus sought a purpose
behind time's arrow *and* time's cycle. The immensity of time therefore, had
moral overtones. It would be going too far to argue that the data of
archaeology and ethnology were the sole stimuli to his fascination with time,
transience, permanence and connectedness between past and present. There
were other forceful stimuli to that perception, some deriving from his own
history, and other stemming from less well-understood rhythms through
Victorian society. Yet it is still possible to claim that the discovery of immense
time depth (so great as to be unquantifiable) allowed Haggard the span of
time he needed for his 'natural selection of civilizations': a kind of cyclical
history.

In this sense Haggard's fictional exploration of the abyss of time, while
being understood as romantic fiction by the educated sectors of Victorian
society, also acted to defuse the threat of unintelligibility. Although Haggard
had to turn to 'She: Who Must be Obeyed' to sketch a reading of the deep
past, it was no less plausible than the fictions being written by Lubbock and
Tylor employing the comparative method more effectively than their
imaginations.

### Concluding remarks

Haggard's work represents one way in which the contours of a scientific
prehistoric archaeology were shaped by a recursive relationship between
Victorian society and culture on the one hand, and the empirical
archaeological phenomena on the other. The discovery of deep time, and of
the possibility that memory would be overcome by oblivion (see Beer
1989:12) provided a threat to scientist and artist alike, a threat which was
defused by effectively turning deep past (oblivion) into ethnographic present
(living representations of stages of European race memory). The prehistoric
past became human, and properly the subject of human understanding.

Yet the price of intelligibility and meaningfulness has been very high
indeed. By creating a structure where the retention of conventional meanings

was paramount, the implications of the ontological singularity of prehistoric archaeological records, as records of human action, have never been worked through. The data of prehistoric archaeology remain over-theorized and radically unstable. Although practitioners have properly lamented the 'abuses' of interpretation fostered by colonial powers, advocates of racial superiority or ethnic cleansing, and desperately sought a philosophy of practice which delivered conceptual and categorical stability as well as meaningfulness, the fact remains that the fear of unintelligibility (of oblivion) overcomes all (see e.g. Murray 1992).

An investigation into the cultural history of archaeology is only the first step on a difficult journey to free prehistoric archaeology from its own history, and to renegotiate its place on the cognitive map of the human sciences. Another step requires us to write the history of archaeological epistemology. This history clearly demonstrates that there is a clash between the overt methodology and scientific epistemology of archaeology (what is sometimes, erroneously, called the context of justification) and the covert structures, which establish the grounds of plausible belief (the context of discovery). Thus it is entirely possible that practitioners can, consciously or unconsciously, and even in the face of dramatically disconfirming data, retain frameworks of interpretation or explanation because they cannot think their way through to new frameworks, or because the impact of such changes on the cognitive map held by everyone else would be too great. In the old days historians, philosophers and sociologists of science would have used Thomas Kuhn's vocabulary of crisis, paradigm change, and gestalt shift to describe aspects of this phenomenon. But what we are dealing with here is somewhat different, where everything points to the need for change, but the cultural traditions of a science and the social and political context of its practice prevent this from happening.

Knowledge of these cultural predispositions should help archaeologists to combat such constraints on their imaginations. If we seek liberation through critical self-reflection, it seems unlikely that we are going to be able to switch it off when it goes too deep. But surely this is a positive option when compared with the probability that we reproduce false consciousness, of being trapped in superficially meaningful debates by the inertia of disciplinary tradition. Down this other path lies an archaeology based on profligacy, a view that we can dispense with a potentially different kind of understanding of human action, because the process of gearing up to develop it costs us too much in the way of our understanding of how the present is constituted. But our current interpretations of the archaeologist's project are not natural they are cultural. Armed with this perspective practitioners can reopen an inquiry into alternative prehistoric archaeologies which will alter the conventions of human science and dramatically expand our framework of self-perception. We should not throw away another chance to do this. In this sense it comes back to imagination, and I shall let Rider Haggard have the last word on that:

*Imagination is a power which comes from we know not where. Perhaps it is existent but ungrasped truth, a gap in the curtain of the unseen which sometimes presses so nearly upon us. Who knows its object? It is the hidden power of the spirit which connects the visible with the invisible: which hears the still small voice calling from the infinite...* (The Times, 26 November 1924).

## Acknowledgements
This paper was first presented at a seminar in the Department of Prehistory at the Research School of Pacific Studies, Australian National University in 1983. In 1992 I gave a revised version at a seminar in the Department of Archaeology, University of Cambridge. Subsequent discussions with Gillian Beer, Vanessa Smith and Anne Turner, all of the Department of English at the University of Cambridge, were very useful. Chris Evans of the Cambridge Archaeology Unit (who has also written on related matters), and Laurent Olivier also helped a great deal. The Wenner-Gren Foundation through a Richard Carley Hunt Fellowship, and La Trobe University, provided the financial and logistical support for 13 months in Cambridge during 1991-3. But most of all a belated big thank-you to Bob Dreher.

### References
BAGEHOT, W. 1881. *Physics and Politics, or Thoughts on the Application of the Principles of 'Natural Selection' and 'Inheritance' to Political Society.* 6th edn. London: Kegan Paul.
BANN, S. 1984. *The Clothing of Clio. A Study of the Representation of History in Nineteenth-century Britain and France.* Cambridge: Cambridge University Press.
BEER, G. 1989. *Arguing with the Past. Essays in Narrative from Woolf to Sidney.* London: Routledge.
BURROW, J. 1966. *Evolution and Society.* Cambridge: Cambridge University Press.
—1983. *A Liberal Descent.* Cambridge: Cambridge University Press.
BUTLER, S. 1970 [1872]. *Erewhon.* P. Mudford (ed). Harmondsworth: Penguin.
DEAN, D. R. 1985. 'Through science to despair': Geology and the Victorians. In G. Paradis and T. Postlewait (eds) *Victorian Science and Victorian Values: Literary Perspectives,* pp. 111-36. New Brunswick, NJ: Rutgers University Press.
DUNNELL, R. 1982. Science, social science, and common sense: the agonizing dilemma of modern archaeology. *Journal of Anthropological Research* 38: 1-25.
EVANS, C. 1989. Digging with the pen. Novel archaeologies and literary traditions. *Archaeological Review from Cambridge* 8 (2): 186-211.

HAGGARD, Sir Henry Rider 1891. *Eric Brighteyes.* London: Longmans, Green.

—1893. *Montezuma's Daughter.* London: Longmans, Green.

—1919 [1887]. *Alan Quatermain.* London: Hodder & Stoughton.

—1952 [1913]. *Child of Storm.* London: Macdonald.

—1955 [1887]. *She.* London: Collins.

—1964 [1910]. *Queen Sheba's Ring.* London: Macdonald.

HIGGINS, D. S. 1981. *Rider Haggard: The Great Storyteller.* London: Cassell.

HUXLEY, T. H. 1893. Lectures on Evolution. In *Science and the Hebrew Tradition.* London: MacMillan.

—1894. *Man's Place in Nature and Other Anthropological Essays.* London: Macmillan.

KATZ, W. 1987. *Rider Haggard and the Fiction of Empire: A Critical Study of British Imperial Fiction.* Cambridge: Cambridge University Press.

KERN, S. 1983. *The Culture of Space and Time, 1880-1918.* London: Weidenfeld & Nicolson.

LYTTON, E. B. 1967 [1871]. *The Coming Race.* Facsimile Reprint. Mokelumne Hill, CA: Health Research.

MURRAY, T. 1987. Remembrance of things present: Appeals to authority in the history and philosophy of archaeology. Unpublished PhD. Department of Anthropology, University of Sydney.

—1989. The history, philosophy and sociology of archaeology: the case of the *Ancient Monuments Protection Act* (1882). In V. Pinsky and A. Wylie (eds) *Critical Directions in Contemporary Archaeology,* pp. 55-67. Cambridge: Cambridge University Press.

—1992. The Tasmanians and the constitution of the 'Dawn of Humanity'. *Antiquity* 66: 730-43.

—1993. Dynamic modelling and new social theory of the mid-to-long term. In S. Van Der Leeuw and J. McGlade (eds) *Dynamic Modelling and the Study of Change in Archaeology.* Edinburgh: Edinburgh University Press.

PARADIS, J. G. and T. POSTLEWAIT (eds) 1985. *Victorian Science and Victorian Values: Literary Perspectives.* New Brunswick, NJ: Rutgers University Press.

Phillips, J. 1860. Address. *Quarterly Journal of the Geological Society* 16: xxx-lvi.

PICK, D. 1989. *Faces of Degeneration. A European Disorder, c.1848- c.1918.* Cambridge: Cambridge University Press.

STOCKING, G. W., Jr. 1968. *Race, Culture and Evolution.* New York: Free Press.

—1987. *Victorian Anthropology.* New York: Free Press.

THOMPSON, E. P. 1967. Time, work, discipline, and industrial capitalism. *Past and Present,* 38: 56-97.

WHITE, H. 1973. *Metahistory: The Historical Imagination in Nineteenth-Century Europe.* Baltimore, MD: Johns Hopkins University Press.

*Chapter 5*

# From Sydney to Sarajevo:
# a centenary reflection on archaeology
# and European identity

This paper touches on a number of highly contentious issues spanning much of the gamut of modern discourse about the production and consumption of archaeological knowledge. At one level it is a reflection on some of the consequences of the search for identity in the prehistoric archaeology of Europe. At another level, it is a small contribution to the literature arising from the need for archaeologists (and political scientists) to mark the centenary of the birth of Gordon Childe (see Gathercole *et al.* 1995; Murray 1995a).

Linking both discussions is the broader question of how European societies can defend themselves against archaeology, and vice versa. In this paper I will argue that the best defense for both is for there to be an intensification of debate about disciplinary ontology and epistemology which might be effectively described as foundational issues for archaeology, as well as for the development of a strong commitment to theory building and assessment. I will observe that although archaeologists have been actively discussing foundational issues under the guise of 'theoretical archaeology' for some three decades now, little headway has been made in developing archaeological theory (an exception being material culture theory). Agreement about the constitution of the disciplinary core of archaeology is also now further away than ever before. Over the same time archaeologists have begun to pay more attention to (and to take increasing responsibility for) the ways archaeological knowledge is used outside the discipline, a factor that has placed further strain on the links between theory and practice.

In recent years much attention has been paid to exploring the ways in which archaeological knowledge has been created within a complex social and cultural web. These analyses have been focused on particular passages of disciplinary history (e.g. Murray 1990), on shifting interpretations of particular sites or contexts (e.g. Baker 1993; Tomaskova 1995), on the politics of gender in archaeology (e.g. Gero and Conkey 1991), on the politics of doing archaeology among indigenous peoples (e.g. McGuire 1992; Murray 1993), and on the role of archaeology in serving the state (e.g. Arnold 1990;

Diaz-Andreu 1993; Dietler 1994; Fowler 1987; Gathercole and Lowenthal 1990). The general conclusion of such studies has been the same – that we need to more effectively understand that archaeologists (and the knowledge they produce) influences, and is influenced by, the societies in which they practice. This recognition sharpens the contrast between a field of study, which is responsive to the needs of its publics and its practitioners, and a discipline with strong traditions of materialist analysis.

Archaeologists are by no means the first to appreciate that people make science and history, and that they do so in complex and frequently paradoxical ways. Generations of history students have had this point driven home in historiography classes, and historians and sociologists of science have explored the rich fields of scientific endeavour, as have historians of anthropology (e.g. the references listed in Murray 1990; Stocking 1987). Even (or is it, especially?) literary criticism has broadened its understanding of cultural context to include a consideration of science (e.g. Beer 1989; Paradis and Postlethwait 1985; Said 1985). These long-standing discussions have explicitly confronted issues of subjectivism, and the powerful role of the present in 'constructing' our knowledge of the past by determining what it is meaningful and valuable for us to know. Granted that such discussions must, by their very nature, be inconclusive it is worth noting that discussions of these matters, particularly as they are expressed in national and ethnic mythologies, have taken on a special urgency over the last decade (e.g. Friedman 1992a, 1992b; Wolf 1994).

Discussions of the role of interpretation in post-processual archaeology have reflected this notion of a hegemony of present over past (through the agency of the theory dependence of observation), but they have tended to avoid a detailed consideration of the consequences of an 'over determination' of archaeological data by interpretation, or of its corollary, the 'under determination' of archaeological interpretation by data. In this reading archaeology is 'of' the present, no matter that it is 'about' the past. This basic tenet is held to support the conclusion that as objective knowledge of the past is impossible, the best we can hope for is an 'open field of discourse' about a whole gamut of possible pasts (and presents). There has been some argument among proponents about whether post-processual archaeology is either strongly or weakly relativist, or strongly constructivist, but matters remain inconclusive. Nonetheless it is a rare thing to have clear and tightly argued discussion of the question of whether archaeological data can constrain archaeological interpretation (an exception being Wylie 1992b).

It would seem that one of the key tasks of 'theoretical archaeology' in this account of archaeological epistemology is to keep such discourse interesting, relevant, accessible, and culturally significant – especially to those who pay our salaries, manage archaeological sites and recovered material culture, or visit sites and museums. While it is never totally a matter of 'giving the people what they want', indeed there has occasionally surfaced a strong didactic tone of 'tell the people what they need', much of the discourse of both processual and post-processual 'theoretical archaeology' have been about locking archaeological interpretation and disciplinary problematics into the web of discourses which define the present. It is also worth noting that not much innovative thinking about the constitution of the present has been possible when the strategy seems to be to confirm the validity or insightfulness of this or that view as a guide to interpreting the past, so that the interpretive primacy of the present is unchallenged by its application to what we think of as the past. The high probability of some circularity of reasoning has not gone unnoticed and has led to talk of mirrors, and the inherent unreliability of archaeological interpretation.

However, and surely this cannot come as any surprise, a special kind of concern is expressed about the 'misuse' of archaeological concepts and categories, especially in matters associated with the political consequences of racial and ethnic differences 'established' or 'confirmed' by archaeologists (see in particular Kohl 1993; Slapsak 1993). This is an old worry which clearly predates the concerns raised by the horrors of Nazi race theory, or even of the use of a Teutonic past in Wilhelmine Germany (e.g. Kossinna 1911; McCann 1988; Veit 1989). Many observers (see especially Trigger 1989) have remarked that the rise of nationalism last century was at least as strong a constitutive force for archaeology as was the rise of colonialism and imperialism. But while we can all appreciate the awful implications of 'misuse' of concepts and categories central to the identity of archaeology itself, it is a very much more difficult business to control such instruments when they are so widely shared within society, or when their very ambiguity gives archaeologists tremendous freedom of interpretive movement. These are foundational matters of the greatest consequence, considering the fact that they lie at the heart of our discipline, and the damage they can do to the rest of society.

But this growing appreciation of the power of context, and our understanding of the power of the present in constructing the past, has yet to spawn sophisticated explorations of foundational issues of disciplinary identity, ontology, or epistemology. Added to this, a growing democratization of access to the archaeological past, and the declining authority of archaeologists as the natural interpreters of the meaning of archaeological things (e.g. McManamon 1991; Murray 1996a), has further heightened fears that archaeologists might lose control over the concepts and categories they routinely deploy in analysis. But for the most part, over the last decade 'theoretical archaeologists' have had their attention focused elsewhere.

Over the same period archaeologists have also grappled with the methodological question of how archaeological data constrain archaeological interpretation. Typically, with some notable exceptions such as Fotiadis (Watson and Fotiadis 1990) and Wylie (1989, 1992a, 1992b), what has passed for careful consideration of the matter has been the usual farrago of position taking about the theory dependence of observation, the employment of ill-digested browsings of the literature of the sociology of science, and some (even for archaeology) extraordinarily incoherent discussions of realist, relativist, and 'indigenised' epistemologies.

There have been calls for both more and less middle range theory (e.g. Cowgill 1993; Saitta 1992; Schiffer 1988; Trigger 1991). Very occasionally we note the assertion of there being archaeological theory and archaeological epistemology, and even more rarely we note the proposition that this theory and this epistemology might be something which we might usefully work towards, so that we might establish new frameworks to ascribe meaning and value to archaeological things. But most of the time we are treated to the spectacle of archaeologists conventionalizing interpretation, by adopting whatever is in vogue in social theory and social philosophy, and producing abstractions which have decreased, not increased, our contact with the objects of our study. This has developed into the primary concern of 'theoretical archaeology'.

It is worth noting that this enterprise has produced outcomes diametrically opposed to those, which were originally thought to flow from the more overt discussion of theory building in archaeology, which began during the 1960s. An appreciation of the values of theoretical knowledge was at that time thought to expand our explanatory and interpretive repertoire, and to add new areas of human action, which could be properly considered as being within the purview of archaeology. The case for archaeological theory was made by exposing the essential aridity of a discipline obsessed by the empirical and by a consideration of all the things which could not be done because of the nature of the archaeological record.

However, it was not intended that such theoretical explorations and the attempts to build archaeological theory, which were thought to develop naturally from them, should become ends in themselves. At that time it was felt that the aim of archaeological theory was to improve our understanding of the objects and contexts which comprise the empirical domain of the discipline, not an enterprise which is primarily concerned with multiplying readings of the past while never developing them sufficiently so that they can be effectively grounded in archaeological things. In this reading the abstractions of contemporary 'theoretical archaeology' are both the cause and effect of the transformation of the field into simply discourse about itself.

Part of the reason for the cult status of theory has stemmed from the cult status of some of the individuals involved, an aspect of disciplinary sociology effectively lampooned by Flannery. Another part flows from the fact that 'theoretical archaeology' is perceived as being a low-risk high return publishing strategy in comparison to the time-consuming business of analysing sites and contexts and creating data. But the greater part of the reason stems from three linked factors. First, as the field of disciplinary activity has relentlessly expanded we have found that much of what underwrote the core of archaeology prior to the 1960s simply does not survive careful scrutiny in an increasingly competitive interpretive and explanatory environment. Second, we have discovered that the business of convincingly grounding ideas and approaches in the past (no matter how much we might believe in them as guides to our understanding of the present) has proved to be very difficult indeed. Third, we have found that along with our capacity to disagree about how to interpret or understand the past, we have also developed very divergent views about the objectives of doing archaeology. Thus core arguments about disciplinary epistemology and ontology have been subsumed into the discourse of 'theoretical archaeology'.

All of these factors have transformed archaeology into 'an open field of discourse' in which interpretations vie for trade among the various interest groups which make up producers and consumers of knowledge. There can be no doubt that modern archaeology has become far more inclusive of the interests and perspectives of an increasingly diverse cohort of practitioners, as well as more responsive to the interests of others who have to consume the knowledge we produce, or who are more directly affected by the conduct of archaeological research. In this reading although much archaeological reasoning may be essentially circular, and knowledge claims made by its practitioners correspondingly weak, at least it represents a serious attempt to make archaeological things meaningful to people in the present. Thus archaeology can remain relevant and useful, and debates between practitioners about such highly abstract frameworks of interpretation might be taken to indicate the vitality of our discipline.

From a different perspective these are all signs of a discipline in very serious trouble, still in the process of defining itself after the collapse of previous orthodoxies in the 1960s. In this alternative reading archaeology has become conceptually unstable, easily swayed by fashion, and unable to convincingly engage interpretive perspectives (which slosh back and forth across the discipline like the tides), with the archaeological data they purport to explain. 'Theoretical archaeology' has developed into the vehicle which imports such new perspectives from traditional source areas, while at the same time offering critique of the previous approaches which newer imports are designed to replace. Such perspectives have rarely been developed to the point where an active engagement with the objects of analysis is possible. Discussion of their virtues usually takes place in terms of a restatement (by the importing archaeologists) of strengths and weaknesses noted by the practitioners of other disciplines (philosophy, history, anthropology). It is also recognized that the nature of such perspectives makes it highly unlikely that they ever could be developed beyond such superficialities, for two reasons. First, because it seems clear enough that they would require major reshaping before they could convincingly connect with the materials they are supposed to help us comprehend – thereby emphasizing the differences between past and present. Second, because the foraging strategies of theoretical archaeologists (see Chippindale 1993) require constant movement of the 'last week it was Hayden White, this week Heidegger, next week Bergson (?)' kind. Thus we have a discipline, which might be plugged into contemporary discourse about humanity, but it has paid a grievous price for the privilege of reinforcing the hegemony of contemporary social theory.

In this reading many of the perspectives, which have been tried in recent decades, might have strengthened the bonds between archaeology and the source areas of those perspectives, but they have not built archaeological theory. Nor have they (again, with the exception of material culture theory) made much of a contribution to the disciplines from which they were borrowed. Thus history, social philosophy, and anthropology have remained essentially unaffected by this process of borrowing, beyond the increased security of having the preeminence of short-term views of humanity legitimized by the application to archaeology.

But to expect that such engagement or development should be the primary criteria of archaeological theory is simply to misunderstand the practice of 'theoretical archaeology' as it has come to be. To focus too much (or at all) on such matters is thought by some to privilege empirical over theoretical knowledge. Furthermore, to recognise that there are real benefits for the development of archaeological theory which might flow from accepting that data do constrain interpretive perspective, is thought to recommit our discipline to the production of a dehumanized past that is methodologically virtuous, but conceptually stale.

While it is true that many members of the profession have been suffering from 'theory fatigue' since the 1960s, and this sometimes surfaces in grouchy or world-weary comments on yet another 'startling and original' analysis of foundational issues in the discipline (e.g. Adams 1991; Watson 1991), the fact remains that the bulk of us still (pathetically perhaps) hope for something to take the pain of crisis away and lead us forward to the pleasant fields of normal science. This yearning for the disciplinary paradigm still prompts archaeologists to read 'theoretical archaeology', but it can also represent the widespread (but patently false) belief that this paradigm will come from outside our discipline and not grow from within it, as a result of the sustained engagement of theory with the empirical.

Thus the traditions of 'theoretical archaeology' as they have developed over the last couple of decades appear to make it more (not less) difficult to build archaeological theory, and to provide new (more convincing) bases for disciplinary definition than the essentially nineteenth century agenda the bulk of us still seem committed to following.

Contemporary archaeology is full of such paradoxes. It has been observed, correctly, that notwithstanding a real eagerness to adopt new techniques and systems of analysis, the vast bulk of archaeologists still go about their business as if all this theoretical turmoil was happening on Mars. The increasing number of outstanding examples of intellectual vacuity marketed by Anglo-American publishers as the contributions to 'theoretical archaeology', can lead to calls for dispensing with such posturing by putting an end to foundational analysis in archaeology (e.g. Watson 1991). However, it is probably fair to say that the bulk of practitioners understand that if we don't actively consider the philosophy of archaeology then we'll have to put up with what philosophers want to prescribe for us (e.g. Wylie 1992a), and to go back to the bad old days and endure more lessons about how not to commit the fallacy of affirming the consequent (e.g. Morgan 1973; Salmon 1982). We shall also miss the essential point, that disciplines are characterized by more than arguments about their epistemology. The philosophy of archaeology and the exploration of foundational issues are our concern and our responsibility.

In some situations the choice between philosophically ill-informed archaeologists and archaeologically ill-informed philosophers might seem like no choice at all, but there can be no doubt that archaeologists will have to seize the responsibility for such foundational discussions if they are going to grow the archaeological theory we so desperately require. Certainly a deeper understanding of the significance of our task in developing an archaeological perspective on humanity can only spring from a contemplation of archaeological ontology and epistemology, as well as an understanding of the social and cultural context of the knowledge we produce. It is equally true that as we experience the tension which will result from an exploration of the taken-for-granteds of archaeological practice, and try to persuade the consumers of the knowledge that we produce that these explorations have implications for them too, we will need to emphasize that our discipline is not just an assortment of methods directed at conventional problems about humanity, but also the basis of new enquires about the human condition, new frameworks of knowledge, and a new ground for thoroughly re-examining the instruments we use to interpret the world.

In this brief paper I link these complex issues surrounding the building of archaeological theory to the broader objective of developing credible archaeological responses to the misuses of archaeological concepts and categories which are frequently associated with the rise of ethnicity politics. I will observe that archaeology needs to find that difficult middle ground between the possibility of repression, which might stem from an appeal to the authority of science, and the equally real prospect of practitioners sacrificing their power to defend society from such misuses through a loss of control over what Eric Wolf has identified as 'perilous ideas' (Wolf 1994). I will argue that it can only find this ground through the building of archaeological theory and through a thoroughgoing reassessment of foundational issues of disciplinary identity. At the root of this exercise is a very general consideration of the role archaeology plays in the establishment of identity, the creation of national and ethnic mythologies, and the restoration of a link between history and the plasticity of humanity. Significantly these same issues are of increasing concern to historians and to socio-cultural anthropologists (e.g. Friedman 1992a, 1992b; Wolf 1982, 1994).

Other archaeologists have explored these issues before now, and some, notably Shennan (1989) have seen in questions raised by the use of concepts such as ethnicity and identity that practitioners find it extremely difficult to be critically self-reflective about core elements of our interpretative armoury which are also central to our comprehension of the present. It is vitally important that we understand that concepts and categories such as identity, ethnicity, culture, and race are expressions of disciplinary metaphysics and epistemology, and which are, therefore, very much foundational matters that are properly our concern.

But there is always the question of our ability to step back from the forces which create our subjective experience as archaeologists, and to critique the validity of such concepts and categories from an archaeological perspective. As other commentators have noted, although archaeologists and anthropologists occasionally reveal their disquiet over the use of ethnicity, race, and culture, the fact remains that they are widely seen by the general public as almost having the status of 'natural knowledge'. In this we encounter the prospect that archaeological concepts and categories are themselves deeply embedded in much bigger configurations of knowledge which at first seem to be well beyond our control (e.g. Wolf 1994). Connected with this is the real question, also noted by Shennan and, more recently by Dietler (1994), of whether much of the conceptual core of contemporary archaeology could survive such reflection. Related to this is the very real question of whether the public authority of the discipline would whither away if the instability and circularity of archaeological interpretation when it is so far abstracted from the objects of analysis, became more widely known.

Archaeologists have dealt with these issues before, and the discipline has survived the process. Towards the close of the paper I will briefly revisit two papers written by Gordon Childe (1933 and 1934) as part of his response to the use of archaeology by Nazi race theoreticians. My purpose here will be to describe the strategy Childe used in his attempt to discredit Nazi 'race science', and then consider whether this strategy would serve as a basis for identifying and rejecting current misuses of archaeological concepts.

Needless to say that with all this on the agenda, my discussion has tended towards the rhetorical and the general, an outcome well within the traditions of 'theoretical archaeology'! Having said this, perhaps a more accurate description of my purpose here is to argue that all of these elements should be on the same agenda and to briefly explore some of the consequences of this new configuration.

## Ethnicity and identity, Europe and Australia

*And one of the ways of manifesting ethnicity is now to don a camouflage suit and grab an AK 47* (Wolf 1994: 1).

I have stressed that this reflection was prompted by more than the Childe centenary, and by depression brought on by a contemplation of the current state of archaeological theory (see Murray 1995b). Archaeologists as members of society have to respond to a multitude of social and cultural pressures, but few have been so enduring or so potentially damaging as the issues raised by the use of the 'perilous' concepts of race, language, culture, and ethnicity. I am hardly the first to observe that the foundations of archaeological knowledge lie deeply buried in links which were thought to exist between the nations and ethnic groups, and in our desire to establish identity through the passage of racial and ethnic history (see Harris 1968; Stocking 1968, 1987; Trigger 1989). Since the nineteenth century there has been a tension between the historicism of this project and the universalism, which underwrote models of social and cultural evolution, but there has been a general understanding that such concepts and categories were fundamental to the creation of a human past. Again, I am hardly the first to observe that there has been a tension between the development of archaeological and anthropological interpretations of such concepts and categories, and more widespread popular notions about identity and ethnic history which are long standing and extremely powerful forces for social mobilization. Over the last four years we have seen this power blossom once again, and we have seen archaeologists struggle to come to terms with it.

Prior to 1992 much had been made of the possibilities of European union, of a powerful new player in the 'new world order', of the collapse of frontiers and old thinking, and of the dawn of a properly European civilisation. By the end of 1992, it became clear enough that whatever had been predicted (and it was difficult enough to sort substance from shadow after a concerted media blitz of 'Europe-making'), it was something of a false dawn. Nothing since then has occasioned a revision of that conclusion.

Perhaps we had been led to expect too much: that countries would cease to subvert the sovereignty of others and stop inciting ethnic rivalries for economic gain; that in straitened economic times governments (and the populations they both represent and guide), would keep in mind the big picture and not head for the bunker of survival at the cost of others; that European societies would turn outward rather than inward. But then again all this talk about whether Europe really existed or whether it was simply a region of the mind, whether Europe created itself or was created by all that was non-Europe, spawned such a tidal wave of geography and metageography that one was entitled to become suspicious that we were in the midst of a publishing and marketing phenomenon. At times it seemed clear that the process of Europe-making had been hijacked by the promoters of the Europe-event. In this sense even abject failure can be turned to economic, political, and of course academic benefit.

With the wisdom of hindsight pundits have declared that the warning signs had been there all along, signs some of us had obviously either ignored or wished away. It was subsequently observed that postcolonial Europe had seemed to be tending towards exclusion rather than inclusion for some time, evidenced by the creation of trade blocs and the tightening of immigration controls. Fascists were back on the streets, and history was being rewritten to capture the minds of a generation of people who had been conspicuously let down by their governments. A Europe with a rising percentage of its population with no jobs, not much education, and with hardly any stake in the future faced a more serious problem with identity than most observers had been prepared to acknowledge. This was made all the more serious by the ambiguous consequences of the 'end of the Cold War', which for some meant the end of internationalism, and for others meant the collapse of traditional forms of social mobilization such as class, and their gradual replacement by new social configurations which give rise to the search for identity. As McDonald observes: 'at the core of this is the question of identity: the struggle against anonymity, the struggle to generate meaning' (McDonald 1994: 19). With the wisdom of hindsight we can identify the existence of some familiar oppositions between nationalism and internationalism, and between historicism and universalism underlying the fear of a future, which has begun to seem almost completely uncertain.

One of the most ambiguous consequences of the beginnings of the new world order was a very overt return of notions of ethnic essentialism, from a place where everyone had thought (or hoped) that they had gone to die after 1945. It would be quite wrong to argue that all forms of identity politics (particularly the politics of ethnicity) take the same shapes or have the same consequences, but over the last three years Europe and Africa together have provided some spectacular examples of its more extreme forms. One of the most disturbing aspects of ethnicity becoming a major focus of social mobilization is that it enshrines essentialist doctrines which seek to define the experience of place in history as the experience of particular ethnic groups. Thus the politics of exclusion, which underwrite such doctrines, have to make regular and direct appeals to the past for the authority to undertake action in the present (see also Kohl 1993; Shennan 1989; Slapsak 1993; Smith 1989). Of greatest concern is the fact that the proponents of such doctrines do not now require the participation of archaeologists to manufacture such histories, as they can rely on older analyses, folk tales, and the fact that the very concepts and categories used by archaeologists are also used by them. This obviously places tremendous pressure on archaeologists to either support or oppose such activities, and to risk a loss of authority either by demonstrating the weakness of archaeological knowledge claims through an active critique of those concepts and categories, or by surrendeti.ng objectivity by supporting their misuse so that political or social goals might be attained.

But Europe and Africa are by no means alone in turning towards ethnicity or identity politics. In Australia 1992 was also characterised by much discussion of national identity, but (perhaps typically enough) its context was different from that in Europe. By the late 1980s Australia had firmly become a multicultural society, which officially described itself as an immigrant nation. But 1992 marked the beginning of a broadening and re-evaluation of Australian history and three linked forces came into play to create the context for this great change.

First, there was the matter of Aboriginal land rights and the recognition of there being Aboriginal history before the arrival of the Europeans. The High Court of Australia brought down its judgement in the case of Eddie Mabo versus the Government of Queensland and recognized the existence of native title in Australia. In so doing it reversed two hundred years of legal doctrine, which had underwritten the dispossession of Aboriginal people, and provided the basis for legislative remedies that put the country on the path of a national reconciliation. The recognition of prior occupancy (and *de facto* ownership), which was enshrined in Federal legislation with the passage of the Native Title Act, linked closely with a developing understanding of the fact that the great diversity of the Aboriginal experience of colonization overlaid the great diversity of Aboriginal history during the preceding 60,000 years. History began to matter a great deal both to Aboriginal and non-Aboriginal Australians (e.g. Attwood 1992; Rowse 1993).

Second, wrapped up with the discussion of Aboriginal land rights and the possibility of reconciliation was the rebirth of a national debate about the constitution of Australia. Much of this debate centered on the issue of whether Australia would remain a constitutional monarchy (with the Queen of England as Head of State), or whether it should develop as a republic. Amongst the heated discussion (which continues) there has been an explicit recognition that the development of multiculturalism in Australia might demand the evolution of constitutional forms away from those adopted from Westminster in the late nineteenth century, when the majority of the population was of Anglo-Irish descent.

Third, a national debate about the place of Australia in Asia, which had been brewing for the last several decades, was escalated sharply by being linked to the push for constitutional reform and the rekindled interest in Australian history, which flowed from the debate about the Republic and the passage of the Native Title Act. Here debate turned on the notion that as a result of immigration, and a re-evaluation of Australia's historical links with Asia, Australia could redefine itself even more completely in a way which recognized its European past while stressing its Asian future.

Needless to say that any one of these three forces alone has the capacity to create anxiety about identity. Taken together they have tended to speed up the exploration of new forms of social mobilization, which share many common elements with those taking shape in Europe or North America. A number of ethnic conflicts, particularly those centered on the countries that have succeeded the former Yugoslavia, have had a considerable impact on Australian society, but these are yet to flow through to the practice of archaeology there. Where Australian archaeology has been most affected is in its relationships with Aboriginal people, particularly in terms of there being much stronger pressure to make its practice relevant to their interests. This pressure has taken many forms ranging from requirements for detailed and meaningful consultation between archaeologists and Aboriginal people about the conduct of research, through to the establishment of complete Aboriginal control over Aboriginal heritage. I have discussed the positive and negative outcomes of this fundamental change in our practice elsewhere (e.g. Murray 1996a, 1996b).

Although it would be silly to equate the experience of archaeologists in the Balkans, for example, with those in Australia, a common thread does exist in the sense that both groups (either willingly or unwillingly) share the field of interpretation with others whose political agendas underwrite their use of archaeological information, and the sites and contexts which comprise the 'heritage' of nations or peoples. If we accept the positive aspects of such sharing, for example the relativist notion that knowledge about the past can take many forms and serve many ends, does this mean that we are powerless to critique more negative outcomes? To go further, if ideas such as ethnicity are common cultural property (even though they may have different 'local' definitions), what value can be placed on our claims that misuses are occurring?

## Briefly revisiting Childe and the Nazis

I have remarked that these are old problems for archaeology, but I have questioned whether archaeology in its current state can defend its concepts and categories from misuse. Given the focus on Gordon Childe mentioned earlier, I want to examine how Childe defined race, language, and culture in a way which first established that the concepts were useful (though dangerous), and then went on to demonstrate how the Nazis had perverted them. Apart from several instances where he was content to be sarcastic (especially about Himmler the poultry farmer), Childe's argument in the two papers selected for discussion (1933, 1934) was based on an historical account of the development of the concepts, and on establishing a clear distinction between popular belief and the authority of science. However, overarching both strategies is an account of what human history signifies as evidence of the plasticity of humanity, of the commonality of human history, rather than as evidence of isolation, timeless essence, and separate development.

There is no need to recapitulate the elements of the historical account of race, language, and culture as Childe ranged widely across geography, philosophy, history, government, philology, genetics and physical anthropology to demonstrate the genesis and development of such ideas. Above all he was concerned to demonstrate that they had changed through investigation and through the further development of the problems. Establishing the pedigrees of the ideas and the problems was one way of confirming the authority of science, another way was to indicate the vast gulf between popular belief and scientific knowledge.

*The suppression of thought during the Dark Ages was justified by an appeal to supposed revelations, vouchsafed to individuals, and the interpretations thereof. The latest onslaught on the freedom of the spirit appeals to alleged scientific facts. The justificatory documents actually exist in the public world - in museums and in the fields - open to every competent observer to examine, analyse and compare. But these documents can no more be profitably studied without laborious preparatory training than can the movements of the stars or the behaviour of electrons* (1933: 410)

Childe hammered home the point of the authority of the science of archaeology by his use of language. Phrases such as 'systematic study' and 'exact terminology' go to establish that an archaeologist's use of such common concepts has 'defined a given term in a different way to vulgar speech and sometimes even differently to colleagues in allied disciplines. The layman may well be pardoned if he takes these technical terms at their face value, but the resultant confusion may have disastrous effects' (1933: 410).

Childe well recognized that if there was such a yawning gap between scientific discussion and popular belief, then it was incumbent on the specialist to share such knowledge with society. Although he did (rightly) criticize the fact that the popularizers of science were still content to rehash outdated notions of race, language, and culture (1934: 68), the fact remained that such ideas and such arguments were very much more difficult and complex than the public imagined. Did the public therefore require training in archaeology in order to rebut Nazi ideology? No, but they needed to be made aware that its pretense to scientific rectitude was a sham.

In an important sense Childe was describing a process where popular notions were transformed by science (or rationality as Childe frequently emphasized) into something quite different to what the Nazis were claiming. Improved communication was obviously part of the prescription for changing such outmoded attitudes, but it did not deal directly with a more fundamental problem, which perhaps had more to do with outlook than logic.

*Moreover, it is not only in Germany that sentimental considerations are liable to disturb the objectivity of scientific judgement. Amongst an imperial people ruling over subjects of diverse hue the racial theory of history has a powerful emotional and economic appeal. Only one who has obtained his ambition and security can afford to disregard that fact* (1934: 68)

At the heart of Childe's rebuttal of Nazi race 'science' was a commitment to changing outlook through the popularization of the archaeological perspective on human history. In Childe's view it was demonstrable that cultures are heterogeneous and contradictory, and that establishing ethnicity (as it is currently defined) was extremely difficult. Above all are the notion of contact and the flow of information and ideas as a positive force in human history.

*Objectively studied Prehistory will rather emphasise how much more precious and vital is the growth of the common tradition that leads up to civilisation than the idiosyncrasies and divagations of any separate groups, however brilliant. To attempt to cut oneself or one's community off from this lifegiving tradition, is to commit spiritual suicide. To admit as good only what is Celtic, or Germanic or Indian, as exclusive nationalism would demand, is unscientific and unhistorical* (1933: 418).

## Concluding remarks

Would Childe's mix of providing an overarching meaning of human history, and a respect for the values of scientific objectivity, work for the contemporary archaeologist seeking to rebut misuses of archaeological concepts? I have my doubts. While it is true that establishing where interpretations do not fit the facts might work in those cases where a direct connection between interpretation and the empirical can be made, it is equally true that such cases are either rare or of little consequence to the overarching interpretations which are being offered.

Certainly the need to respond to Childe's appeal to scientific objectivity and the greater authority of science over popular discourse would sharply polarize the contemporary archaeological community. What might well survive is the strength of his appeal to the commonality of human history, but this would (again) seem to be more a matter of outlook than something which could be convincingly demonstrated against determined opposition. I do not want to labour the point, but what can we do?

Perhaps the honest way forward is for practitioners to demonstrate the circularity and logical weaknesses of many knowledge claims made both by advocates of ethnic essentialism, and by archaeologists. Although this obviously runs the risk of exposing the shortcomings of contemporary archaeology, it might also serve to remove the appeals to scientific authority that are frequently made under its auspices (by both groups). In addition, it would seem that such a demonstration might empower both archaeologists and others to search for more convincing bases on which to mount such interpretations, perhaps even to the extent of building the theories which are so obviously absent. In this sense the destabilization of the hegemony of the present might well have a liberating effect on the minds of practitioners.

On the other hand such a demonstration might serve to prompt us to seek meanings in human history which are not so open to the abuse of these perilous ideas, which might be easier to build theory about, and which might allow us a greater ability to produce convincing archaeological definitions of our concepts and categories. Above all such a demonstration might help us to reflect on the value of our nineteenth century inheritance and the naturalness of our conception of the purposes of archaeological knowledge. Perhaps it is fitting in an era where more than ever before our destinies are held in common that we also seek a balance to our longstanding interest in the histories of peoples, perhaps in the histories of places.

## References

ADAMS, W.Y. 1991. Comment on Richard Watson (What the New Archaeology has accomplished). *Current Anthropology* 32: 281.

ARNOLD, B. 1990. The past as propaganda. Totalitarian archaeology in Nazi Germany. *Antiquity* 64: 464-478.

ATTWOOD, B., 1992: Introduction. In B. Attwood and J. Arnold (eds) *Power, Knowledge and Aborigines*, pp. i-xvi. Bundoora, Vic: La Trobe University Press in association with the National Centre for Australian Studies, Monash University.

BAKER, F., 1993: The Berlin Wall. Production, preservation and consumption of a 20th century monument. *Antiquity* 67: 709-733.

BEER, G. 1989. *Arguing with the Past: Essays in Narrative from Woolf to Sidney*. London: Routledge.

CHILDE, V.G. 1933. Is prehistory practical? *Antiquity* 7: 410- 418.

—1934. Anthropology and Herr Hitler. *Discovery* 15: 65-68.

CHIPPINDALE, C. 1993. Ambition, deference, discrepancy, consumption. The intellectual background to a post-processual archaeology. In N. Yoffee and A. Sherratt (eds) *Archaeological Theory. Who Sets the Agenda?* pp. 27-36. Cambridge: Cambridge University Press.

COWGILL, G. 1993: Distinguished lecture in archaeology: beyond criticising New Archaeology. *American Anthropologist* 95: 551-573.

DIAZ-ANDREU, M. 1993: Theory and ideology in archaeology. Spanish archaeology under the Franco regime. *Antiquity* 67: 74-82.

DIETLER, M. 1994. 'Our ancestors the Gauls': archaeology, ethnic nationalism, and the manipulation of Celtic identity in modern Europe. *American Anthropologist* 96: 584-605.

FOWLER, D. 1987. Uses of the Past: archaeology in the service of the state. *American Antiquity* 52: 229-248.

FRIEDMAN, J. 1992a: Myth, history, and political identity. *Cultural Anthropology* 7: 194- 210.

—1992b: The Past in the Future: history and the politics of identity. *American Anthropologist* 94: 837-859.

GATHERCOLE, P. and D. LOWENTHAL (eds) 1990. *The Politics of the Past.* London: Routledge.

GATHERCOLE, P., IRVING, T. and G. MELLEUISH (eds) 1995. *Childe and Australia.* St Lucia, Qld: University of Queensland Press.

GERO, J. and M. CONKEY (eds) 1991. *Engendering Archaeology. Women and Prehistory.* Oxford: Blackwell.

HARRIS, M. 1968. *The Rise of Anthropological Theory.* New York: Crowell.

KOHL, P. 1993. Nationalism, politics, and the practice of archaeology in Soviet Transcaucasia. *Journal of European Archaeology* 1: 181-190.

KOSSINNA, G. 1911. *Die Herkunft der Germanen.* Wurzburg.

LLOSA, M.V. 1993. *Fiction: the Power of Lies.* Bundoora, Vic: La Trobe University

MCCANN, B. 1988. The National Socialist perversion of archaeology. *World Archaeological Bulletin* 2: 51-54.

MCDONALD, K. 1994. Identity politics. *Arena* (june-july): 18-22.

MCGUIRE, R. 1992. Archaeology and the First Americans. *American Anthropologist* 94: 816-836.

MCMANAMON, F.P. 1991. The many publics for archaeology. *American Antiquity* 56: 121-130.

MORGAN, C. 1973. Archaeology and explanation. *World Archaeology* 4: 259-276.

MURRAY, T. 1990. The history, philosophy and sociology of archaeology. The case of the *Ancient Monuments Protection Act* (1882). In V. Pinsky and A. Wylie (eds) *Critical Directions in Contemporary Archaeology*, pp. 55-67. Cambridge: Cambridge University Press.

—1993. Communication and the importance of disciplinary communities. Who owns thepast? In N. Yoffee and A. Sherratt (eds) *Archaeological Theory. Who sets the agenda?*, pp. 105-116. Cambridge: Cambridge University Press.

—1995a: Gordon Childe, archaeological records, and rethinking the archaeologist's project. In P. Gathercole, T. Irving and G. Melleuish (eds) *Childe and Australia*, pp. 199-211. St Lucia, Qld: University of Queensland Press.

—1995b: On Klejn's agenda for theoretical archaeology. *Current Anthropology* 36: 290-292.

—1996a: On coming to terms with the living. Some aspects of repatriation for the archaeologist. *Antiquity* 267: 217-220.

—1996b: Towards a post-Mabo archaeology of Australia. In B. Attwood (ed) *In the Age of Mabo: History, Aborigines and Australia,* pp. 73-87. Sydney, NSW: Allen & Unwin.

PARADIS, J.G. and T. POSTLETHWAIT (eds) 1985. *Victorian Science and Victorian Values: Literary Perspectives.* New Brunswick, NJ: Rutgers University Press.

ROWSE, T. 1993. *After Mabo. Interpreting Indigenous Traditions.* Melbourne, Vic: Melbourne University Press.

SAID, E. 1985: Orientalism Reconsidered. *Race and Class* 27: 1-15.

SAITTA, D. 1992. Radical archaeology and middle-range methodology. *Antiquity* 66: 886-897.

SALMON, H.M. 1982. *Philosophy and Archaeology.* New York: Academic Press.

SCHIFFER, M.B. 1988: The structure of archaeological theory. *American Antiquity* 53: 461-485.

SHENNAN, S. 1989. Introduction. Archaeological approaches to cultural identity. In S. Shennan (ed) *Archaeological Approaches to Cultural Identity*, pp. 1-32. London: Routledge.

SLAPSAK, B. 1993. Archaeology and contemporary myths of the past. *Journal of European Archaeology* 1: 191-195.

SMITH, A.D. 1989: *The Ethnic Origins of Nations*. Oxford: Blackwell.

STOCKING, G.C. 1968. *Race, Culture, and Evolution*. New York: Free Press.

—1987. *Victorian Anthropology*. New York: Free Press.

TOMASKOVA, S. 1995. A site in history. Archaeology at Dolni Vestonice /Unterwisternitz. *Antiquity* 69: 301-316.

TRIGGER, B. 1989: *A History of Archaeological Thought*. Cambridge: Cambridge University Press.

—1991. Distinguished lecture in archaeology: constraint and freedom - a new synthesis for archaeological explanation. *American Anthropologist* 93: 551-569.

VEIT, U. 1989: Ethnic concepts in German prehistory. A case study on the relationship between cultural identity and archaeological objectivity. In S. Shennan (ed) *Archaeological Approaches to Cultural Identity*, pp. 35-56. London: Routledge.

WATSON, PJ. and M. FOTIADIS 1990. The razor's edge: symbolic-structural archaeology and the expansion of archaeological inference. *American Anthropologist* 92: 613-629.

WATSON, R.A. 1991. What the New Archaeology has accomplished. *Current Anthropology* 32: 275-291.

WOLF, E.R. 1982. *Europe and the People Without History*. Berkeley, Ca: University of California Press.

—1994. Perilous Ideas: race, culture, people. *Current Anthropology* 35: 1-12.

WYLIE, A. 1989. Matters of fact and matters of interest. In S. Shennan (ed) *Archaeological Approaches to Culture and Identity*, pp. 94-109. London: Routledge.

—1992a. On scepticism, philosophy, and archaeological science. *Current Anthropology* 33: 209-213.

—1992b: The interplay of evidential constraints and political interests. Recent archaeological research on gender. *American Antiquity* 57: 15-35.

*Chapter 6*

# Epilogue: the art of archaeological biography

*Personal loss reminds us, albeit too late, that people do archaeology, reconstruct prehistory, present papers, squabble over interpretations, and teach other people to do the same, but, we hope, a little better. And these same people have biases, preconceived notions, personal experiences and agendas-dare one call it a subjective element - that must be comprehended at some level if we are to treat the whole past fairly* (Reid 1991: 195).

## Introduction

The fifty-eight essays that comprise *Encyclopedia of Archaeology: The Great Archaeologists* represent a very broad cross-section of the ways in which archaeologists are writing archaeological biography. No one who has contemplated the vast numbers of biographies devoted to such scientific luminaries as Charles Darwin, Isaac Newton, and Albert Einstein can be at all surprised that such a variety of approach and purpose can be possible. Although there has been a long tradition of biography writing in archaeology (see, e.g., Bowden 1991; Drawer 1985; Thompson 1977; Hunter 1975; Piggott 1985; Woodbury 1973), there has been little overt discussion of how one should go about doing it and about what role the knowledge that is produced should play in the business of 'doing' archaeology.

Douglas Givens (1992), in one of the very few discussions of biography and the history of archaeology, has usefully summarized the types of data archaeologists need to collect if they are to do both their subject and their readers justice. He has also understood that the process of biography writing involves choices that should flow naturally from an understanding of the purposes of such biographies. Givens stresses the importance of 'getting inside' the subjects while not 'falling in love' with them, of understanding the interactions between the subject and colleagues and disciplinary structures, and of coming to an assessment of the contribution made by the subject to the advancement of knowledge, both professional and public.

In this collection archaeologists have deployed all the methodologies described by Givens, but they have done so from a wide variety of perspectives and interests. It is clear that some authors, especially those dealing with subjects either long dead or already admitted to the canon of 'great archaeologists', have no difficulty in establishing a justification for a biography of their subject. Archaeologists such as Johann Winckelmann, William Camden, John Aubrey, and Gordon Childe are justly famous as pioneers and acute thinkers about problems that we regard as central to our discipline. Other authors, especially Geoff Bailey, Lewis Binford, Anick Coudart, Roland Fletcher, Clive Gamble, and Peter Rowley-Conwy, clearly understand that their biographies contain significant elements of autobiography – in the sense that their subjects clearly had a strong personal as well as professional influence on their lives as archaeologists. An important part of the justification for biographies of these and other individuals whose work remains highly influential in present practice (e.g., Robert Adams and Mats Malmer) is the chance to focus analysis on the work of an individual and to create a sense of development in thought and approach. Still others, such as Leo Klejn's treatment of Gustaf Kossinna and Heinrich Schliemann, are designed to correct misunderstandings or imbalances in evidence and argument that are widely held among archaeologists and the general public.

These approaches to defining the purpose of a biography (and the wide range of possible positions that lie between and around them) are entirely appropriate. Givens (1992) and Jacob Gruber (1966) have argued that the role of individuals in archaeology is best appreciated through the vehicle of biography and that the actions and motivations of individuals are a significant element in the practice of disciplines. This is part of the sentiment that motivated J. Jefferson Reid in his editorial (1991) and the decision by the Society of American Archaeology to actively promote the study of the history of archaeology. As a result of this developing focus on the role of individuals in the making of archaeology (and of the construction of pasts) much greater attention has been paid to taking oral testimonies and to encouraging archaeologists to properly archive their records for future generations. Mainstream journals such as *Antiquity* introduced the notion of autobiographical statements from significant archaeologists on the occasion of their formal retirement (Daniel and Chippindale 1989), and *Current Anthropology* has developed an approach to oral history through long interviews with archaeologists such as Leo Klejn, in which the subject is given every opportunity to present a statement about their life as an archaeologist (see, e .g., Taylor 1993). These new forms of autobiography supplement a rich tradition of autobiography writing in archaeology, the most notable exponent of which was Mortimer Wheeler (1955, 1966, 1976).

There is much to be said for this focus on the individual as the means of understanding how archaeologists create and work with formal disciplinary structures (such as journals, learned societies, university departments, and museums), and with formal 'external' structures such as legislation, government agencies (both domestic and international), and non-government organizations and lobby groups. It is equally true that such a focus can also allow us access to informal disciplinary structures that might be based around gender, political affiliations, friendship, or shared experience. Reading the biographies of Robert Adams, David Clarke, Eric Higgs, Francois Bordes, and Lewis Binford written by archaeologists who themselves have strongly influenced my own approach to the subject brought home very strongly the crucial role of tradition and the 'chain of connection' between oneself and one's 'ancestors', an important facet of disciplinary history in Australia that was discussed at some length by the late Sir Grahame Clark (Clark 1989). A focus on the individual can thus reinforce the 'corporate' nature of any discipline – it can emphasize that disciplines are social as well as scientific institutions.

This particular aspect of the history of archaeology, as a means of socializing budding practitioners into the social norms of the discipline, is particularly powerful at a time when the discipline of archaeology is experiencing a marked decline in its sense of community (see, e.g., Murray 1993). But this account of the role of biography in writing the social history of archaeology does not need to emphasize only the conservative elements of such biography writing, conservative in the sense of socializing beginners in what might be hollow or outmoded social institutions. Biography writing is also very valuable in developing alternative images of such social institutions and in helping to reshape the notion of community in archaeology.

### A developing sense of problem

When this project was conceived in 1992 archaeologists were already in the process of converting the history of archaeology from a marginal pursuit into a mainstream activity, a process hastened by the appearance of several interesting biographies (see, e.g., Green 1981; Hawkes 1982; McNairn 1980; Trigger 1980) and 'autobiographical' statements (see, e.g., Daniel and Chippindale 1989; Willey 1988). Since then the history of archaeology, whether in the form of biographies, the analysis of the institutions of the discipline, or through the production of general national histories, has become firmly part of the mainstream (Murray 1990; Pinsky 1990;Trigger 1985, 1989, 1994).

It has been said often enough that disciplines get the disciplinary histories they deserve. I have previously observed that each new account of the archaeologist's project, from the nineteenth century onward, has led to a rewriting of disciplinary history by the advocates of new approaches (Murray

1987). There is an obvious reason why this should happen, and it has to do with justifying behaviour that might be construed as being destabilizing or 'unhelpful' by other practitioners. One way of doing this is to establish that your view has a respectable historical pedigree. Even better is to claim that the urgency of your drive for reformation is fuelled by an understanding that archaeologists have for too long done things incorrectly, or have not done some important things at all, and you are now about to set things straight. There are some excellent examples of this use of history to underwrite disciplinary reformation – Camden's detailed critique of Geoffrey of Monmouth; Hugh Falconer attacking William Buckland and George Cuvier over their suppression of debate about the antiquity of humankind; David Clarke's introduction to *Analytical Archaeology*; and Daniel Miller's survey of post-1960s archaeology in *Artifacts as Categories* (1985) are just a few.

Clearly these are, in George Stocking's terms, 'presentist' histories, although I think that we have all spent rather too long debating the differences between such histories and ones that are perhaps a little less adversarial in their treatment of preceding views. In this sense, because all historians of archaeology have views about the nature and purpose of the archaeologist's project, all histories reflect those views and are, therefore, 'presentist'. Notwithstanding Glyn Daniel's avowed opposition to theory, his histories of archaeology are paeans of praise to empiricism and humanism. Bruce Trigger's more comprehensive coverage is driven by his special concerns, which surface most clearly in those chapters dealing with processual and postprocessual archaeology (1989).

My own interest in the history of archaeology is avowedly presentist. This does not mean that I must inevitably tumble into the pitfalls of Whig history, because the history of archaeology I am particularly interested in requires a strong sense of context to be of any value at all. My interest is in establishing how the edifice of modern prehistoric archaeology – its agendas, concepts, categories, patterns of socialization, and institutions – became established, and the processes that underwrite its transformation. A focus on the subtleties of how research agendas are created, how different groups within archaeology play out their competing interests, and how practitioners lie to themselves (and to their publics) about the kinds of knowledge they produce and consume requires an intense engagement with individuals and with disciplinary structures (see, e .g., Murray 1990).

A related interest is to understand what role the history of archaeology will play in moves to reform modern archaeology in the light of pressure for increasing diversity in approach and purpose among archaeologists and among those members of the general public who consume our product. This diversity has been discussed in terms of the differences between processual and postprocessual archaeology (see, e.g., Binford 1983; Hodder 1991). It is always dangerous to generalize about such complex matters, but in recent years an increasing polarization of opinion within (and outside) archaeology makes it possible to take the broad brush and see the essence of debate as lying within structured sets of oppositions – although these are frequently not very well thought through (see, e.g., Wylie 1992a). The first opposition might be between a disengaged, positivist archaeology on the one hand and a politically engaged, intensely social science on the other. The second reflects concern about the inherent conservatism of disciplines and refers to a choice between an archaeology that is conservative of traditional approaches to the study of human beings in the past and an archaeology that is responsive to the needs of an increasingly diverse cohort of producers and consumers of archaeological knowledge in the present.

These oppositions mask a vast amount of internal variation, which is partially captured by the steadily increasing growth of subdisciplinary specializations such as distributional archaeology and archaeometry. By the same token proponents of new approaches to archaeology (such as feminist archaeology) have rightly rejected life on the margins of 'specialization' and have sought to bring their perspectives center stage and into the mainstream (see, e. g., Gero and Conkey 1991; Hanen and Kelley 1992; Wylie 1992b). It is worth noting that feminist archaeology has also begun to devote much more attention to exploring its history, not just for the sake of disinterring forgotten lives and reputations, but also as a means of better understanding structures of disciplinary oppression as they have played themselves out in the past (see Claasen 1994; Gilchrist 1991; McBryde 1993; Phillips 1995).

Then there are forces for change that arise from divergent understandings of archaeological ontology, which have been a feature of only the last twenty-five years (see, e.g., Binford 1981; Bailey 1983; Murray 1987, 1995). These new understandings about time in archaeology and of the structural properties of archaeological records lie well outside the cultural traditions of our discipline, and they pose challenges that go to the heart of the purpose of archaeological knowledge (see, e.g., Barrett 1994, Chapters 6 and 7; Hodder 1991, Chapter 5; Shanks and Tilley 1987, Chapter 5). In this sense an understanding of our conceptual inheritance not only underscores the magnitude of the challenge, it also helps to set current disputes between processual and postprocessual archaeology in their proper (i.e., very limited) context.

These great debates within archaeology, and the different histories of archaeology they will give rise to, are also beginning to profoundly change the relationship between archaeology and society. It is easy enough to say that these changes, too, will require new histories of archaeology, but there are real questions about the ways in which these divergent histories will relate to each other.

The most significant area of activity in this field has to do with explorations of the relationship between archaeology and the foundation and maintenance of nation-states in the nineteenth and twentieth centuries (see, e.g., Arnold 1990; Diaz-Andreu 1993; Dietler 1994; Fowler 1987; Kohl 1993; Kohl and Fawcett 1995; McCann 1988; Slapsak 1993; Veit 1989). During that time archaeology not only became a 'science' and a legitimate discipline in its own right, it also became pre-eminently popular. The bases of its popularity and authority rested on the fact that practitioners were able to persuade people that it could do two crucial things. First, it could extend the history of nations into prehistory, thus establishing the antiquity of nations or ethnic groups. Consequently, the archaeological record of Europe could be made meaningful and valuable as evidence of continuity or succession, of diffusion or innate genius. Second, and this is a related point, it could overcome the possibility that a high human antiquity implied that human prehistory was unknowable, that oblivion would overcome memory. Although there were arguments about the applicability of the three-age system, about *ex oriente lux* versus *le mirage oriental*, about whether Neanderthals were ancestral to modern human beings, in fact about almost anything, no one after 1840 argued that the prehistoric past was unknowable (see also Trigger 1989).

Much has been written about the things that gave credibility to the new science of prehistoric archaeology. The link to geology and palaeontology with stratigraphy and faunal analysis (see, e.g., Grayson 1983; Van Riper 1993), the use of classification that allowed patterns of difference and similarity in material culture across space and time to be established (see, e.g., Graslund 1987), and the spectacular series of discoveries that just seemed to keep on happening, have all been discussed. However, much less has been written about more important elements that increased plausibility. Here I refer to primarily cultural elements such as the theories, presuppositions, prejudices, or pre-existing frameworks of understanding that guided problem selection. These things did not in themselves create archaeological knowledge. But they did something far more important-they created the need for the knowledge and they supplied the meanings of that knowledge.

However, this is only a small part of the point. Far more important is the fact that such entities were to all intents and purposes immune from an encounter with the empirical. It is fashionable to argue that this immunity was granted as a result of the theory dependence of observation, in other words that the empirical was so constructed by the theoretical that it would be logically circular (hence impossible) for it to be turned against itself. But this analysis only touches the surface, because it does not address the fact that practitioners, despite all their huffing and puffing about science, never sought such an encounter (see Murray1990). Weber has also noted the tendency for nineteenth-century archaeology and anthropology to adopt the mantle of science and for 'its social assumptions and normative values (to pass) as objective judgements' (1974: 273).

It might be argued that this point about links between epistemology and metaphysics in nineteenth-century archaeology has little to offer contemporary archaeology, but such an argument would be wrong. Archaeologists are now having to live with the consequences of this pact concluded between archaeologists and society in the nineteenth century, particularly the widespread (but in most cases patently false) belief that archaeology can prove the antiquity of ethnic identities. The ideas of race, language, and culture that have done so much to configure archaeology and anthropology since the mid-nineteenth century are now 'perilous' (Wolf 1994), in the sense that they have a great capacity to cause harm to human lives and human freedoms. There is no mistaking the tenor of the times when nation-states are beginning to fragment into polities built around a range of different sources of identity, but there is also no mistaking the absolute centrality of 'the past' in the constitution of these new identities (see Friedman 1992; Gathercole and Lowenthal 1990; Rowlands 1994; Shennan 1989; Smith 1989).

It is obviously vital that archaeologists communicate with society about the ways in which knowledge about the past is built up and the 'tolerance limits' that should be set on archaeology's statements of interpretation. However, it is worth noting that the core social assumptions and normative values of archaeologists are still largely unexplored, and the ways in which these values articulate with archaeological data to produce plausible accounts of 'the past' are the subject of intense, if not particularly well-informed, debate. This goal of critical reflection about the intellectual inheritance of contemporary archaeology is made the more difficult by the fact that links between the empirical data of archaeology and the ideas, theories, hypotheses, models, or guesses we have about them are very weak indeed (see Murray 1996a).

Our current histories, whether they are based on the analysis of individuals, or of something more general, have played a part in our drive for critical reflection. For example, in the matter of exploring new frameworks for understanding the archaeological past, mainstream histories of nineteenth-century European archaeology (e.g., Daniel 1943, 1971, 1975; Trigger 1989) have tended to argue that by and large the central discourse of that archaeology was between proponents of universalist accounts of human history (what Trigger calls evolutionist archaeology) and those more concerned with exploring the particularism of culture history. The fact that discourse about history writing formed around these antinomies is at least as old as the conflict between Vico and Herder gives the debates a respectable antiquity as well as a kind of timelessness, as if the eternal verity of this discourse is established. Consequently an impression of naturalness is conveyed, an impression that the primary determinants of archaeological discourse should be thus – of processualism taking up the cudgels of universalism, and postprocessualism restoring the balance.

This is a plausible account. But when we look a little harder at this period we see that far from there being a consensus about the boundaries of discourse, both Glyn Daniel and (to a lesser extent) Bruce Trigger have masked some highly significant variation. The reason for this masking is that both authors have produced histories of contemporary archaeology, not histories of thinking about archaeology or histories of the social and cultural contexts of archaeological thought. As such these histories are teleological, and those bits of the story that seem to have no clear connection with the current state of affairs are either bowdlerized or excised. Such histories of the victors are commonplace in anthropology and archaeology, especially when so many of one's disciplinary ancestors would seem crazed if not just politically incorrect by today's standards. Sven Nilsson's statements about the reality of trolls and the bestial character of the Lapps made in his great *Primitive Inhabitants of Scandinavia* (1868) are a case in point. These aspects of Nilsson tend not to appear in accounts about his extremely significant role in the history of archaeology.

My point here is that the ferment within contemporary archaeology will require us to constantly return to the history of our discipline in order to 'denaturalize' current conceptions of the nature and purpose of archaeological knowledge, to demonstrate that these are not eternal truths and that there are other archaeologies possible. I have already discussed some of the implications of our need to work harder at explaining the 'tolerance limits' of archaeological interpretations to the people who have to go out and live with them, but there are other external forces that will also require a re-evaluation of our intellectual inheritance.

Chief among these is the now problematic relationship between archaeologists and Indigenous peoples in the 'settler societies' of the United States, Canada, Australia, South Africa, and New Zealand (see, e.g., McGuire 1992; McManamon 1991; Murray 1996b, 1996c). In recent years Indigenous peoples have made it quite clear that they regard much of what archaeologists do, and the ways they set about doing it, to be deeply colonialist. We should be absolutely clear that there are no easy ways to resolve these tensions, but it seems obvious enough that archaeologists will have to reflect deeply about the impact their practice has on Indigenous groups and to become more firmly part of the very difficult process of reconciliation within settler societies. Some practitioners might take this to mean that they should abandon science or any pretence to objectivity in their practice, and to do this as an act of contrition for the fact that too few of us have until recently given much thought to these aspects of 'doing' archaeology. Others take the more balanced view that decolonizing archaeology does not mean abandoning a quest for objectivity, far from it. In fact, the most successful way to begin the process of decolonizing archaeology is to reflect critically about archaeological practice (especially in light of feedback from indigenous people), to retain a commitment to objectivity, however mitigated this might be (see, e.g., Murray 1996a; Wylie 1992a), and to recognize that this is a process without end.

There are a great many hidden histories of archaeology, not just those of nationalism, colonialism, or of the oppression of women. For example, demands for increasing access to 'the past' might also mean that we need to rethink the impact of professionalization on a field of study that once had many amateur contributors (see, e.g., Griffiths 1996; Levine 1986). Some (see, e.g., Phillips 1995) have suggested that there is a close link between the exclusion of amateurs and the marginalization of women in twentieth-century archaeology and that the notion of the 'great archaeologist', which to an extent this volume represents, celebrates the domination of the full-time, professional, mostly male archaeologist. This argument has some force, but it seems clear enough that if archaeology continues with the process of being re-imagined by its practitioners and by the societies that support it, then new subjects for archaeological biography will be found and our 'old reliables', such as Gordon Childe, can have some company in the disciplinary pantheon.

## Concluding remarks

It has been my goal to argue for both radical and conservative roles for biography writing in archaeology and to stress its very great value in helping us to understand the social and cultural elements of archaeological knowledge. If the picture I have produced is one of a discipline in a ferment of change, but also in a ferment of self-discovery, then this is, in my view, a fair portrait of a discipline at last coming to terms with the differences between 'the past' and 'doing archaeology'. I have placed considerable stress on the need for archaeology to respond positively to calls for a democratization of access to 'the past' and for the fact that groups once marginalized or simply overlooked by practitioners will (with justification) seek to create their own histories of archaeology to validate their contemporary aspirations. This shift in focus from the maintenance of a history of the victors to histories of those once thought either insignificant or vanquished does not in any way mean that the discipline of archaeology should collapse into a disabling relativism, or into a series of mutually incomprehensible discourses about 'the past' that have to resort to political means to establish which view of 'the past' is plausible or meaningful.

There can be no doubt that this more open view of archaeological knowledge confronts practitioners with new challenges, but at least we have the minimal satisfaction that this is a convincing demonstration of the continuing relevance of the discipline. But we should also be quite clear that this openness requires archaeologists as practitioners to place great emphasis on the power of empirical archaeological data to constrain interpretation, and to resist strongly the notion that 'anything goes' in this field. It also enjoins them most particularly in the very difficult business of building archaeological theory that might link ideas and observables, or at least, allow us to establish what the 'tolerance limits' of such ideas within archaeology might be (Murray 1996a; Trigger 1991; Wylie 1992a).

To hold fast to the notion that understanding the interaction between our ideas about 'the past' and our ability to convincingly ground those ideas in archaeological phenomena should be a major goal for our discipline might be thought unreasonably restrictive. But surely this is mistaken, and there is a world of difference between saying that only one view of 'the past' must prevail and adopting a more nuanced position that many 'pasts' are possible but that archaeologists should seek to develop perspectives so that they more meaningfully intersect with archaeological phenomena. In this reading there are pasts, such as some that are grounded in religious belief, that do not depend for plausibility on the degree to which they illuminate or are illuminated by archaeological phenomena. This is entirely appropriate. Advancing the cause of theoretical development, and of accepting the basic premise that archaeological phenomena constrain archaeological interpretation, in no way necessitates the removal of other forms as satisfying frameworks for understanding 'the past'. What it does do is to allow us to clearly distinguish between systems of knowledge and to take action accordingly.

It is often thought that this approach to archaeological epistemology acts to repress or oppress marginal groups within society, but the striking aspect of our current situation is that the very act of being more transparent about the significant elements of archaeological epistemology places the conceptual core of our discipline under much greater threat than do these ostensibly marginal perspectives on the nature and purpose of archaeological knowledge. The sharp disjunction between the methodological and epistemological rhetoric of mainstream archaeologists (especially in their appeal to science or to contemporary social theory to underwrite the authority of their statements) and what a close analysis reveals about practice indicates that much of the plausibility of contemporary archaeological interpretation lies in the link between the institutions of archaeology and the ideology of the dominant culture. It seems self-evident that as our interests in 'the past' grow and diversify, and if archaeology is not to collapse into a welter of disabling relativisms relying upon coercion, trickery, ignorance, or cultural prejudice to underwrite the plausibility of archaeological interpretations, then an acceptance of the power of the empirical to constrain interpretation is inevitable.

I think, perhaps naively, that if we establish that archaeological perspectives have histories and that our disciplinary culture is not *sui generis*, then it surely follows that this understanding might be a powerful force for liberating the archaeological imagination so that we might do a better job of constructing an archaeology that is more directly related to the structural properties of its data, and an archaeology that is better able to inform its public about the nature of the knowledge being claimed about 'the past'. I also think, again perhaps naively, that the new perspectives on humanity that will flow from this changed psychology of research might actually produce pasts that can form the basis of an effective critique of how we construct presents.

But it is always important to remember that people 'do' archaeology and that people consume our product. While there are powerful formal and informal frameworks that structure our behaviour as archaeologists, and the expectations of our consumers, there is no doubt that biography provides a unique and powerful point of access into those structures.

**Note**
David van Reybrouck very kindly read and commented on a draft of this essay. He reminded me of the importance of obituaries as an additional source of information about many of the matters considered here and drew my attention to two editorials by Douglas Givens in the *Bulletin of the History of Archaeology*, May and November 1995.

**References**
ARNOLD, B. 1990. The Past as Propaganda: Totalitarian Archaeology in Nazi Germany. *Antiquity* 64: 464-478.
BAILEY, G. N. 1983. Concepts of Time in Quaternary Prehistory. *Annual Reviews in Anthropology* 12: 165-192 .

BARRETT, J. C. 1994. *Fragments from Antiquity*. Oxford: Blackwell.

BINFORD, L. R. 1981. Behavioral Archaeology and the 'Pompeii Premise'. *Journal of Anthropological Research* 37: 195-208.

—1983. *Working at Archaeology*. New York: Academic Press.

BOWDEN, M. C. B. 1991. *Pitt Rivers: The Life and Archaeological Work of Lieutenant-General Augustus Henry Lane Fox Pitt Rivers, DCL, FRS, FSA*. Cambridge: Cambridge University Press.

CLAASEN, C. (ed) 1994. *Women in Archaeology*. Philadelphia: University of Pennsylvania Press.

CLARK, J. G. D. 1989. *Prehistory at Cambridge and Beyond*. Cambridge: Cambridge University Press.

DANIEL, G. E. 1943. *The Three Ages: An Essay on Archaeological Method*. Cambridge: Cambridge University Press.

—1967. *The Origins and Growth of Archaeology*. Harmondsworth, UK: Penguin.

—1971. From Worsaae to Childe: The Models of Prehistory. *Proceedings of the Prehistoric Society* 37: 140-153.

—1975. *A Hundred and Fifty Years of Archaeology*. London: Duckworth.

DANIEL, G., and C. CHIPPINDALE (eds) 1989. *The Pastmasters: Eleven Modern Pioneers of Archaeology*. London: Thames & Hudson.

DIAZ-ANDREU, M. 1993. Theory and Ideology in Archaeology: Spanish Archaeology under the Franco Regime. *Antiquity* 67: 74-82.

DIETLER, M. 1994. 'Our Ancestors the Gauls': Archaeology, Ethnic Nationalism, and the Manipulation of Celtic Identity in Modern Europe. *American Anthropologist* 96 (3): 584-605.

DROWER, M. S. 1985. *Flinders Petrie: A Life in Archaeology*. London: Gollancz.

Evans, J. 1943. *Time and Chance*. Oxford: Clarendon.

FOWLER, D. 1987. Uses of the Past: Archaeology in the Service of the State. *American Antiquity* 52: 229- 248.

FRIEDMAN, J. 1992. The Past in the Future: History and the Politics of Identity. *American Anthropologist* 94 (4): 837- 859.

GATHERCOLE, P. and D. LOWENTHAL (eds) 1990. *The Politics of the Past*. London: Unwin Hyman.

GERO, J. and M. CONKEY (eds) 1991. *Engendered Archaeology: Women and Production in Prehistory*. Oxford: Blackwell.

GILCHRIST, R. 1991. Women's Archaeology? Political Feminism, Gender Theory and Historical Revision. *Antiquity* 65: 495-501.

GIVENS, D. R. 1992. The Role of Biography in Writing the History of Archaeology. In J.E. Reyman (ed) *Rediscovering Our Past: Essays on the History of American Archaeology*, pp. 51-65. Aldershot, UK: Avebury.

GRASLUND, Bo. 1987. *The Birth of Prehistoric Chronology: Dating Methods and Dating Systems in Nineteenth-Century Scandinavian Archaeology*. Cambridge: Cambridge University Press.

GRAYSON, D. K. 1983. *The Establishment of Human Antiquity*. New York: Academic Press.

GREEN, S. 1981. *Prehistorian: A Biography of V. Gordon Childe*. Bradford-on-Avon, UK: Moonraker Press.

GRIFFITHS, T. 1996. *Hunters and Collectors*. Cambridge: Cambridge University Press.

GRUBER, J. 1966. In Search of Experience: Biography as an Instrument for the History of Anthropology. In J. Helm (ed) *Pioneers of American Anthropology, the Uses of Biography*, pp. 3-27. Seattle: University of Washington Press.

HANEN, M. and J. KELLEY 1992. Gender and Archaeological Knowledge. In L. Embree (ed) *Metaarchaeology, Reflections by Archaeologists and Philosophers*, pp. 195-225. Dordrecht: Kluwer.

HAWKES, J. 1982. *Mortimer Wheeler: Adventurer in Archaeology*. London: Weidenfeld and Nicolson.

HODDER, I. 1991. *Reading the Past*. 2nd edn. Cambridge: Cambridge University Press.

HUNTER, M. 1975. *John Aubrey and the Realm of Learning*. London: Duckworth.

KOHL, P. 1993. Nationalism, Politics, and the Practice of Archaeology in Soviet Transcaucasia. *Journal of European Archaeology* 1 (2): 181-190.

KOHL, P. and C. FAWCETT (eds) 1995. *Nationalism, Politics, and the Practice of Archaeology*. Cambridge: Cambridge University Press.

LEVINE, P. 1986. *The Amateur and the Professional: Antiquarians, Historians, and Archaeologists in Victorian England 1838-1886*. Cambridge: Cambridge University Press.

McBryde, I. 1993. In Her Right Place ...? Women in Archaeology: Past and Present. In H. Du Cros and L. J. Smith (eds) *Women in Archaeology: A Feminist Critique*, pp. xi-xv. Canberra: Department of Prehistory, Research School of Pacific Studies, Australian National University.

MCCANN, B. 1988. The National Socialist Perversion of Archaeology. *World Archaeological Bulletin* 2: 51-54.

MCGUIRE, R. 1992. Archaeology and the First Americans. *American Anthropologist* 94 (4): 816-836.

MCMANAMON, F. P. 1991.The Many Publics for Archaeology. *American Antiquity* 56 (1): 121-130.

MCNAIRN, B. 1980. *Method and Theory of V. Gordon Childe*. Edinburgh: Edinburgh University Press.

MILLER, D. 1985. *Artifacts as Categories*. Cambridge: Cambridge University Press.

MURRAY, T. 1987. Remembrances of Things Present: Appeals to Authority in the History and Philosophy of Archaeology. Unpublished PhD, Department of Anthropology, University of Sydney.

—1990. The History, Philosophy and Sociology of Archaeology: The Case of the *Ancient Monuments Protection Act* (1882). In V. Pinsky and A.Wylie(eds) *Critical Directions in Contemporary Archaeology*, pp. 55-67. Cambridge: Cambridge University Press.

—1993. Communication and the Importance of Disciplinary Communities: Who Owns the Past? In N. Yoffee and A. Sherratt (eds) *Archaeological Theory: Who Sets the Agenda?* pp. 105-116. Cambridge: Cambridge University Press.

—1996a. From Sydney to Sarajevo: A Centenary Reflection on Archaeology and European Identity. *Archaeological Dialogues* 1: 58-74.

—1996b. On Coming to Terms with the Living: Some Aspects of Repatriation for the Archaeologist. *Antiquity* 267: 217- 220.

—1996c. *Mabo and Re-Creating the Heritage of Australia*. Working Papers in Australian Studies, Sir Robert Menzies Centre for Australian Studies, University of London.

PHILLIPS, P. 1995. Hidden from History: The Participation of Women in Six British Archaeological Journals 1900- 1950. B.A. (Hons.) thesis. School of Archaeology, La Trobe University.

PIGGOTT, S. 1985 (1950). *William Stukeley: An Eighteenth-Century Antiquary*. 2nd edn. London: Thames and Hudson.

PINSKY, V. 1990. Introduction: Historical Foundations. In V. Pinsky and A. Wylie (eds) *Critical Directions in Contemporary Archaeology*, pp. 51-54. Cambridge: Cambridge University Press.

REID, J. J. 1991. On the History of Archaeology and Archaeologists. *American Antiquity* 56 (2): 195-196.

ROWLANDS, M. 1994. The Politics of Identity in Archaeology. In G.C. Bond and A. Gilliam (eds) *Social Constructions of the Past: Representations as Power*, pp. 129-143. London: Routledge.

SHANKS, M. and C. TILLEY 1987. *Social Theory and Archaeology*. Cambridge: Polity Press.

SHENNAN, S. 1989. Introduction: Archaeological Approaches to Cultural Identity. In S. Shennan (ed) *Archaeological Approaches to Cultural Identity*, pp. 1-32. London: Unwin Hyman.

SLAPSAK, B. 1993. Archaeology and Contemporary Myths of the Past. *Journal of European Archaeology* 1 (2): 191-19 5.

SMITH, A. D. 1989. *The Ethnic Origins of Nations*. Oxford: Blackwell.

TAYLOR, T. 1993. Conversations with Leo Klejn. *Current Anthropology* 34 (5): 723-735.

THOMPSON, M. W. 1977. *General Pitt-Rivers: Evolution and Archaeology in the Nineteenth-Century.* Bradford-on-Avon, UK: Moonraker Press.

TRIGGER, B. G. 1980. *Gordon Childe*. London: Thames and Hudson.

—1985. Writing the History of Archaeology. A Survey of Trends. In G. Stocking Jr. (ed) *Objects and Others, Essays on Museums and Material Culture*, pp. 218-235. Madison: University of Wisconsin Press.

—1989. *History of Archaeological Thought*. Cambridge: Cambridge University Press.

—1991. Distinguished Lecture in Archaeology: Constraint and Freedom - a New Synthesis for Archaeological Explanation. *American Anthropologist* 93: 550- 569.

—1994. The Coming of Age of the History of Archaeology. *Journal of Archaeological Research* 2: 113-136.

VAN RIPER, A. B. 1993. *Men Among the Mammoths*. Chicago: University of Chicago Press.

VEIT, U. 1989. Ethnic Concepts in German Prehistory: A Case Study on the Relationship between Cultural Identity and Archaeological Objectivity. In S. Shennan (ed) *Archaeological Approaches to Cultural Identity*, pp. 33-56. London: Unwin Hyman.

WEBER, G. 1974. Science and Society in Nineteenth Century Anthropology. *History of Science* 15: 260-283.

WHEELER, R. E. Mortimer 1955. *Still Digging: Interleaves from an Antiquary's Notebook*. London: M. Joseph.

—1966. *Alms for Oblivion: An Antiquary's Scrapbook*. London: Weidenfeld and Nicolson.

—1976. *My Archaeological Mission to India and Pakistan.* London: Thames and Hudson.

WILLEY, G. R. 1988. *Portraits in American Archaeology: Remembrances of Some Distinguished Americanists*. Albuquerque: University of New Mexico Press.

WOLF, E. R. 1994. Perilous Ideas. Race, Culture, People. *Current Anthropology* 35 (1): 1-12.

WOODBURY, R. B. 1973. *Alfred V. Kidder.* New York: Columbia University Press.

WYLIE, A. 1991. Gender theory and the archaeological record: why is there no archaeology of gender? In J. Gero and M. Conkey (eds) *Engendering Archaeology*, pp. 31-54. Oxford: Blackwell.

—1992a. On 'Heavily Decomposing Red Herrings': Scientific method in archaeology and the ladening of evidence with theory. In L. Embree (ed) *Metaarchaeology, Reflections by Archaeologists and Philosophers*, pp. 269-288. Dordrecht: Kluwer.

—1992b. The interplay of evidential constraints and political interests: recent archaeological research on gender. *American Antiquity* 57 (1): 15-35.

*Chapter 7*

# Excavating the cultural traditions of nineteenth century English archaeology: the case of Robert Knox

### Introduction: the need for new histories of archaeology

During the last three decades archaeologists have devoted a great deal of time (and perhaps even more *angst)* to discussing core elements of disciplinary philosophy. Much of this discussion has tended to focus on epistemological and logical matters – issues of knowledge production and justification, and a continuing exploration of the nature of archaeological reasoning. In recent years the focus on epistemology has been broadened by the adoption of perspectives drawn from the history and sociology of science, and inquiries have been stimulated into the question of what makes archaeological accounts of the past plausible. A consideration of plausibility has led to more detailed investigations of the links between archaeology, and the society which sustains its practice. This, in turn, has greatly increased the significance of the history of archaeology as a primary source of perspective about disciplinary traditions and the 'culture' of archaeology (see e.g. Wylie 1989; 1992a; 1992b; Murray 1996; 1999; 2001; 1995).

My interest in exploring new histories of archaeology is the direct result of a desire to establish how the edifice of modern archaeology – its agendas, concepts, categories, patterns of socialisation, and its institutions, became established, and the processes which have underwritten its transformations. Other justifications for this interest range from the banal – it's a fascinating enterprise, to the more complex – we need to understand more about how people use pasts to support or construct presents – some which we should support, others we should oppose. I will elaborate a little further on this point, because it helps to explain why I am undertaking research into the fascinating (but frequently repugnant) anthropology of Robert Knox.

Archaeology became a highly popular discipline in the nineteenth century mainly because people were persuaded that it could do two things. First, that archaeology could extend the history of nations into prehistory, and thus establish the antiquity of nations or ethnic groups. Consequently the archaeological record of Europe could be made meaningful and valuable as evidence of continuity or succession, of diffusion or innate genius. Second, and this is a related point, because archaeology was widely believed to be capable of overcoming the possibility that a high human antiquity implied that human prehistory was unknowable, that oblivion would overcome memory. A detailed examination of these claims clearly indicates that the primary basis of persuasion had as much to do with appeals to unexamined presuppositions about human nature and human history, as it did with much-hyped notions of scientific method.

Mainstream histories of nineteenth century European archaeology (e.g. Daniel 1943; 1971; 1975; Trigger 1989) have tended to argue that by-and-large the central discourse of that archaeology was between proponents of universalist accounts of human history (what Trigger called evolutionist archaeology), and those more concerned with exploring the particularism of culture history. This is an exciting account, but close inspection reveals that far from there being a consensus about the boundaries of discourse, in fact the opposite was the case. A close analysis of the debates, which surrounded the foundation and institutionalisation of archaeology and anthropology in mid nineteenth century England, reveals the existence of much hidden history (Weber 1974; Murray 1987; Stocking 1987).

Robert Knox's search for a scientific English anthropology that was both polygenist and anti-evolutionist provides an excellent case in point, because it also reveals the complex linkages between anatomy, ethnology and philosophy that were created by those who adhered more to the 'Great Chain of Being' than to Darwinism. Although distinctly marginal to contemporary philosophical orthodoxies, the transcendentalism of *naturphilosophie* played a significant role in the development of ethnology (particularly in the construction of the concept of culture). A close analysis of Knox's *The Races of Men* reveals something of the spirit that drove this alternative anthropology. Furthermore, the conflict between these alternative anthropologies and archaeologies in mid nineteenth century England gives us an opportunity to explore the ways in which the participants sought support from science and society, and the conditions under which that support was given.

### A voice from the margins: Robert Knox

Robert Knox was born in Edinburgh on the 4th of September 1793. After a brilliant school career, he graduated from medicine in 1814. Knox's first choice was to pursue a research career in human anatomy, but on the 16th June 1815 he was gazetted 'Hospital Assistant to the Forces', as the British army mobilised to meet the threat posed by Napoleon's return from Elba.

A few days after the Battle of Waterloo he was sent to Brussels to tend the wounded. It was here that he first saw the practical differences between British and French medicine. In his view the standard of surgery amongst the

British was deplorable, and Knox was later to remark that this experience convinced him of the necessity of sound anatomical training for safe surgery. After returning to England with a party of wounded Knox was gazetted to the 72nd Regiment (later the Seaforth Highlanders), and in April 1817 sailed for the Cape of Good Hope.

Knox was directly involved in the Kaffir War of 1819, the by-product of which was a plentiful supply of crania and major bones collected from the battlefields. But he was to gain far more than an expanded comparative collection during his time at the Cape. Knox's biographer, Henry Lonsdale, believes that it was the experience of the Kaffir War and the general political situation in the colony that formed Knox's views about the inherent differences between the human races and the inevitable antagonisms that arose from the perception of such differences:

> *...when so visibly under his cognizance antagonistic races of men were playing their game of humanity - the Saxon encroaching and the Caffre daring and impetuous in repelling the foe. ...so many forces gathered on an African plateau, and there manifesting to those who could observe the characteristics, the tendencies and antagonisms of race* (Lonsdale 1870: 12).

Knox returned to Edinburgh in 1821, on half pay from the army, and began to write papers for major Scots journals. Late in 1821, Knox took the major step of his intellectual life and went to Paris. There were many reasons to leave Edinburgh. His teacher John Barclay had stressed the importance of the work of the French comparative anatomists Xavier Bichat and Pierre Beclard. Knox's experience of the standard of British medical care at Brussels had left him with the impression that the French were far more advanced in the field of general medicine, but there is much we do not yet know about his life in Paris. Lonsdale mentions that Knox joined the Freemasons in Paris on the 22nd of April 1822, but makes no comment about what this meant to him. The French Freemasons were strongly anti-clerical and politically Liberal during the reign of Louis XVIII, and it seems likely that Knox must have held similar opinions (which would been well outside the political mainstream in England and Scotland at that time).

Politics aside, Knox was in Paris to work and make contact with the French medical community. He first became associated with Baron Larrey, Napoleon's friend and Chief Surgeon. Through Larrey Knox met and befriended the luminaries of the Parisian scientific elite – George Cuvier, Etienne Geoffroy Saint-Hilaire, and Henri De Blainville. He also formed close ties with the new generation of researchers – Etienne Serres and Pierre

Beclard. Geoffroy Saint-Hilaire gave the second part of his epoch-making lectures on *Philosophic Anatomy* in 1822, while Knox was in Paris, and they had a considerable impact on him. Cuvier had already published his great works *Recherche sur les ossemens fossiles de quadrupèdes* (1812) and *Le Règne animal distribué d'après son organisation* (1819), making him the foremost scientist of his time. Knox always had high praise for Geoffroy Saint-Hilaire and Cuvier, describing them as 'the men who have most contributed to the development of the true relation of Anatomy to the Science of Living Beings'.

Armed with an appreciation of the relationship of fossils to geological time (from Cuvier) and grounding in the tenets of 'transcendental anatomy' (from Geoffroy Saint-Hilaire and Serres), Knox returned to work in Edinburgh late in 1822. Recognition soon followed when he was elected a Fellow of the Royal Society of Edinburgh, and a Councillor of the Wernerian Society. Knox's new work clearly shows the influence of his time in Paris in that he was now much more concerned with the elucidation of the relationship of structure and function in organisms – a concern that also motivated the work of Cuvier and Geoffroy Saint Hilaire.

A measure of this success came in 1825 when John Barclay offered him a partnership in his School of Anatomy – over the heads of his assistants. Knox accepted willingly and proceeded to lecture after the fashion of his senior partner. Like Barclay, he valued the work of the early French anatomists Bichet and Beclard, and also included the work of contemporary researchers, particularly from the Continent. Knox taught his pupils comparative anatomy – not for its own sake, but to elucidate the laws of the 'organic whole', illustrating his lectures with preparations of the rudimentary organs in the human embryo and tracing their development. Following Cuvier, he also used fossils to demonstrate the principles of comparative anatomy and to indicate the brief antiquity of human beings when compared with the age of the earth. Knox became an even more popular lecturer than Barclay, and soon had the largest anatomy class ever assembled in the United Kingdom. When Barclay died Knox took over control of the school.

His capacity for work was phenomenal. Not only did he lecture to medical students, but he also instituted 'Saturday Lectures' for the learned general public. These consisted of lectures on Zoology, Comparative Anatomy, Physiology and Ethnology. In them he stressed the implications of Cuvier's work on fossils, and Geology for the Mosaic Cosmogony, and the importance of Geoffroy Saint-Hilaire's 'transcendental anatomy', which he felt had extended Cuvier's view of the past into the future. Knox was not loath to question the statements of revealed religion on the origin and nature of life.

This was too much for Edinburgh, dominated by the Presbyterian Kirk and the conservative professors of the University. They tolerated Knox writing his treatises on comparative anatomy for the learned societies, but it was altogether different for him to lecture to his students and general public about his ideas on the age of the earth and the origin of life. It was even worse that he applied his theories to human beings, and his slighting references to the character of the Saxon race were not welcomed. England was intellectually dominated by the philosophy of William Paley and the Natural Theologists, and Knox's public statements marked him as politically and intellectually unreliable. It is indicative that one of Knox's major rivals, Sir Charles Bell, had accepted Paley's *Evidence of Christianity* without questioning the doctrine of final causes. Knox was beginning to accumulate very powerful enemies.

In the 1826-27 session of the anatomy school Knox faced a novel problem, and the solution which presented itself was to be his downfall. Knox's regular source of corpses, the Dublin and London Resurrectionists, were unable to supply enough bodies to meet the dissection requirements of his school. Unlike the French situation, where corpses were supplied to registered schools of dissection by the government, the United Kingdom had no such provisions. William Burke and William Hare came to his rescue. These men had hit upon a novel idea; they murdered Edinburgh citizens and sold the corpses to Knox. Actually, that Knox was their client was pure chance – they had originally intended to deal with Alexander Munro, one of the Professors of Anatomy at the University.

In the trial that followed their arrest, the whole gory affair received wide publicity. In the public mind, Knox was guilty of complicity to murder – but the court cleared him of this charge. He was effectively reprimanded for not taking due care in ascertaining the provenance of the corpses, and an independent inquiry, conducted by members of the academic community, came to the same conclusion. It is not hard to understand why his colleagues, who were engaged in much the same traffic, gave him no support. Knox's political unreliability made him a perfect scapegoat.

Knox managed to struggle on with his anatomy school, but by 1842 his financial condition was grave, making it necessary for him to sell his school and to begin a new career writing for the medical press and giving public lectures. From this time onwards Knox did no more original scientific work, a fact which forced his later works to rely much more on polemic than on substantive research.

### A closer look at *The Races of Men*

The intent of *The Races of Men* (1850) is best understood by linking Knox's ideas about transcendental anatomy with the taxonomy of Georges Cuvier.

Together, these can be effectively contrasted with the English debate that Stocking has correctly identified as being conditioned by religious and humanitarian issues. These issues were kept separate from science on the Continent (Stocking 1973; 1987).

Although he often professed himself as being uncomfortable with the business of conveying complex philosophies to the general public, there can be little doubt that Knox was uniquely suited to his new situation. His anatomical researches and the fieldwork he conducted during his stay in South Africa formed a stock of first hand information that few race theorists possessed. His anatomical and morphological work also provided a stronger base for taxonomical statements than virtually any other theorist of his time. The depth of his scientific knowledge is certainly not demonstrated in *The Races of Men* (1850), however two articles in the *Lancet* (Knox 1855a; 1855b) give a clearer picture of his abilities.

*The Races of Men* has two major facets. The first is the theory and method of Knox's classifications. The second is the political implications which Knox drew from his theory. Obviously these divisions are fundamentally artificial given that the precepts and conclusions of one closely influenced the conduct of the other. Knox characterised the nature of his work unambiguously:

> *I disclaim all pretention of attempting a complete history of mankind, even from the single point of view from which I contemplate history. No materials exist for such a history. Of man's origin we know nothing correctly, we do not know when he first appeared in space; his place in time, then, is unknown* (1850: 1).

Knox began by stressing the importance of the physical character and constitution of human beings which he considered to be the basis of his taxonomy: 'Men are of various Races; call them Species if you will; call them permanent varieties it matters not' (1850: 2). But physical structure was not to be the only classifiable characteristic: 'Now the object of these lectures is to show that in human history race is everything' (1850: 2f).

Knox admitted that he had no real facts to speak of, but happily stated his belief that the human races possess organic differences as well. Responding to the idea that cultural differences are mostly environmental rather than innate (the view taken by many Monogenists, or believers in a single human origin), Knox declared: 'The mind of the race, instinctive and reasoning naturally differs in correspondence with organizations'. For him human beings are instinctive, the mind is not a *Tabula Rasa* and the qualities of race form the qualities of that instinct (1850: 3). For Knox the classification of mere physical externals would no longer suffice, the minds and cultures of different races

117

would become classifiable as well. The lessons of history all point in a single direction: 'human history cannot be a mere chapter of accidents', and race should now be much more than a physical designation. For Knox: 'race or hereditary descent is everything, it stamps the man' (1850: 5).

Knox's method was to identify contemporary races (which he believed had existed for centuries without change), and then to work back to the partially known and then the totally unknown. For Knox races existed because they differed from each other widely, and moral and cultural differences were not a particular response to education, religion, or climate. They were also not caused by any general laws governing intra-specific variation (which had been proposed by James Cowles Prichard). Races were fixed and innate; they were not convertible into other races over time in response to changed circumstances of life but were the product of the eternal laws of nature:

> As a living and material being, the history of man is included in a history of the organic world ... He has specific laws regulating his form, but these are in perfect accordance with nature's works. By the unity of organization he is connected with all life, past, present and to come (1850:6).

There are thus two human histories, the zoological and the intellectual – the former basically regulating the latter. Further than this, human beings, like the animals, must be found to occupy a particular portion of space and time. This is very important when Knox sought to reject the notion of 'hybrid fertility' in that it allowed him to argue that each of the races had a separate geographical origin, outside of which the race cannot hope to perpetually survive. Much of The *Races of Men* is taken up demonstrating this special 'natural' relationship between homeland and race, as a fundamental tenet of his Polygenism (the view that each of the human races had a separate origin).

Implied in this 'new view' of race taxonomy is a criticism of the methods of Blumenbach and Prichard. Knox asserted that they had classified only physical and cultural externals and not sought an understanding of process. In his view anatomy and linguistics could only ever hope to be causally related to the fundamental principles of physiology and embryology. The influence of Geoffroy Saint Hilaire and Serres is obvious in his commitment to the principles of transcendental anatomy, 'which alone of all systems, affords us a glimpse and a hope of a true "theory of nature"' (1850: 11f). The great philosophical problems raised by a search for understanding the nature and meaning of being human would be confronted in such a search for operative fundamentals. The theory of human progress, that was to become so much in vogue after Darwin, was certainly not one of these operative fundamentals. For Knox no law of progress operated in nature. The doctrine of unity of organisation and the existence of a 'Scale of Being' – found so often amongst the *Naturphilosophers* is strongly present in Knox's basic perceptions of the nature of life.

But if such an ordered atmosphere exists, how was Knox able to counter the factor of intra-specific variation? Knox resorted to natural law, again building his typologies from the ontogenetic to the phylogenetic. In his view every living individual grows up influenced and regulated by two contending principles. The law of unity of organization ever ready to retain the embryonic form, and the law of deformation. Knox argued that nature, being an ordered and exact entity, constantly leans to the former in the development of every individual, guaranteeing the individuality of species. Without such a 'balance of power' between the two forces Knox felt that we should have no distinct species of human beings or animals on the earth, because the laws of deformation or unity would perpetually alter every form and nothing could be recognized.

Thus out of the great deterministic scheme of nature arises the law of specialisation, leading to the perfection of the individual. But there were inconsistencies in this argument, even for Knox, who still had to argue for the Scale of Being, and consequently for the temporal mutability of all species: 'in time there is probably no such thing as species: No absolutely new creations ever took place ... (1850: 16). For Knox it became a question of the perspective of time. In the short-term he felt he could lay down rules for the immutability of species, but as a transcendental anatomist he was obliged to think the opposite.

The uncertainty of Knox's statements on these vital questions was a response to the fact that the solutions to two absolutely fundamental questions were beyond the sphere of human enquiry. The first was the origin of life on the globe, and the second was the nature of the secondary laws that governed the endless manifestations of primitive forms over time. Knox did not accept the implications of uniformitarian geology for biology, because for him such changes in form could not have been gradual and continuing without rest. Instead he favoured Cuvier's catastrophist scenario, which made such organic change temporally discontinuous. If species were to continuously change in response to organic variation, the careful order of nature would be in chaos. It was a difficult intellectual step from the role of the taxonomist and the creation of order, to the perception that such taxonomies were certainly not universal over time or space.

Knox moved from such general concepts into the particular area of his work, the influence of race on the course of history. In fact, apart from the statement of general physiological principles, Knox's assessment of the physical characteristics of races was scant to say the least. In fact he classified his races on the basis of the most superficial similarities or dissimilarities. Nonetheless Knox forcefully argued his point that there were clearly definable races within the body of the European population:

> *But the object of this work is to show that European races, so called, differ from each other as widely as the Negro does from the Bushman, the Caffre from the Hottentot, the Red Indian of American from the Esquimaux* (1850: 34f).

However, Knox's basic method turned out not to be a discussion of physical differences, but the endowment of their historical actions with racial qualities.

After an examination of the historical conduct and the cultural and social aspects of the various European races, Knox felt able to derive mental, moral and physical characteristics that were to function as the type for the classification of each race. Next came a demonstration of the immutability of race. For Knox all races followed the laws of hereditary descent, children not differing in form from their parents, with nothing, save extinction, changing the operation of such laws. Knox proceeded with his mainly cultural analysis of the human races: 'the results of the physical and mental qualities of race are naturally manifested in its civilisation, for every race has its own form of civilisation' (1850: 45). Knox's discussion of each race was formulaic. First, expose the logical and evidential faults of previous commentators. With recourse to history, reject the claims of monogenism and reject any non-natural arguments or special pleading. Second, establish the geographical area of origin, and the history, language and culture of the race in question. Occasionally, tucked away in the geographical section, there might be some startlingly superficial physical assessment of the race in question (e.g. 1850: 56).

But Knox did not intend to classify every human, not even most of them. His far from satisfactory discussion was merely one small aspect of his object. Far more important was for him to characterise the races as permanent and unvaried. Thus Knox for the great part of the work sought to answer two related questions: first, do races ever amalgamate? Second, can a human race ever permanently change its locality?

Both questions raised a host of related queries particularly the means by which we could identify the obstacles to a race changing its original locality. Much of Knox's argument about these matters turned on his account of human hybridity. In this Knox adopted the orthodox polygenist view that human beings could never create reproductively self supporting hybrids and that nature produces no such hybrids either among human beings or other animals. For the polygenists when hybrids did appear, by accident or through human intervention, they would soon cease to be, because they are either non-productive, or one or other of the pure breeds would speedily predominate and the weaker would subsequently disappear. Time was important here too because it was argued that in the short term hybrids may reproduce, but over time there would be an inevitable reversions to type.

Armed with this account of hybridity Knox moved to a discussion of the possibility of races changing their original locality. For Knox it was a law of nature that species have their geographical as well as their temporal place in nature, with species being seen as an expression of a geographical locality, with its totality of ecological factors. On this basis Knox argued that races which 'invade' or populate other geographical areas are doomed, because either the climate will beat them, or the lack of vitality engendered by the new environment will destroy the race and its culture through physiological and psychological degradation from type. However, this account of the role of climate forced Knox to consider a question inherently dangerous for a polygenist – to what extent did climate influence the human mind and body?

In true style Knox resorted to natural law. Climatic influences cause accidental deformities and as such are *not* transmissible by descent, with deviations from form being checked by laws of form that are checked by the law of unity of organization, and the law of deformation. The first law related to the tendency of nature to reproduce the specific form instead of the variety, while the second states that aberrations are infertile or otherwise non-viable. There is an obvious logical circularity here, but it is worth noting that much the same problems were being experienced by Knox's monogenist opponents. Although part of the problem can be sourced to the structure of the theories being deployed by the antagonists, an equally important problem was the quality of the data in the period before systematic fieldwork. Both sides were plagued by the fact that most of the reports from overseas correspondents that were faithfully repeated time and again in the course of the monogenist-polygenist debate were little better than hearsay or misinformation.

Knox's answer to the second central question, whether a human race ever permanently changes its locality, flowed directly from his assumptions about ecology and racial fitness. It was an answer with quite distinct political implications, especially for the makers of British imperial policy. In Knox's view the inherent drive of the Anglo-Saxon, for instance, may lead them to conquer and settle other areas, but such settlements could have no permanent existence. For Knox races were so inherently different and antagonistic, that even if these ecological factors were not in play, people could never settle peacefully in different race areas. For the Continental theorists *The Races of*

*Men* broke little new ground, but in Britain Knox's arguments were not in the least well received. To replace the determinism of God with the determinism of nature – which had no 'fundament moral principles' was a shocking thing to many. That Knox could make 'scientific' statements that purported to prove that 'with a deepening colour vanishes civilisation, the arts of peace, science, literature and abstract justice... ', was just too much. Apart from such considerations, the real question with Knox's polygenism was in his concept of species.

Knox regarded species, races and permanent varieties as one and the same. How was he able to do this? The answer lies in his 'reconciliation' of the principles of transcendental anatomy and the fixity of species proposed by Cuvier. Knox makes the nature of his reconciliation quite clear:

> *...that although the species forming a genus do certainly, when arranged as I shall presently show exhibit difference so slight as to be barely perceptible, still they remained distinct throughout all times, the answer was that permanent varieties only were contemplated and not species; that permanent varieties were the product of accidental birth, and the present varieties of the races of man ...thought permanent were the product of accidental circumstances* (1850: 107).

One important factor that was necessary for such a concept of species was the provision of a vast stretch of time to allow such laws the universality of operation they required. Cuvier's catastrophist geology was extended beyond the classification of fossils and linked by Knox to the concept of the Laws of Parallelism. These were first developed by the German transcendentalists and the French comparative anatomists and embryologists and stated that all 'living animal forms have an obvious consanguinity, are constructed on one plan, and physiologically identical forming one great chain of being' (1850: 166f). There is more than an ounce of faith in Knox's account of species, but it had the virtue of being quite consistent with the fundamental of his racial taxonomy:

> *How specialities arise we know not, but as they constitute the realisation of nature's great plan, we must hold by them, in fact there being no other guide for him in acquiring knowledge of the living world* (1850: 590).

For Knox the final difference between human beings and other animals finds ultimate form in the embryo. Knox proposed a developmental framework that indicated a progression in the complexity of forms from a microscopic point through all forms of life to its ultimate expression in the human archetype, the European. Knox did not believe Negro was an arrested embryological form of the white, rather that this race was totally different, a form that obeyed its own laws of development. Thus in terms of the archetype, the Negro was not the same as the white and it was thought by Knox to be nonsense to propose convertibility – the forms were distinct not different. Knox's logical trail is not hard to follow from here. Species are expressions of embryological distinctiveness and so the Negroes are evidently specifically different from the white. However, when Knox applied such a scenario to the taxonomy of life he concluded that the Negro was developmentally closer to the European than to the ape (mainly for cultural reasons).

Put in taxonomical terms, Knox placed all human races in the same family. All life was subject to the same origin – no species are ever created but in the progression of time all forms runs their course as aspects of the same life force and organization. At the end of time the Scale of Being becomes a unitary expression of life. Thus Knox was able to reconcile varietal difference with specific distinctiveness. Species are distinct entities in themselves only in a temporal sense, but the laws that govern the nature of species are constant through time. Such order was an expression of the organization and determinism – the highest aspect of it was the law of extra-specific reproduction. For Knox the hybrid, the 'sin against nature', had to be rejected because he felt that such 'permanent sporting' was destructive of the true mechanistic, materialist conception of nature that he espoused.

If Negroes were developmentally distinct from whites then there could not be any possibility of inter-racial reproductive fertility. Such a simple scenario might persuade some, but Knox faced serious difficulties applying his concept of species to real-world situations. For example, if readers were to allow that his concept of species explained the differences between black and white, how were they to relate this to the picture of racial antagonism and inherent difference that Knox had painted for Europeans. Knox seriously could not, and did not, propose that a Celt was specifically different to the Saxon – or did he? In the end Knox's account becomes very vague, turning towards flights of philosophical fantasy which (I suspect) must have bewildered a good number of his audiences in the salons and lecture halls of the north of England.

Retracing the logical twists and turns of Knox's transcendentalist account of the nature and meaning of human variety and the significance of history reveals many of the preoccupations, ambiguities, and contradictions of his time. It is a relatively straightforward matter to identify the points where Knox's logic fails and the special pleading begins. It is also easy to highlight inconsistencies in his treatment of archaeological, historical and ethnological data, and observe that Knox was able to manipulate data of highly variable quality to support his overall program. However, while we should acknowledge these problems and clearly identify his specious arguments about race (many of which remain common currency), it is important to see *The Races of Men* as an excellent example of philosophies of transcendentalism, which were eventually silenced by Darwinism. Written fifteen years before Lubbock's *Prehistoric Times* (1865) Knox's book broached questions of continuity and identity which were to become so important during the remainder of the nineteenth century, and which have returned with such force with the end of the Cold War and the onward march of globalisation.

## Some temporary conclusions

Knox's polygenism, his anti-clericalism, and his anti-Darwinism set him against the most powerful members of the British scientific establishment. But Knox was also (along with Paul Broca and James Hunt) intensely interested in building an anthropology that genuinely integrated perspectives from all of what we now consider to be the four fields of anthropology. Knox's vision of British anthropology was lost when James Hunt lost his battles with Lubbock, Huxley and others in the British Association for the Advancement of Science and in the Anthropological Society of London (see Murray 1987: ch 6; Stocking 1971; 1987).

These kinds of battles happen frequently enough in science, but it is important in the present context for us to consider the consequences of losing. In Knox's case, his racist anthropology (and its great, if fleeting, popularity) was simply ignored by later disciplinary historians such as Burrow (1966), a point first noted by Stocking (1968). Knox was expunged from the disciplinary memory as a disreputable embarrassment, a horrid wrong turning on the path to truth.

I have revived the sad history of Robert Knox in this paper because he is a good example of how histories of archaeology (and anthropology) are presentist, either by design, or simply because they reflect hegemony whatever ideological presuppositions practitioners labour under at any point in time. I have also presented this brief excursion into disciplinary history to support a much more critical attitude being adopted by some archaeologists to putative links between race, language and culture (see e.g. Shennan 1989; Veit 1989; Kohl and Fawcett 1995; Murray 1996; Jones 1997; Diaz-Andreu 1998; Harke 1998).

I have noted elsewhere that a gap between the methodological rhetoric and practical performance of archaeologists is particularly strong when matters of religious belief or ideological commitment come into play (Murray 1990). The reaction of the British scientific elite to Knox's anthropology provides a clear illustration of this phenomenon. James Cowles Prichard, Lubbock and others did indeed accept that archaeologists could profitably explore the links between race, language, and culture as a basis for writing the prehistory of Europe. But in killing off Knox's anti-evolutionism, and his insistence on the permanence of racial type, they also effectively attacked the foundations of the link between race, language, and culture, which was so useful to them. The crucial point here is that neither the victors nor the vanquished in the struggle for British anthropology recognised this. It is worth noting that recently we have been forcefully reminded that this is an unresolved dilemma (see e.g. Slapsak 1993; Dietler 1994; Kohl & Fawcett 1995; Jones 1997).

There is no doubt that much of the opposition to the work of was spurred by a rejection of his radical, anti-Christian, anti-imperial politics, and the fear that his insistence that human beings were no different to any other species in the natural world would essentially dehumanise society. The victorious archaeology and anthropology of Lubbock and Tylor (although sharing many of Knox's perceptions) was conservative of sensibilities, as well as being sound Liberal politics. This, not the propaganda that it was necessarily better science, was the reason for its success (Murray 1990).

**References**

BURROW, J. W. 1966. *Evolution and Society*. Cambridge: Cambridge University Press.
DANIEL, G. 1943. *The Three Ages: An essay on archaeological method*. Cambridge: Cambridge University Press.
—1971. From Worsaae to Childe. The models of prehistory. *Proceedings of the Prehistoric Society* 37: 140-153.
—1975. *One Hundred and Fifty Years of Archaeology*. London: Duckworth.
DIAZ-ANDREU, M. 1998. Comment on Heinrich Harke 'Archaeologists and Migrations. A Problem of Attitude?' *Current Anthropology* 39 (1): 28-29.
DIETLER, M. 1994. Our Ancestors the Gauls'. Archaeology, Ethnic Nationalism, and the Manipulation of Celtic Identity in Modern Europe. *American Anthropologist* 96 (3): 584-605.
HARKE, H. 1998. Archaeologists and Migrations. A Problem of Attitude? *Current Anthropology* 39 (1): 19-45.
JONES, S. 1997. *The Archaeology of Ethnicity. Constructing Identities in the Past and Present*.London: Routledge.
KOHL, P. and C. FAWCETT 1995. *Nationalism, Politics and the Practice of Archaeology*. Cambridge: Cambridge University Press.
KNOX, R. 1850. *The Races of Men*. London: Henry Renshaw.
—1855a. The Azteque and Bosjeman Children. Now Being Exhibited in London and on the Races they are Presumed to Belong. *Lancet* 1: 357-360.
—1855b. Introduction to Inquiries into the Philosophy of Zoology. *Lancet* 1: 625-627.

MURRAY, T. 1987. Remembrance of Things Present. Appeals to authority in the history and philosophy of archaeology. Unpublished PhD. Department of Anthropology, University of Sydney.

—1990. The history, philosophy and sociology of archaeology. The case of the *Ancient Monuments Protection Act* (1882). In: V. Pinsky and A. Wylie (eds) *Critical Directions in Contemporary Archaeology,* pp. 55-67. Cambridge: Cambridge University Press.

—1996. From Sydney to Sarajevo. A Centenary Reflection on Archaeology and European Identity. *Archaeological Dialogues* 1: 55-69.

—1999. The Art of Archaeological Biography. In T. Murray, T. (ed) *Encyclopedia of Archaeology: the Great Archaeologists,* 2 vols, pp. 869-883. Santa Barbara: ABC CLIO.

—2001. On 'normalizing the Palaeolithic: an orthodoxy questioned. In R. Corbey and W. Roebroeks, (eds) *Studying Human Origins. Disciplinary History and Epistemology,* pp. 29-44. Amsterdam: University of Amsterdam Press.

SHENNAN, S. 1989. Introduction: archaeological approaches to cultural identity. In S. Shennan (ed) *Archaeological Approaches to Cultural Identity,* pp. 1-32. London: Unwin Hyman.

SLAPSAK, B. 1993. Archaeology and contemporary myths of the past. *The Journal of European Archaeology* 1 (2): 191-195.

STOCKING, G. W. Jr. 1968. *Race, Culture and Evolution.* New York: The Free Press.

—1971. What's in a name? The origins of the Royal Anthropological Institute, (1837-1871). *Man* (ns) 6: 369-390.

—1973. From chronology to ethnology. James Cowles Prichard and British Anthropology 1800-1850. In the reprint edition of J. C. Prichard *Researches into the Physical History of Man,* (1831), pp. ix-cx. Chicago: University of Chicago Press.

—1987. *Victorian Anthropology.* New York: Free Press.

TRIGGER, B. G. 1989. *A History of Archaeological Thought.* Cambridge: Cambridge University Press.

VEIT, U. 1989. Ethnic concepts in German prehistory. A case study on the relationship between cultural identity and archaeological objectivity. In S. Shennan (ed) *Archaeological Approaches to Cultural Identity,* pp. 35-56. London: Unwin Hyman.

WEBER, G. 1974. Science and society in nineteenth century anthropology. *History of Science* XV: 260-283.

WOLF, E. R. 1994. Perilous Ideas. Race, Culture, People. *Current Anthropology* 35 (1): 1-12.

WYLIE, A. 1989. Matters of Fact and Matters of Interest. In S. Shennan (ed) *Archaeological Approaches to Cultural Identity,* pp. 94-109. London: Unwin Hyman.

—1992a. On scepticism, Philosophy, and Archaeological Science. *Current Anthropology* 33 (2): 209-213.

—1992b. The interplay of evidential constraints and political interests. Recent archaeological research on gender. *American Antiquity* 57 (1): 15-35.

—1995. Alternative histories. Epistemic disunity and political integrity. In P.R. Schmidt and T.C. Patterson (eds) *Making Alternative Histories,* pp. 255-272. School of American Research, Albuquerque: University of New Mexico Press.

# Chapter 8

# On 'normalizing' the Palaeolithic: an orthodoxy questioned

In recent years some archaeologists have been considering the issue of whether archaeological data can constrain archaeological interpretation (see e.g. Murray 1987, 1996; Wylie 1992, 1995). Of course these discussions have also considered the related questions of whether data should constrain interpretation, or what reliability we might attach to knowledge claims based on interpretations which ignore such constraints. It would be fair to say that practitioners are far from agreement on any or all of these significant matters, not least because fundamental questions concerning disciplinary epistemology and ontology remain largely undiscussed and unresolved.

One such question has to do with the murky relationship between our understanding of 'archaeological data' and our comprehension of the structural properties of archaeological records (e.g. Murray 1997; Patrik 1985). On the surface it seems self-evident that interpretation should be constrained by evidence. However, in practice archaeologists have either wittingly or unwittingly accepted that it is natural for schemes of archaeological interpretation to be at odds with the structural properties of the archaeological phenomena being interpreted, usually because such phenomena are considered to be intractable partial remnants of extinct cultural systems (e.g. Maschner and Mithen 1996: 9-10). It is also significant that this freedom from such fundamental constraints occasions little comment beyond a generalized perception that if archaeologists were to accept such constraints, their capacity to explore the meanings of archaeological things in conventional terms would be fatally compromised, and that they would produce boring and valueless knowledge.

De Boer and Lathrap (1979) have characterized this conflict between making meanings and the constraints which can be imposed on the nature of archaeological phenomena as a kind of choice:

*Either they [archaeologists] must become practitioners of an over extended uniformitarianism in which past cultural behaviour is 'read' from our knowledge of present cultural behaviour or they must eschew their commitment to understanding behaviour altogether and engage*

*in a kind of 'artefact physics' in which the form and distribution of*
*behavioural by-products are measured in a behavioural vacuum* (De
Boer and Lathrap 1979: 103).

They conclude that this is in fact a 'familiar quandary of choosing between
a significant pursuit based on a faulty method or one which is
methodologically sound but trivial in purpose' (De Boer and Lathrap 1979:
103). This shows that making meanings in conventional behavioural terms
(however unreliable they might be) is of far greater moment than searching
for other frameworks that might produce more reliable knowledge of the
archaeological past. What makes these unconstrained (and potentially faulty)
interpretations plausible has little to do with their connection to evidence and
much more to do with our expectations of what an intelligible human past
should be like. Thus, a practical distinction is (wittingly or unwittingly)
maintained between accepting the constraints of evidence as 'data' or specific
pieces of information, and accepting that the nature of archaeological
phenomena might threaten modes of interpretation and explanation, which
have developed over the last 200 years.

I have previously noted in an extended discussion of the discovery of high
human antiquity in the mid-nineteenth century (Murray 1993) that the major
conceptual consequence of that discovery was the distinct (and threatening)
prospect of evidence of human action in deep prehistory being unintelligible
in terms of the social theory of the time. In that previous context I developed
the argument further by establishing that this threat has been, (and continues
to be) met by the process of 'normalization'. This process has taken many
forms, sometimes involving a redescription of aberrant evidence in
conventional terms (thus defining the threat out of existence), or by setting
up interpretative instruments which are so abstracted from the evidence that
the two cannot be effectively brought into contact, or by simply pretending
that the problem evidence does not exist.

The notion that evidence should constrain interpretation only in certain
circumstances and not others, and that 'meaningfulness' is the most important
goal for archaeologists, provides us with good reasons to look more closely
at what makes archaeological knowledge claims plausible. It also affords us
the opportunity to think more deeply about archaeological epistemology,
especially about whether practitioners can (or should) continue to abandon
science in favour of cultural tradition. Explorations of disciplinary
epistemology and identity obviously raise significant issues about the nature
of archaeological theory, and the extent to which archaeologists can (or want
to) transform borrowed theory (whatever its source) to interact more
effectively with archaeological phenomena.

Those archaeologists interested in understanding the complex issues raised by a discussion of constraints also explicitly recognize the very real connections between unexplored cultural prejudice and oppression – whatever its social expression (see e.g. Murray 1996; Wylie 1995). This recognition can be shared by other practitioners seeking to make archaeology more inclusive of perspectives drawn from the margins of society, the dispossessed, the powerless, and the victims of prejudice, although these groups frequently see science as supporting such oppression rather than being an important resource for liberation.

My purpose in this chapter is to continue with an exploration of the plausibility of archaeological knowledge claims, and to seek to support the view that archaeologists need to think more deeply about the process of 'normalization' in their practice. I will do this by demonstrating the value of the history of archaeology as a point of entry into a more general project of describing the disciplinary culture of archaeology, and of tracing the links between the traditions of this culture and the plausibility of archaeological knowledge claims (see also Kelly and Hanen 1988). In these discussions I am particularly interested in understanding how the clear rift between the methodological rhetoric of archaeologists (the acceptance that evidence constrains interpretation) and the reality of practice (such constraint only occurs at the most superficial level) can be masked by practitioners. Above all, I will be seeking to support the argument that it is not necessary to separate the process of critical self-reflection from the business of doing science, and that the liberation of the oppressed might well involve us taking a very much harder look at the traditional grounds for establishing meaningful questions and answers in archaeology (see Murray 1992: 740-741; and especially Wylie 1995: 271-217).

## Disciplinary history: plausibility and tradition

Since the birth of the 'new' archaeology in 1962, archaeologists have been engaged in gradually intensifying debate about the fundamentals of the discipline. At first, archaeologists concentrated on disciplinary epistemology, if only to argue that it had to fall into line with 'scientific' epistemology if knowledge claims were to have any reliability. This rediscovery of positivism has been transformed over the last 30 years by changing fashions in the philosophy of science, and by an increasing understanding that a focus on epistemology (particularly the context of justification of archaeological knowledge claims) was not telling us very much about why archaeologists approach the past as they do, and what expectations practitioners (and others) have of interpretations and explanations. A broadening of discussion into 'foundational' matters has stimulated inquiry into what makes knowledge claims made by archaeologists plausible, and has led to more detailed investigations of the links between archaeology and the society which sustains its practice. This, in turn, has greatly increased the significance of the history of archaeology – as a primary source of perspective about disciplinary traditions and the 'culture' of archaeology.

Further, in highlighting the complex relationships between archaeology and society, we have also come closer to understanding the role archaeological knowledge has come to play within the general field of the human sciences, particularly in the writing of history and in the practice of anthropology. These two disciplines have, since the nineteenth century, set the standards archaeologists have attempted to achieve when interpreting past societies or explaining change in human history. At this time, the cutting edge of debate about the nature of archaeological knowledge is located precisely at the question of whether this traditionally close relationship should be re-evaluated and whether we need to rethink the traditional location of archaeology on the cognitive map of the human sciences.

There are many reasons for the pressure to re-evaluate, but the most important have to do with the impact of research into the nature of archaeological records as records of human action, and the impact of research into the history of archaeology. Over the last 30 years archaeologists have been forced to confront the fact that traditional readings of archaeological ontology do not square with modern research into the formation of archaeological sites, and our understanding of how human behaviour can be 'read' from such contexts. These views are a major departure from those, which have shaped archaeology, since its establishment in the first half of the nineteenth century, precisely at the same time that the disciplines of history and anthropology also took their modern forms (Levine 1986; Trigger 1989). It is now well understood that a crucial element of any re-evaluation of the nature of archaeological knowledge will be the history of contemporary orthodoxy, if only to establish that current views about the nature of that knowledge are cultural and not natural.

The first half of the nineteenth century has been identified as one of the most significant periods in the history of archaeology for three linked reasons. First, it was during this period that high human antiquity was established and links with the natural sciences) were regularized (e.g. Grayson 1983; Van Riper 1993). Second, the use of ancient material culture to plausibly 'reconstruct' the histories of ethnic groups (and newly created nations) was widely accepted (Trigger 1989). Third, archaeology was 'enrolled' by anthropology to provide empirical examples of the stages of human social and cultural evolution, thereby increasing the plausibility of social evolutionary theory.

Existing histories of archaeology do not carry analysis any further than this, because they explicitly accept an orthodox reading of relationships between archaeology, anthropology, and history. But as George Stocking has noted, there are many unwritten histories of nineteenth century anthropology and archaeology, which revolve around people or ideas which both disciplines have attempted to expunge from their collective memories (Stocking 1987).

**Humanizing the Palaeolithic**

The establishment of a high human antiquity is rightly regarded by most historians of archaeology as one of the crucial passages in the history of the discipline (see e.g. Burrow 1966; Daniel 1959, 1971, 1975; Grayson 1983; Schnapp 1996; Van Riper 1993). According to Grayson and Van Riper, the science of prehistoric archaeology was firmly established between the years 1858 and 1870. Furthermore, the archaeological demonstration of social and cultural evolution was – according to Gruber and Harris at least – crucial to the successful foundation of anthropology (Gruber 1965 and Harris 1968).

In this re-examination I offer no new facts concerning the events surrounding the excavation of Brixham Cave, or the Somme Gravels. Nor will I be breaking new ground by arguing that Evans, Prestwich, Lubbock, Tylor and others gave meaning to the material culture found at those places by claiming that traditional Tasmanian Aboriginal society had been (to all intents and purposes) the living representation of the Palaeolithic (see e.g. Murray 1992). Furthermore, I most certainly will not be claiming that the use of ethnographic analogy as a source of inference about human prehistory began with the need to interpret the meaning of high human antiquity. Historians of archaeology have already demonstrated that inferences drawn from ethnographic analogy were a central feature of both antiquarianism and archaeology. Indeed, the fact that ethnographic analogy continued to provide the crucial source of inference for this new class of archaeological data provides a focal point for the re-examination.

I will, however, produce a partial analysis of the significance of a continued use of ethnographic analogy by stressing the fact that the practice of this new prehistoric archaeology systematically violated the scientific canons laid down by its practitioners (without any significant reduction in the plausibility of their statements). A more complete analysis, which considers the consequences of un-dimensionable human antiquity until the advent of radiometric chronologies in the 1950s and 1960s (a century later), has appeared elsewhere (Murray 1987, 1997).

There is no doubt that the establishment of a science of prehistoric archaeology was considered to be a major advance in human knowledge.

Indeed, even Armand de Quatrefages and Sir John Lubbock, both adversaries on central issues concerning the study of mankind, found a measure of commonality in their enthusiastic welcome for the new science. Quatrefages stated:

> *To plunge into this obscurity with the hope of finding in it any certain land-marks, and to discover facts of which even legends say nothing, would thirty years ago have appeared a senseless enterprise. It is, nevertheless, the work accomplished by one of the most recent sciences, Prehistoric Archaeology* (original emphasis, Quatrefages 1879: 131).

And Lubbock wrote:

> *Of late years, however, a new branch of knowledge has arisen; a new science has, so to say, been born among us, which deals with times and events far more ancient than any of which have fallen within the province of the archaeologist* (Lubbock 1865).

Much had been achieved since the 1830s, but by common consent the greatest achievement of the European antiquaries, the students of language and society, and the natural historians, was that a methodology had been developed which rescued understanding of the prehistoric past from the realms of speculation. Anthropologists such as Quatrefages (1875) and Topinard (see Hammond 1980) might disagree among themselves, and collectively diverge from the positions taken by supporters of ethnology such as Lubbock or palaeontologists such as Boyd Dawkins, or even antiquaries such as John Evans, but all shared the optimistic and scientist mood of the moment – a celebration of the possibility of rational knowledge of the past, where imagination did not 'usurp the place of research' (Lubbock 1865:1). In this new regime previously insoluble problems in ethnology would acquire solutions. Boyd Dawkins captured some of the growing sense of confidence in this new methodology.

> *Archaeology, also, by the use of strictly inductive methods, has grown from a mere antiquarian speculation into a science; and its students have proved the truth of the three divisions of human progress familiar to the Greek and Roman philosopher, and expressed in the pages of Hesiod and Lucretius – the Ages of Stone, Bronze and Iron. The subdivision of the first of these into the older, or Palaeolithic, and newer, or Neolithic, by Sir John Lubbock, is the only refinement which has been made in this classification* (1874: viii).

While it is true that the authors of the new anthropologies and synthetic prehistories did not necessarily regard knowledge of the prehistoric past as having the same certainty or credibility as geology, physics, or chemistry (often choosing to substitute 'light' for 'knowledge'), they were absolutely clear that sciences such as geology could, if used by archaeologists, guarantee a fair measure of credibility. If the archaeologist added the information about prehistoric 'conditions of existence' and diet which had been procured through inferences and inductions based on geological, palaeontological and ethnographic knowledge, the broad agenda of prehistoric archaeology could be defended against the attacks of those who were not persuaded that rational knowledge of the prehistoric human past was possible.

Contrasting the certainties of palaeontology with the less definite knowledge produced by archaeology, and admitting that 'in the present state of our knowledge the skeleton of a savage could not always be distinguished from that of a philosopher' (Lubbock 1872: viii), Lubbock still felt it possible to argue that sufficient data remained to give a reliable basis for the reconstruction of prehistoric human action because it could be interpreted through uniformitarian propositions:

*But on the other hand, while animals leave only teeth and bones behind them, the men of past ages are to be studied principally by their works; houses for the living, tombs for the dead, fortifications for defence, temples for worship, implements for use, and ornaments for decoration* (Lubbock 1865: 2; see also Boyd Dawkins 1874: viii).

The methodological rhetoric of the new synthetic prehistories emphasized that plausible understanding could now only be derived from the description and analysis of the material facts of human action, geological time, environmental and ecological context, and human physical form, as well as the ethnographic and ethno-linguistic evidence for the history of human society and language. This was considered to be a solid foundation for the activities of a new science. Current shortcomings in the database were not thought to be so severe as to place the entire enterprise in jeopardy.

For example, referring to the lack of precise, absolute, chronology for prehistoric humans (an essential feature of nineteenth-century scientific history), Quatrefages saw no reason to argue that shortcomings in the database should be made good through the time-honoured agents of *a priori* assumptions, imagination, and final causes:

*Let us observe, in the first place, that here we can have no dates properly so called. They exist only in history. Now primitive man can have no history in the scientific sense of the word. Most great religions have endeavoured to fill this gap. But my readers are aware that I have refused all considerations drawn from such a source, and that I intend to bring forward here none but the results of experiment and observation* (Quatrefages 1879: 129-130).

Once again, not all authors of synthetic prehistories and anthropologies agreed with Quatrefages about what this rejection of *a priori* assumptions would entail. While workers such as Lubbock, Lyell, Huxley, Falconer, and Tylor displayed a similar caution towards accepted approaches to understanding human nature, in practice they could not accept that all aspects of knowledge about human nature were negotiable (see e.g. Bartholemew 1973; Lyell 1863). Lubbock, in particular, was quite prepared to accept that a science of prehistoric archaeology would cast doubt on previous understandings such as the extent of human antiquity, and the causes of human physical and cultural change and variation, but this did not include a rejection of monogenism or an acceptance of the program of anthropology outlined by James Hunt and Paul Broca, a program which anthropologists such as Quatrefages and Topinard, despite their own differences of opinion, fully accepted (Burrow 1966; Stocking 1973).

Notwithstanding disagreements about core ontological issues, especially the importance of mind as the basis for distinguishing human from animal, propagandists of the science of prehistoric archaeology collectively sought justification for the new enterprise from histories of research into prehistory and human palaeontology. Significantly, these same people were propagandists for other sciences such as geology, ethnology and anthropology. The intellectual links of prehistoric archaeology were clearly established. These histories were written both by natural historians, whose primary interest was in geology and palaeontology, and by antiquaries, who sought to link the advances made in the classification of prehistoric material culture with the new interpretative and explanatory possibilities provided by the natural historians, the physical anthropologists, the ethnographers, and the philologists.

This history writing had several goals. First, to justify the importance of the new science by demonstrating that it had a long history marred by a failure to recognize the value of remnant material culture and/ or stratigraphic contexts. Second, to justify the methodological credentials of geology, palaeontology and prehistoric archaeology by portraying them as having been rescued from obscurity by the power of nineteenth century science, and of prehistoric archaeology as having been rescued by the certainties of geology and palaeontology. Importantly, this form of presentist history (Stocking

1968) was being produced for most other human, earth, and life sciences during the same period (see e.g. Bowler 1976; Mayr 1982).

Just as the participants in the new science were generally agreed on the essentials of the history of prehistoric archaeology, so they were agreed that its methodology must be based on firm empiricist principles. Although there was a greater emphasis on the use of 'strict inductions' than on inference, analogy and deduction, these aspects of methodology were acceptable as long as they could be securely grounded in the empirical data. In the event, as I have said, some practitioners found it more difficult to banish every aspect of apriorism from their activities than others. They also found it difficult to empirically assess the truth-value of their premises, despite the fact that the premises of ethnology and anthropology were a major source of conflict. Consequently, there was every justification for banishing the power of the *a priori* from the investigation of human affairs. The twin bogeys of authority, and the metaphysics of final causes and essences, were seen as the elements of unreason, powerful forces hindering the development of a science of human society that would help humans to attain the Enlightenment goal of a good and just society based on an appreciation of the laws governing human action through all space and time.

Henceforth, prehistoric archaeology, whether conducted under the aegis of ethnology or anthropology, would pursue the positivist path of a search for law. It would defend itself against prejudice and unreason, for in unreason lay the seeds of a return to an understanding of the prehistoric past that owed more to the rationalism of moral philosophy and to presuppositions about the nature of society than to an objective description and explanation of the empirical facts. Just like the geologists, biologists, ethnologists and anthropologists, the practitioners of prehistoric archaeology well understood the potentially unpalatable conclusions of their science, after all they engaged in long and bitter conflict among themselves about these issues. However, the rhetoric demanded that the search for truth should be held more important than a rearguard action in the defense of unreason – a charge they frequently leveled against each other.

Another aspect of the methodological rhetoric stemmed from the new data discovered by natural historians and archaeologists. It was widely felt that through a multiplication in the quantities and range of material facts, and through the development of true theory (read the Three Age System) prehistoric archaeology was considered to have won its spurs as a nineteenth-century science. Again, while there were definite differences of opinion as to whether prehistoric archaeology could be seen to be the link between geology and history, an argument favoured by Boyd Dawkins (Boyd Dawkins 1880, especially chapter 1) or whether it found its true home within the human sciences, the argument favoured by Lubbock, Evans, Quatrefages, Pouchet and Vogt, there was no doubt that the new science was not considered to be a threat to the cognitive map of nineteenth century science. The knowledge derived from a scientific investigation of human prehistory had definite connections to other forms of knowledge about human action and human history.

For instance, both the ethnologists and the anthropologists argued that the facts of human socio-cultural variation, the facts of human physical difference and similarity, the facts of philology, and the facts of prehistoric archaeology, would provide clear support for a discipline that would synthesize the mounting array of information about human beings into a science of which humans were the sole subject. Although practitioners of prehistoric archaeology were to express support for either ethnology or anthropology during this period, often for moral and political, rather than purely scientific reasons, there was general agreement among them about the importance of using prehistoric data to assist the process of recasting universal human history in terms of empirically justified scientific laws. In sum, the methodological rhetoric of prehistoric archaeology emphasized rigorous epistemology and the connections between knowledge derived from the interaction of methodology and database, and other sources of knowledge about human beings and the phenomenal world.

Earlier in this chapter I claimed that there were distinct differences between this rhetoric and everyday performance. I have claimed that this difference is most apparent in the epistemology of the new science – a strong emphasis on induction, with implicit approval of deduction, as long as the premises could be assessed for their truth-value. However, not only were the observation statements produced by practitioners heavily dependent on theory, those theories were undeveloped to the point that there were no generally agreed means of testing them.

Grayson's comprehensive account of the establishment of a high human antiquity has demonstrated that this major turning point in the history of archaeology also had a great impact outside the discipline (Grayson 1983; see also Van Riper 1993). Clearly, developments in geology, palaeontology and biology both potentiated and justified the validity of claims for the presence of stone tools in unimpeachably old strata. It had an even more profound impact on the study of human beings. The prospect of an almost unimaginably deep human history was simultaneously threatening and liberating – threatening because it broke down the distinctions between humans and other animals and because a conceptual vacuum now existed which had to be filled, liberating because the restrictions of the old chronology had been lifted, and the search for an understanding of human nature could be pursued over a longer time span (see also Murray 1993).

The discovery of stone tools in unimpeachably old strata raised two questions: what kind of human being made them, and how long ago? Lubbock, among others, followed standard ethnological practice by providing a solution to the former question based on comparative ethnography, and a standard of empirical practice by substituting the methods of geology for an appeal to 'untrustworthy tradition'.

Both Lubbock and Tylor needed a 'human face for the Palaeolithic', because the standards of proof and interpretation established by ethnology and anthropology required such an image. Palaeolithic man would be only the most ghostly of shadows without the Van Diemener, and both Lubbock's and Tylor's (and, of course, Morgan's) systems demanded more than that. Notwithstanding this, both Lubbock and Tylor were adamant that the Van Diemeners could not be considered to be 'frozen moments' from the Palaeolithic.

However, even taking into account the claims that there were no direct analogies between current savages and the humans of the Palaeolithic, and that to some extent palaeolithic society could be theoretically reconstructed on the basis of psychic unity and the reconstruction of conditions of existence, the practical result was that the Van Diemeners and the South Americans did become the fossil representatives of the Palaeolithic, precisely because they were the meaningful (reliable) image of the terms in which the prehistoric past was to be known.

By providing a meaningful image of Palaeolithic humanity, evolutionary archaeology and anthropology not only effectively denied a history to contemporary 'savages', they also made an understanding of the Palaeolithic effectively synchronous with the present. The vast time scale had disappeared for the very 'reason that it was undimensionable by any of the ethnological or anthropological theories then available.

In addition, there were the difficulties of quantifying time itself. It was all very well to speak of a vast and near limitless antiquity, but archaeologists had to begin to set limits if only to conceptualize processes of change and variation operating in the Palaeolithic more clearly. Unfortunately, uniformitarian geology, once the arbiter of time, had fallen prey to the ravages of an even more scientific discipline, that of physics. Burchfield has charted the effects of Lord Kelvin and others on prevailing Lyellian determinations of the age of the earth (Burchfield 1974, 1975). Working from the Second Law of Thermodynamics Kelvin and his followers successfully pared down age estimates, effectively shrinking the time span of prehistoric archaeology into the bargain and giving free rein to a variety of geochronological methods.

Lubbock summarized most of them (Lubbock 1865: 380-411). There was the evidence for changes in vegetation, derived from the Danish sites. Then there was the data of changes in the Swiss lake levels, Horner's calculation of deposition rates on the Nile, and Morlot's drift cone. All were soundly criticized by him for being inconclusive, and of using circular logic. The most conclusive evidence for chronology, to Lubbock's mind at least, stemmed from changes in the climate of Western Europe. Notwithstanding these techniques for establishing chronology, the practitioners of prehistoric archaeology were basically incapable of reaching agreement about the time depth of European prehistory. In the face of these difficulties they returned to classifications based on changes in palaeofaunas and material culture, and the relative chronologies they potentiated (Daniel 1975; Oakley 1964). These were, in essence, developments of the Three Age System. Although de Mortillet could trick them out with universal meaning as the material products and indicators of positivist laws of progress and psychic unity, the fact remained that as prehistoric archaeology retreated into classification as a means for establishing relative chronology, the synchronic variation of material culture would begin to pose and potentiate puzzles and problems of its own (see Daniel 1975; Peake 1940). The seeds of a return to historicism were sown.

## Finding a place for archaeology in the human sciences

If we focus on the methodological rhetoric of the new science of prehistoric archaeology, the traditional claims for a link between the foundation of the science and the establishment of a high human antiquity lose some of their force but gain a great deal of texture. Clearly, the linking of palaeontology and geology to archaeology allowed practitioners to claim a scientific reliability for their reconstructions of human life during the Palaeolithic. I do not dispute that practitioners believed their own positivist rhetoric (there is no need to accuse them of deception). Nonetheless, a careful analysis of this passage of the history of archaeology reveals a structure of assumption about the nature and significance of archaeological knowledge, which established that archaeological representations of human action should mirror those of contemporary social theory. Significantly, these *a priori* assumptions violated the positivist epistemology of the practitioners. Moreover, this disjunction between rhetoric and practice went, for the most part, unremarked by either practitioners or consumers of archaeological knowledge (see also Murray 1989). What interests me is why these practitioners sought meaning in terms of contemporary 'savages', why others found their accounts plausible, and the consequences of this framework of interpretation for the future conduct of prehistoric archaeology.

In the first half of the nineteenth century the short time-scale prehistories of Nilsson (1868) and Worsaae (1849) provided exemplars of how the historical and ethnological significance of archaeological data could be expanded beyond the earlier formulations of Camden, Speed, Aubrey and Stukeley. This expansion was the result of two responses to the sense of the new prehistories: first, the enrolment of archaeological data by the proponents of a more general inquiry into the nature of humankind, which at this time was encompassed by ethnology; second, the use of ethnological method and underdeveloped ethnological theory by the practitioners of prehistoric archaeology.

These two responses, which collectively exhibit a kind of symbiotic relationship, were justified with ease. The data of prehistoric archaeology took their rightful place alongside ethnography, physical anthropology, and philology, barely causing a ripple in the terms of the central preoccupations of ethnology. Indeed, no radical recasting of the terms of pre-existing debates was deemed necessary by any of the disputants as a result of the incorporation of the archaeology of the 1840s and 1850s. This incorporation was made even easier by the fact that the archaeologists themselves, through their need to write plausible prehistory, effectively pre-processed archaeological data through the application of ethnological methodology and theory. The ascription of cause, part-and-parcel of the explanation of change and variation, was facilitated and justified by the use of ethnological databases such as ethnography and physical anthropology.

The discovery of a high human antiquity has been considered by historians of archaeology and anthropology to have had a dramatic effect on the structures which guided the terms of the more general inquiry into the nature of human beings (Burrow 1966; Daniel 1959, 1971, 1975, 1976; Grayson 1983; Gruber 1965; Harris 1968; Laming-Emperaire 1964; Oakley 1964; Peake 1940; Stocking 1968, 1971; Vogt 1975; Weber 1974). But how great an effect? Were the archaeological data of a deeper prehistoric past to be enrolled in the same way as the 'short-span' data provided by Nilsson, Wilson and Worsaae? Or were the new data of such a different order that the theories which fostered explanation and gave meaning to the purported inductions of the early prehistorians would simply fail to convince? Could prehistoric archaeologists continue to maintain that symbiotic relationship with ethnology, and later, anthropology, and thus gain plausible and justifiable grounds for the reconstruction and explanation of human action in the deep prehistoric past? How would induction fare in the drive to explain human nature so far (temporally) removed from the present?

It transpired that the evidence of high human antiquity was indeed enrolled and drafted into the service of ontological antinomies which, expressed in the form of dualisms, had lain behind both the eighteenth century universal histories and the return of historicism – human unity or diversity, mind and body, nature and culture. Throughout the last half of the nineteenth century, discussions in the metropolitan anthropological and ethnological societies of London, Paris and elsewhere linked archaeology and ethnology into a 'historical anthropology' where the archaeological past became an arena in which debates about human nature assumed both ontological and moral dimensions. One of the better examples of this is found in the later chapters of Lubbock's 1865 *Prehistoric Times* (Lubbock 1865 cf. Van Reybrouck 2001).

During this period, first ethnology and later anthropology provided the theory which presupposed the bulk of the observation statements made about human action in the prehistoric past. In so doing, they also established the exemplars of practice, standards of proof, and the objectives of prehistoric archaeology. Yet ethnology itself was changed through the discovery of high human antiquity, as well as by a resurgence of interest in physical anthropology that was in part caused by the discovery of fossil human skeletal material (Boule and Vallois 1946). Ethnology and, later, anthropology determined the degree to which anomalous archaeological data could influence the terms of those long-standing ontological antinomies mentioned above. To this extent, the change of emphasis from evolutionary archaeology to cultural historical archaeology later in the nineteenth century reflected changes in the orientations of anthropology and ethnology.

Ethnology and anthropology both provided core aspects of a complex interdisciplinary matrix for the reconsideration of long-standing ontological oppositions, while their practitioners simultaneously claimed, through the rhetoric of positivism and empiricism, that they were entirely opposed to metaphysics. Of course the traditions of anthropological and antiquarian research in the major European centres of research all created distinct local varieties of ethnology, anthropology, and prehistoric archaeology, many of which persist to the present day. One of the best examples of this is provided by the contentious history of 'anthropology' in Britain during the time when James Hunt was using the Anthropological Society of London as a forum for introducing Broca's reading of anthropology as a higher-level integrative discipline. The venom with which Lubbock and his followers opposed Hunt's plans has been well discussed (Stocking 1971).

The archaeological evidence of a deeper human prehistory was enrolled, by the practitioners of ethnology and anthropology, for two reasons. First, the new data was evidence of human action, and if theories of human nature were to have any kind of temporal validity then they had to account for it. Second, this new class of evidence was more empirically reliable than much of the ethnographic evidence previously incorporated (Harris 1968; Stocking 1983).

Practitioners of prehistoric archaeology, most of them natural historians (read geologists and palaeontologists), retained the symbiotic relationship with ethnology and anthropology for the same reasons as before. Although great time-depth opened the possibility that human beings could be investigated as part of the animal world, in practice the primary question came to be the grounds of distinction between animals and human beings. As these differences were thought to stem largely from language, rationality and culture, the natural loci for the discussion of these issues was anthropology and ethnology.

Enrolment of archaeology by ethnology and the use of ethnology by archaeologists occurred through an extension of the scope of prehistoric archaeology beyond the bounds of the cultural, ethnic or racial histories established by Nilsson and Worsaae, themselves the product of the power of ethnology. High human antiquity and the possibility of human prehistory that would not be interpretable through the structures of culture history expanded ethnology as well as prehistoric archaeology. Importantly, the palaeontological and geological investigation of the superficial strata of Western Europe, a research program which had been active while the Three Age System was still in its Scandinavian infancy, spawned a class of data which found their nineteenth century meanings within ethnology and anthropology (Cf. Van Reybrouck 2001).

The cumulative effects of several factors are considered to have guided this process of enrolment, and the extension of symbiosis, and I shall only list three of them here. First, the unfamiliarity of the new evidence effectively increased a dependence on the *a priori*, as practitioners struggled to make it meaningful. Second, the great uncertainty surrounding the quantification of the new time scale. Vast it may be, but how vast? In practice, undimensioned time made the truthfulness of the 'inductions' difficult to establish and to justify. Third, the use of ethnographic analogy, and uniformitarian assumptions, to support meaningful interpretation of the unfamiliar, and the potentially unintelligible.

The approaches developed by prehistorians and anthropologists such as Lubbock and Tylor stimulated the growth of anthropology and recast the relationships between archaeology and anthropology. Importantly, Lubbock, Tylor, and others argued that this new approach, based on empiricism, eclipsed rationalism as the primary basis on which plausible understanding of the prehistoric past could be achieved.

Implicit in their arguments is the claim that the discovery of a high human antiquity not only led to the writing of a different kind of prehistory, but also contributed to the replacement of ethnology by anthropology as the most general of the generalising human sciences. During the 1860s and 1870s it began to be widely felt that the contemplation of human action over great time spans, and the consideration of the process whereby humans evolved in mind as well as in body, cast the conflict over human unity or diversity in a new light (see Burrow 1966; Stocking 1971; Weber 1974).

No longer could that conflict be resolved by the observation of contemporary races and the reconstruction of their histories. A broader framework of observation and theory building was clearly needed, and anthropology was thrust forward, by James Hunt, Paul Broca and Edward Tylor to do this. Despite the clear failure of anthropology to produce this theory during the 1860s and 1870s (the heyday of its most universal reading), it was to remain an integrative, holistic concept, still appealed to but lacking the meta-theory which would allow the integration of disparate databases.

Clearly, the enrolment of archaeological data by the proponents of the fledgling science of ethnology was a critical part of the process whereby meaning and value were ascribed to the prehistoric data. To this extent, potentially unintelligible evidence of prehistoric human action was 'normalized' or 'naturalized' by history and by ethnology, and rendered meaningful. Without the plausibility of that previous accommodation, the data of a deeper human prehistory would have posed interpretative and explanatory problems of great magnitude.

Grayson may well be correct to the extent that puzzles and problems were generated by the discoveries in England and France, and that these provided the empirical focus for prehistoric archaeology, but it is apparent that these were not the only problems to be confronted by the archaeologists and natural historians. Further, it is also clear that the conceptualization of those puzzles and problems, and the solutions considered by practitioners to be justifiable, did not only arise from the data themselves. I have outlined other, more critical, theoretical and disciplinary sources and contexts.

Significantly, while the *use* of these structures was never debated, there were frequent disputes between practitioners arising from differing interpretations of archaeological data which sprang from divergent positions on core ontological and epistemological antinomies (see e.g. Argyll 1869; Gillespie 1977). Archaeological data were enrolled by all sides, and the factor of enrolment tended to focus the forms of understanding within contemporary versions of long-standing debates. The discovery of a deep human antiquity may have necessitated adjustments to the structures, as the participants sought to make their own perspectives primarily determining, and those of their opponents, contingent, but there was never a thought that in some way or other archaeological data were better understood outside that framework.

The point here is that all sides needed archaeological data. Further, to be useful to either position, those data had to be interpreted and explained through the ontological and epistemological structures of those opposed positions. Archaeological data themselves could not disrupt those structures, to the extent that their value as interpreters of the present state of humanity would be questioned. In an important sense, archaeological data could only acquire meaning and value within the terms of such structures, using the theories of ethnology and anthropology as orientation points on the map of the mid-nineteenth century 'human' sciences. What is significant here is the strong sense in which popular frameworks for establishing the meanings of archaeological phenomena (which in the past had included the Bible and folklore, but also included a matrix of normative assumptions about human nature, culture, and the meaning of human history) were both subsumed by, and objectified as, the sciences of archaeology and anthropology.

A critical part of my argument here rests on the distinct discrepancies between the methodological rhetoric of practitioners and their practical performance in justifying the claims to scientific status for the new discipline. All participants in the debate about the constitution of the proper study of man, such as ethnologists, anthropologists, monogenists, polygenists, and supporters and detractors of the Darwinian thesis, accepted that the methodology of prehistoric archaeology was scientific, and that it would play an important role in establishing the nature of human nature in all its varieties through space and time (Burrow 1976; Stocking 1971; Weber 1974). Furthermore, it was generally agreed that the new science was firmly based on a scientifically reliable methodology and possessed an appropriate database for answering meaningful and valuable questions. For these reasons it was thought that prehistoric archaeology would produce meaningful and valuable knowledge about human beings. Finally, all sides recognized that the knowledge produced through the study of prehistoric archaeology was a potentially important contribution to the repertoire of the more general human sciences, either ethnology or anthropology.

Significantly, knowledge about the prehistoric past, whatever its source or scientific status, had been incorporated into the universal histories of the eighteenth century, and in the first propositions of the science of ethnology earlier in the nineteenth century. The discovery of a high human antiquity did nothing to alter this tradition of connectedness between knowledge of the prehistoric human past and other aspects of knowledge about humans.

Therefore, despite the fact that there was by no means universal agreement among practitioners about the interpretation of prehistoric data (such as the causes of social and cultural change and variation, the extent of human antiquity, the material cultural correlates of mind, ethnicity or race, and the issue of whether human history was progressive), prehistoric archaeology had found its place within the general framework of sciences that both produced knowledge about human beings and provided the basis of the definition of 'humanness' itself.

Archaeological data never led to great changes in the structures which determined the identity of meaningful knowledge about human beings, nor in those which established the canons of meaning itself. Archaeological data gained meaning through existing frameworks of understanding. With the acceptance of the Three Age System, prehistoric data were thought to have been released from the state of superstition and conjecture, where it had been left by Stukeley and others. But were they to acquire a significance equal to that of history or ethnography?

Notwithstanding divergent viewpoints about the proper links between prehistoric archaeology and other fields of inquiry into human nature and the meaning of human history, we have seen that all practitioners were agreed that hypothesis was now to be banished before the onslaught of empirical data, and the prehistoric past was now to be understood through the critical description and analysis of observables. Prehistoric archaeology had become a science because its practitioners had adopted a scientific methodology, and applied it to a range of data that were considered by them to be susceptible to induction. It transpired that the everyday practice of the practitioners of the new science rarely approached the standards set down in the rhetoric. Given the shortcomings of the database, and the fact that ethnological and anthropological theory was still the subject of debate and dispute, it is difficult to see how the practitioners of prehistoric archaeology could have met their own standards. However, these limitations were really only the symptoms of a much more serious problem. Because the time span itself was in dispute (old, but how old?) and because there was no anthropological or ethnological framework to make sense of the meaning of a really long time scale, practitioners adopted approaches which effectively created a prehistoric archaeology which to all intents and purposes banished the consideration of long-span analyses from its day-to-day operations.

I have previously referred to the process of 'normalization' or 'naturalization' whereby potentially disturbing data is defused through a process of reinterpretation or reformulation. Berry (1968) among others has discussed this issue with respect to the impact of Darwinian biology in its association with uniformitarian geology, but despite the work of Grayson (1983), Van Riper (1993), and Stocking (1968), we still lack a vantage point on the operations of this process in prehistoric archaeology. Out of all of the numerous references to 'vast', 'unimaginable' antiquity, 'a period we cannot sum up in years', it is the transformation of the stone tools of Brixham and the Somme – from posing a problem of interpretation to being plausibility interpreted as being made by people similar to Tasmanian Aborigines – that most clearly demonstrates 'naturalization' in action.

Much has been written about the things which gave credibility to the new science of prehistoric archaeology. The link to geology and palaeontology with stratigraphy and faunal analysis (Cf. Grayson 1983; Van Riper 1993), the use of classification which allowed patterns of difference and similarity in material culture across space and time to be established (Cf. Graslund 1987), and the spectacular series of discoveries which just seemed to keep on happening, have all been canvassed. However, much less has been written about more important elements that increased plausibility. Here I refer to primarily cultural elements such as the theories, presuppositions, prejudices, or pre-existing frameworks of understanding that guided problem selection. These things did not, in themselves, create archaeological knowledge (see Stoczkowski 2001). But they did something far more important – they created the need for the knowledge, and they supplied the meanings of that knowledge.

However, this is only a small part of the point. Far more important is the fact that such entities were to all intents and purposes immune from an encounter with the empirical. It is fashionable to argue that this immunity was granted as a result of the theory dependence of observation, in other words that the empirical was so constructed by the theoretical that it would be logically circular (hence impossible) for it to be turned against itself. But this analysis only touches the surface, because it does not address the fact that practitioners, despite all their huffing and puffing about science, never sought such an encounter (Murray 1989). Weber has also noted the tendency for nineteenth century archaeology and anthropology to adopt the mantle of science and for 'its social assumptions and normative values [to pass] as objective judgements' (Weber 1974: 273).

## Concluding remarks

The discovery of high human antiquity provides an excellent example of the potential of the archaeological record to shock practitioners, and of the process of 'normalization' or 'naturalization' which practitioners have traditionally undertaken to bring anomalous information back into the realm of conventional understanding. It is also an excellent example of the close and abiding link between systematic violation of methodological rhetoric and the normative assumptions that underwrite the immunity of interpretation from the constraint of evidence.

In my view this nexus provides the strongest link between the inherent conservatism of archaeological theory (even when it is pretending to be radical), and our inability to rise to the challenge posed by our developing understanding of the ontology of archaeological records. I think, perhaps naively, that if we establish that archaeological perspectives have histories and that our disciplinary culture is not *sui generis*, then it surely follows that this might be a powerful force for liberating the archaeological imagination, so that we might make a better fist of constructing an archaeology which can be both meaningful and more directly related to the structural properties of its data. I also think, again perhaps naively, that the new perspectives on humanity which will flow from this changed psychology of research might actually produce pasts which can form the basis of an effective critique of how we construct presents.

Any history of archaeology should also be a history of the retention of concepts that owe their plausibility to the cultural traditions of the discipline rather than to their usefulness in more directly engaging the archaeological past. But the point here surely should be that to resolve thorny problems related to theory building and disciplinary epistemology will require us to constantly return to the history of our discipline in order to 'denaturalize' current conceptions of the nature and purpose of archaeological knowledge, to demonstrate that these are not eternal truths and that there are other archaeologies possible (see Murray 1999).

Furthermore it is obviously vital that archaeologists communicate with society about the ways in which knowledge about the past is built up and the 'tolerance limits' which should be set on its statements of interpretation. But it is equally obvious that the important work of exploring the core social assumptions and normative values of archaeologists, begun by Gordon Childe and continued during the era of postprocessual archaeology, still has a very long way to go.

**References**

ARGYLL, Duke of, (George Douglas Campbell) 1869. *Primeval Man: an examination of some recent speculations*. London: Strahan

BARTHOLEMEW, M. 1973. Lyell and Evolution: an account of Lyell's response to the idea of an evolutionary ancestry for man. *British Journal for the History of Science* 6: 261-303

BERRY, W.B.N. 1968. *Growth of a Prehistoric Timescale Based on Organic Evolution*. San Francisco: Freeman.

BOULE, M. and H.V. VALLOIS 1946. *Les Hommes Fossiles*. Paris: Masson et Cie.

BOWLER, P.J. 1976. *Fossils and Progress. Palaeontology and the Idea of Progressive Evolution in the Nineteenth Century*. New York: Science History Publications.

BOYD DAWKINS, W. 1874. *Cave Hunting: Researches on the Evidence of Caves Respecting the Early History of Europe*. London: Macmillan.

—1880. *Early Man in Britain and His Place in the Tertiary Period*. London: Macmillan.

BURCHFIELD, J.D. 1974. Darwin and the dilemma of geological time. *Isis* 65: 301-321.

—1975. *Lord Kelvin and the Age of the Earth*. London: Macmillan

BURROW, J.W. 1966. *Evolution and Society*. Cambridge: Cambridge University Press.

DANIEL, G. 1959. The Idea of Man's Antiquity. *Scientific American* 201: 167-176.

—1971. From Worsaae to Childe: the Models of Prehistory. *Proceedings of the Prehistoric Society* XXXVII: 140-153.

—1975. *One Hundred and Fifty Years of Archaeology*. London: Duckworth.

—1976. Stone, Bronze and Iron. In J.V.S. Megaw (ed) *To Illustrate the Monuments*, pp. 35-42. London: Thames and Hudson

DE BOER, W. and D.W. LATHRAP 1979. The making and breaking of Shipibo-Conibo ceramics. In C. Kramer (ed) *Ethnoarchaeology. Implications of Ethnography for Archaeology*, pp. 102-138. New York: Columbia University Press

GILLESPIE, N.C. 1977. The Duke of Argyll, evolutionary anthropology and the art of scientific controversy. *Isis* 68: 40-54.

GRASLUND, B. 1987. *The Birth of Prehistoric Chronology. Dating Methods and Dating Systems in Nineteenth Century Scandinavian Archaeology*. Cambridge: Cambridge University Press.

GRAYSON, D.K. 1983. *The Establishment of Human Antiquity*. New York: Academic Press.

GRUBER, J.W. 1965. Brixham Cave and the Antiquity of Man. In M.E. Spiro (ed) *Context and Meaning in Cultural Anthropology*, pp. 373-252. New York: Free Press.

HAMMOND, M. 1980. Anthropology as a weapon of social combat in late nineteenth century France. *Journal of the History of Behavioural Sciences* 16: 118-132.

HARRIS, M. 1968. *The Rise of Anthropological Theory*. New York : Crowell

KELLY, J. and M. HANEN 1988. *Archaeology and the Methodology of Science*. Albuquerque: University of New Mexico Press.

LAMING-EMPERAIRE, A. 1964. *Origines de l'archéologie préhistorique en France*. Paris: A. and J. Picard.

LEVINE, P.1986. *The Amateur and the Professional: Antiquarians, Historians and Archaeologists in Victorian England*, 1838-1886. Cambridge: Cambridge University Press.

LUBBOCK, J. 1865. *Pre-historic Times as Illustrated by Ancient Remains and the Manners and Customs of Modern Savages*. London: Williams and Norgate.

—1872. *Pre-historic Times as Illustrated by Ancient Remains and the Manners and Customs of Modern Savages*. 3rd edn. London: Williams and Norgate.

LYELL, C. 1863. *Geological Evidences of the Antiquity of Man*. London: John Murray.

MASCHNER, H. and S. MITHEN 1996. Darwinian archaeologies: an introductory essay. In H. Maschner and S. Mithen (eds) *Darwinian Archaeologies*, pp. 3-14. New York: Plenum.

MAYR, E. 1982. *The Growth of Biological Thought. Diversity, Evolution, Inheritance*. Cambridge Mass: Belknap Press.

MURRAY, T. 1976. Aspects of Polygenism in the Works of Robert Knox and James Hunt. Unpublished B.A. honours thesis. Department of History, University of Sydney.

—1987. Remembrance of Things Present: Appeals to Authority in the History and Philosophy of Archaeology. Unpublished PhD. Department of Anthropology, University of Sydney.

—1989. The history, philosophy and sociology of archaeology: the case of the *Ancient Monuments Protection Act* (1882). In V. Pinsky and A. Wylie (eds) *Critical Directions in Contemporary Archaeology*, pp. 55-67. Cambridge: Cambridge University Press.

—1992. Tasmania and the Constitution of 'the Dawn of Humanity'. *Antiquity* 66: 730-743.

—1993. Archaeology, ideology and the threat of the past: Sir Henry Rider Haggard and the acquisition of time. *World Archaeology* 25 (2): 175-186.

147

—1996. From Sydney to Sarajevo: a centenary reflection on archaeology and European identity. *Archaeological Dialogues* 1: 55-69.

—1997. Dynamic Modelling and new social theory of the mid-to-long term. In S. Van Der Keeuw and J. McGlade (eds) *Time, Process, and Structured Transformation*, pp. 449-463. London: Routledge.

—1999. The Art of Archaeological Biography. In *Encyclopedia of Archaeology: the Great Archaeologists*, 2 vols, pp. 869-883. Santa Barbara: ABC CLIO.

NILSSON, S.1868. *The Primitive Inhabitants of Scandinavia*. London: Longmans

OAKLEY, K.P. 1964. The problem of man's antiquity. An historical survey. *Bulletin of the British Museum (Natural History) Geology* 9 (5)

PATRIK, L.E. 1985. Is there an archaeological record? *Advances in Archaeological Method and Theory* 8: 27-62.

PEAKE, H.J.E.1940. The study of prehistoric times. *Journal of the Royal Anthropological Institute* 70: 103-146.

QUATREFAGES, de Breau, J.L.A. 1875. *Natural History of Man*. E.A. Youmanns, trans. New York: Popular Science Library.

—1879. *The Human Species*. London: Kegan Paul.

SCHNAPP, A. 1996. The Discovery of the Past. London: British Museum Press.

STOCKING, G.W. 1968. Race, Culture and Evolution. New York: Free Press.

STOCKING, G.W. Jr 1971. What's in a name? The origins of the Royal Anthropological Institute (1837-1871). *Man* (ns) 6: 369-390.

—1973. From chronology to ethnology: James Cowles Prichard and British Anthropology 1800-1850. In reprint edn of J.C. Prichard, *Researches into the Physical History of Man*, 183, pp. ix-cx. Chicago: University of Chicago Press.

—1983. The ethnographer's magic: fieldwork in British anthropology from Tylor to Malinowski. In G. W. Stocking Jr. (ed) *Observers Observed: Essays on Ethnographic Fieldwork*, pp. 70-120. Madison: University of Wisconsin Press.

—1987. *Victorian Anthropology*. New York: Free Press.

STOCZKOWSKI, V. 2001. How to benefit from received ideas. In R. Corbey and W. Roebroeks (eds) *Studying Human Origins. Disciplinary History and Epistemology*, pp. 21-28. Amsterdam: Amsterdam University Press.

TRIGGER, B.G. 1989. *A History of Archaeological Thought*. Cambridge: Cambridge University Press.

VAN REYROUCK, D. 2001. On savages and simians: continuity and discontinuity in the history of human origin studies. In R. Corbey and W. Roebroeks (eds) *Studying Human Origins. Disciplinary History and Epistemology*, pp.77-96. Amsterdam: Amsterdam University Press.

VAN RIPER, A. 1993. *Men Among the Mammoths*. Chicago: Chicago University Press.

VOGET, F.W. 1975. *A History of Ethnology*. New York: Holt, Rinehart and Winston.

WEBER, G. 1974. Science and society in nineteenth century anthropology. *History of Science* XV: 260-283.

WORSAAE, J.J.A. 1849. *The Primeval Antiquities of Denmark*. London: John Henry Parker.

WYLIE, A. 1992. Between philosophy and archaeology. *American Antiquity* 50 (2): 478-490.

—1995. The reaction against analogy. In M.B. Schiffer (ed) *Advances in Archaeological Method and Theory*, vol. 8, pp. 63-111. New York: Academic Press.

# Chapter 9

# Epilogue:
# why the history of archaeology matters

In recent years the history of archaeology has been enjoying something of a vogue in different research traditions, resulting in a wealth of new studies and publications. In the English-speaking world, our store of biographies and national histories has been considerably expanded by the five-volume *Encyclopedia of Archaeology* (Murray 1999; 2001). The *Bulletin of the History of Archaeology* has provided a much needed forum for research, and the AREA Project – Archives of European Archaeology – has begun to explore a range of resources bearing on the history of archaeology in Europe. At the same time, archaeologists have continued to justify and to advocate the significance of 'novel' approaches to archaeology through partial histories of the discipline (the most recent being those associated with the revival of 'Darwinian Archaeologies' such as Lyman *et al.* 1997). Other agendas have been advanced through the production of alternative histories of national archaeologies (e.g. Patterson 1995), the role of women (e.g. Diaz-Andreu and Sorensen 1998) and amateurs (Kehoe and Emmerichs 1999).

In his comprehensive survey of disciplinary historiography, Trigger (2001) points out that the history of archaeology has become a richly complex field producing knowledge that serves a diverse range of interests. Major synthetic treatments (Trigger 1989; Schnapp 1996) have made firm statements about disciplinary history and identity that have stressed the entanglement of archaeology and society, and the complex and ambiguous roots of the archaeological perspective. A concern with disciplinary identity (particularly for Trigger) has also meant a concern with disciplinary epistemology and metaphysics – in other words, with the nature of archaeological knowledge and of archaeological phenomena. This bridge between disciplinary history and epistemology has also focused attention on the need to explore archaeological institutions (university departments, museums and professional associations) as well as those structures (such as heritage legislation) that help shape the intersections between archaeology and society.

Over the last decade or so historians of archaeology have also focused their attention on methodological matters. Van Reybrouck (2002) is probably right in arguing here that perspectives from the sociology of science have been slow to filter through into mainstream histories of archaeology, but they have been present (see e.g. Fahenstock 1984; Murray 1989; 1998; Trigger 1985; 2001). Indeed, the kinds of methodological introspection found in two older collections (Christenson 1989; Reyman 1992) have recently been further expanded in the papers assembled by Corbey and Roebroeks (2001), where historians of archaeology (and historians of sciences cognate to archaeology) explicitly debate the role of the history of archaeology both within and outside the discipline.

The papers collected here as *Ancestral Archives* advance our understanding of many of the themes and issues that have been at the heart of recent work in the field – methodology, the purposes of history-writing, issues of disciplinary identity, the socio-politics of archaeology (particularly in nationalist and colonialist contexts) and disciplinary epistemology. I shall now look at these in slightly greater detail.

## How and why the history of archaeology

*Ancestral Archives* contributes to a continuing reflection about the how and the why of the history of archaeology. It does so through explicit methodological discussions (e.g. Van Reybrouck 2002, Kaeser 2002), and through practical demonstrations of the value of archival resources (Alexandri 2002; Lewuillon 2002; Ruiz, Sanchez and Bellon 2002; and Roughley, Sherratt and Shell 2002). In the Introduction, Schlanger (2002a) steers a course between the various models of practice that have become available, and makes an important distinction between histories of archaeology that are *for* archaeology and those that are *about* archaeology. In Schlanger's (2002a) view the history of archaeology should play a significant role in developing a coherent philosophy of archaeology, but it should also seek to comprehend archaeology as a social and cultural product in its own right.

This is especially important in discussions about the identity of archaeology. Schnapp's (2002) discussion of the 'evolution' of archaeology from natural history and antiquarianism makes the important observation that archaeology – the study of material remains from the past – does not simply belong to archaeologists. Likewise Nordbladh's (2002) evocative history of Pehr Tham reinforces the notion that antiquarianism was no 'wrong turning' on the path to archaeology, but rather a coherent activity in itself. Recognizing the interests of others, whether they be practitioners of different cognate disciplines, political opponents (Richard (2002) on de Mortillet), members of professional associations (Maischberger (2002) on war-time members of the German Archaeological Institute), or politicians with a keen eye to the rhetorical power of archaeological data (Schlanger (2002b) on

Smuts) emphasizes the fact that archaeological perspectives (either past or present) are strikingly ambiguous.

Understanding ambiguity also helps us to avoid the ultimately sterile oppositions of internalist/externalist and presentist/historicist histories that have tended to dog the histories of other sciences. Here the work of Blanckaert (e.g. 2001) in tracing out the complex lineages of archaeological and anthropological concepts and categories has been especially valuable. Lewuillon's detailed discussion of the iconography of archaeological illustration advances our understanding of the evolution of the observational languages of archaeology during the nineteenth century. This advocacy of sociology of science perspectives by archaeologists has not, however, been matched by much interest in archaeology from historians of cognate disciplines such as anthropology (e.g. George Stocking), let alone historians of science *(cf.* however Van Riper 1993). One hopes that the possibilities demonstrated here will provide sufficient incentive for non-archaeologists to improve this situation.

The contribution of the history of archaeology to contemporary debates about disciplinary theory and epistemology is particularly apparent in discussions about the impact of colonialism and nationalism on archaeological reasoning. Boast's (2002) analysis of Wheeler's research at Arikamedu, and Schlanger's (2002b) account of Smuts' use of archaeology to justify the social order in South Africa, make significant contributions to the exploration of colonial science. This is of course an on-going issue, and histories of archaeology have already begun to play their part in the development of postcolonial approaches, both internal and external, to our discipline. Significantly, one of the best examples of this genre, Griffiths 1996, was written by a historian, and not by an archaeologist. Nonetheless, an exploration of links between archaeology and colonialism will uncover much hidden social history in Europe, particularly with regard to the subjugation of ethnic minorities within European nations (see e.g. Jones 1997; Murray 1989; 1998).

After the flood of research in the 1990s, on the links between archaeology and nationalism, the detailed historical examples presented in *Ancestral Archives* (particularly those by Richard 2002; Alexandri 2002; and Ruiz, Sanchez and Bellon 2002) can be more easily appreciated by practitioners. Certainly these studies give us an opportunity to explore the ways in which archaeologists have sought support from science and society, and the conditions under which that support has been given. Alexandri's (2002) use of archival resources to chart the ways in which archaeological knowledge actually contributed to the formation of community identity in newly independent Greece stands as a major contribution to the field.

Other aspects of disciplinary history can also help us explore the identity of archaeology through an analysis of disciplinary epistemology and metaphysics. Schnapp (2002) eloquently argues for the value of a critical historiography in this role, and the contributions by Van Reybrouck (2002) and particularly Kaeser (2002) focus on the use of perspectives drawn from the sociology of science to make this explicit. Certainly Kaeser's (2002) analysis of the internationalization of archaeology, during the very same period where it was such a powerful force in the creation of national identities, highlights the rhetorical value of a positivist generalizing science based on explicit observational languages and strict logical rules – many of which were more honoured in the breach than the observance.

One of the consequences of the turn towards critical self-reflection in archaeology has been that we now understand more about the power of tradition. Tradition guides the socialization of practitioners (especially in matters related to the goals of archaeology, problem selection, methodology and assessments of the plausibility of knowledge claims). Tradition also structures the terms in which practitioners of disciplines cognate to archaeology establish the meaning or plausibility of archaeological knowledge claims. In this sense tradition oversees both the production and the legitimation of archaeological knowledge (Murray 1987).

Understanding the reasons why interpretations and explanations are found to be plausible or implausible has proved to be a more challenging problem. Work in the sociology of science undertaken during the same period has been of some assistance here, especially in the discussion of the power of disciplines (e.g. Lemaine *et al.* 1976). These discussions have fostered an understanding of two important and different senses of the term 'discipline' – on the one hand a body of specialized knowledge and/or skills, and on the other, a political institution. While there has been no rejection of the former sense as being a critical facet of the identity of disciplines (this was also the primary concern of older-style disciplinary histories), in practice research and discussion has focused on the sense of disciplines as institutions marking out areas of human knowledge and socializing their members.

In this latter sense disciplines act as socializing mechanisms where individual and community values and interests collide, and where practitioners acquire their perceptions of what explanations and interpretations are cognitively plausible, what theories materially advance knowledge of observable and unobservable phenomena, what problems are worth pursuing, and what methodologies are likely to yield reliable knowledge of the phenomena under review. Analysis of the disciplinary 'culture' of practitioners allows us to chart the ways in which social and cultural 'givens' (normative values) can be incorporated, as privileged assumptions, analytically prior to induction by the contributors. Van Reybrouck (2002) and Kaeser (2002) are excellent examples of this approach.

Notwithstanding the value of having new case studies exploring well-defined problems, this collection is particularly useful for two additional reasons. *Ancestral Archives* clearly demonstrates the tremendous potential of micro-scale archival research in the history of archaeology. The bulk of the papers are based on documentary records (personal papers, correspondence, images, catalogues, government archives and those of professional associations and the like) that have hitherto attracted little attention. These show a richness and diversity as resources for history-making both at the level of individual actors (see Nordbladh 2002; Sherratt 2002; Richard 2002; Schlanger and Soulier 2002; Maischberger 2002), and at other more general levels or contexts (Alexandri 2002; Lewuillon 2002; and Roughley, Sherratt and Shell 2002). *Ancestral Archives* also demonstrates the diversity of the national experiences of archaeology, be it in France (Richard 2002), Sweden (Nordbladh 2002), Spain (Ruiz, Sanchez and Bellon 2002), Greece (Alexandri 2002), India (Boast 2002) and South Africa (Schlanger 2002b), where nationalism, colonialism and internationalism (Kaeser 2002) are deeply enmeshed in the development of archaeological perspectives that created distinctive regional traditions of practice, based on a common inheritance of observational languages and concepts. The idea of there being a unity within the diversity of archaeologies past and present has been strengthened by the inclusion of new case studies and sources of information.

## Closing observations

Exploring new histories of archaeology can help us understand how the edifice of modern archaeology – its agendas, concepts, categories, patterns of socialization, and institutions – became established, and the processes that have underwritten its transformations. *Ancestral Archives* contributes to these broad questions of disciplinary identity and epistemology, but it also offers a great deal more.

Discussions of archaeology in nationalist and colonialist situations have strengthened our understanding of the importance of social and cultural context in archaeological reasoning. However, they also stress the importance of archaeology *within* the histories of nations and communities since the early 19th century. In this sense the role of archaeology as a significant social and cultural force (in the second and third worlds, as well as in the first) underscores the point that archaeology does not belong only to archaeologists. Histories of archaeology, whether by archaeologists or others, have the capacity to further enrich our understanding of the origins of communities, ethnicities, nations and empires and of their transformations over the last two centuries.

This is a worthwhile objective, and so is an exploration of the ways in which archaeologists have sought to make sense of the past. Given the social and cultural importance of archaeology and the very real consequences of what might be described as misuses of disciplinary concepts and categories, it is incumbent upon practitioners to speak directly and honestly with our fellow archaeologists, and also with the wider communities that consume our productions. Ranging from the amusing and quirky (Sherratt 2002) to the desperately sad accounts of life under totalitarianism (Maischberger 2002), *Ancestral Archives* contains a wealth of insights and perspectives that will help us achieve these goals.

**References**

ALEXANDRI, A. 2002. Names and emblems: Greek archaeology, regional identities and national narratives at the turn of the 20th century. In N. Schlanger (ed) *Ancestral Archives: Explorations in the History of Archaeology,* pp. 191-199. Special Issue of Antiquity 76: 291.

BLANCKAERT, C. (ed) 2001. *Les politiques de l'anthropologie. Discours et pratiques en France (1860-1940].* Paris: L'Harmattan.

BOAST, R. 2002. Mortimer Wheeler's science of order: the tradition of accuracy at Arikamedu. In N. Schlanger (ed) *Ancestral Archives: Explorations in the History of Archaeology,* pp.165-170. Special Issue of *Antiquity* 76: 291.

CHRISTENSON, A. (ed) 1989. *Tracing Archaeology's Past: the Historiography of Archaeology.* Carbondale: Southern Illinois University Press.

CORBEY, R. and W. ROEBROEKS 2001. Does disciplinary history matter? An introduction. In R. Corbey and W. Roebroeks (eds) *Studying Human Origins. Disciplinary History and Epistemology,* pp. 1-8. Amsterdam: Amsterdam University Press.

DIAZ-ANDREU, M. and M-L. STIG SORENSEN 1998. *Excavating Women. A History of Women in European Archaeology.* London: Routledge.

FAHNESTOCK, P.J. 1984. History and theoretical development: the importance of a critical historiography of archaeology. *Archaeological Review from Cambridge* 3: 7-18.

GRIFFITHS, T. 1996. *Hunters and Collectors: the Antiquarian Imagination in Australia.* Melbourne: Cambridge University Press.

JONES, S. 1997. *The Archaeology of Ethnicity.* London: Routledge.

KAESER, M-A. 2002. On the international roots of prehistory. In N. Schlanger (ed) *Ancestral Archives: Explorations in the History of Archaeology,* pp. 170-177. Special Issue of *Antiquity* 76: 291.

KEHOE, A. and M. EMMERICHS. 1999. *Studies in the Professionalization of Archaeology.* Albuquerque: University of New Mexico Press.

LEMAINE, G., MACLEOD, R., MULKAY, M. and P. WEINGART (eds) 1976. *Perspectives on the Emergence of Scientific Disciplines.* The Hague: Mouton.

LEWUILLON, S. 2002. Archaeological illustrations: a new development in 19th century science. In N. Schlanger (ed) *Ancestral Archives: Explorations in the History of Archaeology*, pp. 223-234. Special Issue of *Antiquity* 76: 291.

LYMAN, R.L., O'BRIEN, M.J. and R.C. DUNNELL (eds) 1997. *The Rise and Fall of Culture History*. New York: Plenum Press.

MAISCHBERGER, M. 2002. German archaeology during the Third Reich, 1933-45: a case study based on archival evidence. In N. Schlanger (ed) *Ancestral Archives: Explorations in the History of Archaeology*, pp. 209-218. Special Issue of *Antiquity* 76: 291.

MURRAY, T. 1987. Remembrances of Things Present: Appeals to Authority in the History and Philosophy of Archaeology. Unpublished PhD dissertation, Department of Anthropology, University of Sydney.

—1989. The history, philosophy and sociology of archaeology: the case of the *Ancient Monuments Protection Act* 1882. In V. Pinsky and A. Wylie (eds) *Critical Traditions in Contemporary Archaeology*, pp. 55-67. Cambridge: Cambridge University Press.

—1998. Excavating the cultural traditions of nineteenth century English archaeology: the case of Robert Knox. In A. Gustafsson and H. Karlsson (eds) *Glyfer och arkeologiske rum - en vänbok til Jarl Nordbladh*, pp. 501-15. Goteborg, Sweden: University of Goteborg.

MURRAY, T. (ed) 1999. *Encyclopedia of Archaeology. The Great Archaeologists*. Oxford/Santa Barbara: ABC-CLIO.

—(ed) 2001. *Encyclopedia of Archaeology. History and Discoveries*. Oxford/Santa Barbara: ABC-CLIO.

NORDBLADH, J. 2002. How to organize oneself within history: Pehr Tham and this relation to antiquity at the end of the 18th century. In N. Schlanger (ed) *Ancestral Archives: Explorations in the History of Archaeology*, pp. 141-150. Special Issue of *Antiquity* 76: 291.

PATTERSON, T. 1995. *Towards a Social History of Archaeology in the United States*. Fort Worth: Harcourt Brace.

REYMAN, J. (ed) 1992 *Rediscovering Our Past: Essays on the History of American Archaeology*. Aldershot: Avebury.

RICHARD, N. 2002. Archaeological arguments in national debates in late 19th century France: Gabriel de Mortillet's *La Formation de la nation française* (1897). In N. Schlanger (ed) *Ancestral Archives: Explorations in the History of Archaeology*, pp. 177-184. Special Issue of *Antiquity* 76: 291.

ROUGHLEY, C., SHERRATT, A. and C. SHELL 2002. Past records, new views: Carnac 1830-2000. In N. Schlanger (ed) *Ancestral Archives: Explorations in the History of Archaeology*, pp. 218-223. Special Issue of *Antiquity* 76: 291.

RUIZ, A., SANCHEZ, A. and J.P. BELLON 2002. The history of Iberian archaeology: one archaeology for two Spains. In N. Schlanger (ed) *Ancestral Archives: Explorations in the History of Archaeology*, pp. 184-190. Special Issue of *Antiquity* 76: 291.

SCHLANGER, N. 2002a. Introduction. In N. Schlanger (ed) *Ancestral Archives: Explorations in the History of Archaeology*, pp. 127-131. Special Issue of *Antiquity* 76: 291.

—2002b. Making the past for South Africa's future: the prehistory of Field-Marshal Smuts (1920s-1940s). In N. Schlanger (ed) *Ancestral Archives: Explorations in the History of Archaeology*, pp. 200-209. Special Issue of *Antiquity* 76: 291.

SCHLANGER, N. and P. SOULIER 2002. A feast for the eyes: celebrating prehistory in the de Mortillet dinners (an iconographic dossier). In N. Schlanger (ed) *Ancestral Archives: Explorations in the History of Archaeology*, pp. 132-133. Special Issue of *Antiquity* 76: 291.

155

SCHNAPP, A. 1996. *The Discovery of the Past: the Origins of Archaeology.* London: British Museum Press.

—2002. Between antiquarians and archaeologists – continuities and ruptures. In N. Schlanger (ed) *Ancestral Archives: Explorations in the History of Archaeology,* pp. 134-140. Special Issue of *Antiquity* 76: 291.

SHERRATT, A. 2002. Darwin among the archaeologists: the John Evans nexus and the Borneo Caves. In N. Schlanger (ed) *Ancestral Archives: Explorations in the History of Archaeology,* pp. 151-157. Special Issue of *Antiquity* 76: 291.

TRIGGER, B.G. 1985. Writing the history of archaeology: a survey of trends. In G.W. Stocking, Jr., (ed) *Objects and Others: Essays on Museums and Material Culture:* 218-315. Madison: University of Wisconsin Press.

—1989. *A History of Archaeological Thought.* Cambridge: Cambridge University Press.

—2001. Historiography. In T. Murray (ed) *Encyclopedia of Archaeology. History and Discoveries,* Vol. 2: 630-39. Oxford/Santa Barbara (CA): ABC-CLIO.

VAN REYBROUCK, D. 2002. Boule's error: on the social context of scientific knowledge. In N. Schlanger (ed) *Ancestral Archives: Explorations in the History of Archaeology,* pp. 158-164. Special Issue of *Antiquity* 76: 291.

VAN RIPER, A.B. 1993. *Men Among the Mammoths: Victorian Science and the Discovery of Human Prehistory.* Chicago: University of Chicago Press.

# Chapter 10

# Archbishop Ussher and archaeological time

According to the chronology developed by Archbishop Ussher, October 1996 marked the 6,000th anniversary of the creation of the earth. In a somewhat tardy recognition of this event I will briefly reflect on some contemporary debates among archaeologists about the nature and significance of archaeological time. As it is impossible to consider issues of chronology or temporality without also considering central elements of archaeological epistemology and ontology, I will make some observations on these matters as well.

### James Ussher and Chronology

James Ussher (1581-1656) lived a life full of learning and political controversy. Indeed he felt that the purpose of his prodigious knowledge was to examine the value of ideas – either ecclesiastical or secular – in terms of their history. He, like William Camden, Sir Robert Bruce Cotton and other British antiquaries of the time, were quite well aware of the political consequences of history and antiquarian study, not the least of which was the closure of the Society of Antiquaries of London by James I (see Piggott 1976; Trigger 1989: 47-48). Ussher clashed with both Charles I and Cromwell, fought constant battles within the Irish Church, and was frequently engaged in learned disputation with purveyors of Popery (once doing so for three days, after which his opponent retired from the field, presumably a shattered man). He saw some of his colleagues and his King go to the executioner's block and, while he sought fame and influence, he did not hesitate to use history to critique what he considered to be abuses in the present. The *Dictionary of National Biography* summed him up in straightforward terms: 'His Augustinian theology commended him to the puritans, his veneration for antiquity to the high churchmen; no royalist surpassed him in his deference to the divine right of kings. All parties had confidence in his character, and marvelled at his learning' (1965: 70).

James Ussher's life and work provides one of the best examples of the link between arcane historical knowledge and the society which both sustains and frequently threatens its production. Although we are slowly becoming more accustomed to appreciating the tremendous gifts made to archaeology by workers such as Lubbock, Falconer, Childe or Grahame Clark (and somewhat better informed about their shortcomings), archaeologists, by and large, know little about Ussher, beyond the fact that he was responsible for the 4004 chronology which was to be found in the margins of that most authoritative of all texts, the King James Bible.

Historians of archaeology (the most prolific and influential being Trigger) have devoted little space to the discussion of the chronology (e.g. Trigger 1989:31), but Grayson (1983: 27-42) and Van Riper (1993: 2-14) have done more to set Ussher in his context. Stephen Gould's (1988: 21-59) study of Thomas Burnet, particularly of *The Sacred Theory of the Earth* (1684), helps us to begin to appreciate the scale of Ussher's (1658) achievement in bringing order to history and authority to the present. By far the best discussion of Ussher is found in Parry (1995) where he is most clearly set in the context of seventeenth century British antiquarianism. Notwithstanding this, and a description of his life, published by Elrington (1848) last century, there is still no full-scale modern study. Parry's elegant consideration can be expanded by reference to the *Dictionary of National Biography*, and Brice (1982). A more nuanced understanding of the relationship between chronology and the history of geology can be fleshed-out by reference to standard works such as Albritton (1980), Berry (1987), the papers in Barnes and Shapin (1979), Jordanova and Porter (1979), and Lindberg and Numbers (1986).

In focusing only on the Biblical chronology and giving scant consideration the rest of Ussher's work, the reasons for the chronology, and the manner of its construction and elaboration, have largely been overlooked by historians of archaeology. Ussher's interest in chronology first bore fruit at the age of sixteen, but it was always pursued as part of a broader inquiry into the history of the Church in Ireland and England, and as a basis for vindicating the purity of Anglican doctrine, by demonstrating its antiquity. Indeed, from 1623 he was encouraged in this research by James I who gave him indefinite leave of absence from his Irish duties to study the antiquities of the English Church. Ussher's chronology was not the product of fancy but of deep learning which had very clear political implications. Furthermore, Ussher and his friends, Camden and Sir Robert Bruce Cotton, understood that the primary focus of antiquarian learning had to be in the production of history and with it a validation of identity.

Ussher's chronology, which was rightly considered to be a marvel of the age, was authoritative for two reasons. First, it was the product of a great scholar steeped in the original sources. Second, it provided a sense of chronological relationship between peoples and between peoples and the great events of human history. Thus, the real importance of the chronology was not so much the amount of time involved in it (although that would become a crucial justification for its demise in the nineteenth century), but in the historical relations it described and validated. Ussher's chronology (which was based exclusively on literary sources) thus allowed for a rational connection to be established between past and present, which also had room for the dictates of revealed religion. This was quite a different task to that undertaken by other antiquaries, or indeed by Ussher himself in other writings, which tended to focus on writing local or national histories built up from monuments, items of material culture and literary sources.

## Archaeologists, Chronology, and Time

Historians of archaeology have described in detail the downfall of the Ussherian chronology in the nineteenth century and its replacement by the Three Age System and the notion of high human antiquity (Graslund 1987; Grayson 1983; Levine 1986; Trigger 1989). It is generally agreed that these new frameworks for ordering chronology and for perceiving the scale of human history were fundamental to the successful creation of prehistoric archaeology as a field of study. There is a great deal of truth in this conventional tale of the triumph of science over superstition, but there is a lot of nonsense as well. Archaeologists have developed new systems for ordering time, and over the last century, they have developed radically new techniques for measuring time as well (see e.g. Albritton 1980; Berry 1987; Burchfield 1990) but until recently they have scarcely changed their frameworks for understanding time (see Murray 1987, 1993, 1995, 1997, 1999, 2001).

Beginning with the work of Bailey (1981, 1983) and subsequently developed by Murray (1987, 1993, 1997), Shanks and Tilley (1987), Barrett (1994), Gosden (1994), Thomas (1996a, 1996b) and most recently by McGlade (1999) and Olivier (1995, 1999, 2001) archaeologists have taken the first tentative steps towards exploring the nature of time in archaeology beyond a consideration of chronology. Significantly, cleavages in outlook, which mirror those found in other aspects of archaeological theory and practice, have begun to emerge.

In the following sections I will describe some of those cleavages and reflect on some of their implications for our understanding of the nature and purpose of archaeology. Although there have always been disputes about chronology in archaeology, even in Ussher's time, there are significant differences between disputes about chronology and the discussions of time and temporality which have surfaced since the late 1980s.

Historians and archaeologists have long understood that matters of temporality are crucial for the construction of history, particularly in terms of questions of origin, the nature of change and variation, the building of trajectories, and in promoting discussions of the tempo of human history. In this essay I do not argue that these traditional concerns have been replaced by new construals of the significance of time in archaeology. However, having said this, I will seek to demonstrate that a reconsideration of the fundamental issues raised by an exploration of the nature of archaeological time should change the ways in which these concerns will play out in the future. Perhaps the clearest example of this change in fortunes is the link, which is now being made between the existence of different conceptions of time in archaeology and the development of divergent accounts of archaeological ontology and epistemology.

This development reflects a broadening of perspective which stems from two sources of inspiration. The first of these has its roots in postmodernism, the archaeological versions of which (generally referred to as postprocessual archaeology) have drawn on an eclectic mix of sociology and social philosophy, hermeneutical perspectives generally associated with the Frankfurt School, material culture theories, and most recently an attempted application of the philosophical project of Heidegger to archaeology.

The second, which continues a long-standing tension in archaeology between natural science and social theory, stems from an improving understanding of the complex nature of archaeological records both in terms of their formation as well as in their interpretation. This second source is most closely associated with the work of Michael Schiffer and Lewis Binford (particularly the fallout from the 'Pompeii premise' debate) (Binford 1981) and the extensions which have been made on this by Bailey (1983) and others that have often gone under the rubric of 'time perspectivism'.

It is customary to discuss these differences in perspective as presenting an either/or choice for archaeologists, for example whether or not to follow the notion that the nature of archaeological records as phenomena is only of minor importance when seeking to interpret those records in terms which accord closely with the form and substance of contemporary social theory. In this essay I specifically reject this view, arguing instead that interpretations of archaeological records must not be seen as separate from the nature of the phenomena which make up those records. Or, to put it another way, no set of archaeological phenomena is totally constructed by the theories or perspectives which are the foundations of its description and/or interpretation. I will seek to justify this view by focusing on both ontological and epistemological considerations; however, before doing so I will describe the two divergent positions in greater detail.

## Some time stories in contemporary archaeology

Archaeologists should be at the forefront of any discussion about time and humanity. They are not, a fact which has been observed by archaeologists who hold very different views about the nature of archaeological theory (see e.g. Barrett 1994; Bailey 1981, 1983, 1987, 1997; Murray 1987, 1993, 1995, 1997, 1999; Shanks and Tilley 1987). All have noted that archaeologists have substituted an obsession with chronology for thinking about time and history, an obsession which attained a particularly bizarre form during the early phases of the new archaeology when a positivist science of universals was directly (and naively) contrasted with the 'particularities' of history (see e.g. Dymond 1974; Trigger 1968). During the last fifteen years alternative images of history in archaeology have been advanced, particularly that of 'total' history which has been linked (in the archaeological literature at least) with the notion of scale and the 'long term' (see e.g. Hodder 1987; Knapp 1992). There has also been a very useful consideration of the role of narrative and of the need to consider temporality (the notion of the 'lived' time of the actors) based on the work of Ricoeur (1984) and others (see e.g. Barrett 1994). Much of this discussion of temporality has also focused on the notion of cultural and social landscapes exhibiting a multiplicity of temporalities and on the idea that these must also be considered if one is to understand social action in the past.

This focus on temporality and its links to history has also been marked by an increased interest in the philosophy of history, particularly in the works of Collingwood and Hayden White (see e.g. Hodder 1991a), and an increased opposition to the perceived dominance of the 'science time' of chronology in the archaeological imagination. Time in this reading is much more complex and interesting than simply acting as a unit of measurement – it is perhaps the central feature of human existence. This opposition takes its most straightforward form in one of Shanks and Tilley's aphorisms:

*4.1 There is no singular time, but temporalities. Time is related to social practice. It is part of the social construction of reality. As with space, it does not simply form a container for action but is a medium giving form to action and establishing action as meaningful. Different structures of temporality are implicated in different practices* (1987: 211).

In this reading time is a social and cultural construct, not some abstraction which can be used to unproblematically order behaviours, or to play a key role in describing the ontology of archaeological records. This focus on exploring the 'social time' of past lives is now being developed to enhance the traditional reconstructivist goals of archaeology. This approach has prompted useful re-evaluations of the archaeology of landscape and of ritual (see especially Barrett 1994; Mizoguchi 1993), and has supported attacks made on the conventional assumption that no social archaeology of the long-term is possible (see especially Shanks and Tilley 1987: Chapter 5).

Other advocates of this view have tended to reinforce the separation of 'science time' and 'social time' by stressing the view that the detailed analysis of archaeological records as phenomena is of secondary importance to the consideration of the material culture, which in part comprises those records. For archaeologists such as Thomas (1996a, 1996b), developing an interpretation of the interactions between people and material culture is the goal of archaeology, a goal which can be readily achieved through the re-constitution of the past within the present, both through acts of empathy (in the style of Collingwood), and through more the conventional means of ethnographic analogy. Significantly much of this developing focus on 'social time' reflects the influence of contemporary social theory and it should in essence be considered as an attempt by archaeologists to reposition the goals of social archaeology to more closely accord with that theory.

It is significant to note that the advocates of a deep engagement with 'social time' have shown little interest in the implications of changing perspectives on 'science time'. Indeed, the two positions on time have been seen to be almost mutually exclusive. But, notwithstanding the interest attaching to notions of temporality and of 'social time', it is apparent that the divide between 'science time' and 'social time' is not nearly as sharp as Shanks and Tilley or Thomas require. The most obvious objection to a sharp separation is that the phenomena accepted as being the objects of analysis by social archaeologists are first constructed as a time series using theoretical perspectives which need not necessarily have anything in common with the perspectives that foster the interpretation of those phenomena. Moving from this mundane point that chronology orders the phenomena that are the subject of interpretation, we also find that 'science time' is much more than simple chronology, in that it also establishes the minimum units for the description and comparison of phenomena, which together constitute that which is to be interpreted or explained, again no matter the theoretical perspective adopted at this stage.

The usefulness of the distinction is further called into question when we consider that all time stories can be more readily affected by 'science time' than by different views of 'social time'. A paradigmatic example of this impact is provided by the upheavals which have followed the introduction of radiometric dating to the European Neolithic and Bronze Age (see e.g. Renfrew 1973). Another more recent example is the practice of 'chronometric hygiene' (see e.g. Spriggs and Anderson 1993), which has a demonstrated potential to fundamentally alter the ways in which archaeological phenomena constituted by radiometric dating can be 're-read'.

Notwithstanding these fairly basic qualifications, the argument that doing social archaeology, and enhancing an archaeological contribution to social theory, requires us to focus our interpretive efforts on constructing and theorising 'social time' has gained currency among practitioners. Of particular interest is the idea that archaeologists might begin to approach a social archaeology of the long-term, which was previously seen as being the preserve of 'science time'. But separating 'science time' from 'social time' does not of itself provide a framework within which archaeologists might go about writing history. Indeed, such a separation is artificial and can make the goal of achieving a social archaeology of the long-term more, rather than less, difficult to achieve.

The artificiality of this separation is partially exemplified by the goal of seeking ever-finer scales of chronological resolution through the development of dating systems, or the refinement of data recovery technologies. Archaeological science has been a constant source of inspiration in this area as new sources of data are created not just by asking different questions but also by developing technologies which allow us to find answers among previously unprospected remains. The same kind of benefits can also flow from a serious engagement with methodologies of data recording and analysis, especially in the field of distributional archaeology (see Ebert 1992; Rossignol and Wandsnider 1992). Although distributional archaeology remains more a method than the basis of a theorised social archaeology, which moves us beyond the basics of cultural ecology, the methods that have been developed to establish chronology in difficult archaeological contexts (such as open sites) merit serious attention. Such approaches might avoid the essential circularity of the opposition of 'science time' and 'social time', but to do this they have to avoid the trap of equating time with chronology.

The other reason why such a theoretical separation between 'science time' and 'social time' will do more harm than good stems from an inconsistency within the 'social' approach as it currently stands. One of the most problematic aspects of conceptually equating time with chronology is that this marginalises significant discussions about the links between history, as prehistoric archaeologists might seek to write it, and issues of disciplinary epistemology. If we accept the epistemological position of 'mitigated objectivism' (Wylie 1992), as both Hodder and Shanks and Tilley have, then the notion that all archaeological data are subjective must be ruled as inadmissible. From this flows, quite properly, the notion that concepts of time are crucial to discussions of process, causality, and identity. Thus, framing interpretation around the 'time of the actors' is always contingent on the fact that 'science time' both constructs phenomena and helps us establish the validity of interpretations. Therefore the empirical character of archaeological records is entirely consequential for both the development and assessment of knowledge claims made by archaeologists, notwithstanding the capitalist roots of 'science time' (Squair 1994). I shall return to this issue below.

Over the same period other archaeologists have sought the basis of an archaeology which addresses both concerns, but does so in way that embraces the idea that the empirical phenomena of archaeology can and should constrain interpretation (see e.g. Bailey 1981, 1983, 1987, 1997; Murray 1987, 1995, 1997, 1999, 2001). In the context of this search the differences between archaeology and palaeobiology are thought to be instructive, because archaeology is characterised by the persistence of core concepts of time and history, while in palaeobiology there has been fundamental change in its modus vivendi over the same period (see e.g. Behrensmeyer and Schindel 1983; Eldredge and Gould 1972; Gingerich 1982). But is this persistence the product of few changes, or have the changes been great but has disciplinary inertia at the conceptual level been a more powerful force?

Advocates of these alternative approaches to temporality (and they are so diverse in their interests and emphases that it is inaccurate to refer to them as a school of thought) have focused on a congeries of changes in our understanding of the nature of archaeological phenomena. All agree that archaeological phenomena can no longer be considered as being the subject of common sense understandings – they are complex phenomena which are the product of both natural and cultural formation processes (see e.g. Schiffer 1987; Stern 1993, 1994). There is a high level of disagreement among archaeologists about whether this effectively means that archaeological records are unintelligible in conventional anthropological terms, and about whether entropy makes reconstructions of the past that can be evaluated in empirical, as well as theoretical terms, at the levels required by social archaeology, simply impossible to achieve (see e.g. Binford 1981; Murray 1987, 1999, 2001; Schiffer 1985).

Equally contested is the question of whether the 'behaviours' that have been the traditional focus of anthropological archaeology have any empirical (as distinct from theoretical) content. Further, it is an open question as to whether the data we seek to understand are simply palimpsests of many 'behaviours' occurring within the envelope of archaeologically observable time, that emit a signal which is superficially intelligible to us, but which might (because it is a time-averaged composite) have little if anything to do with the specific 'behaviours' of the actors. None of these issues, which go right to the heart of the ontology of archaeological records and thus are highly consequential for the building of archaeological theory, is even close to resolution. Therefore, a diversity of views arise when archaeologists seriously consider the power of empirical data to constrain interpretation and, through inductive strategies, to be an active principle in the development of alternative frameworks of interpretation (see e.g. Murray 2001).

Behavioural palimpsests are the creation of both the formation processes of archaeological records and of our capacity to measure time. These phenomena, created by 'science time', may well not exist in the contemporary world, nor is it likely that they would have been apparent at the scale of the 'time of the actors'. While 'social time' might be theorised in terms which do not differ greatly from the conventions of total history, radiometric time would now seem to pose very difficult problems regarding the constitution of process, temporality and causation in archaeology. Bailey has usefully summarised aspects of this issue:

*Above all, new dating methods have demonstrated that human cultural history extends over a timespan of at least two million years. This poses in a new way the issue of how we are to make use of knowledge of the past, what questions we should ask of it, and whether by archaeological investigations of human activities over this timespan, we can learn something new about human nature not available from other sources* (1983: 165).

Most discussion of archaeological time undertaken by archaeologists interested in linking 'science time' and 'social time' has tended to focus on the possibility (or the lack of it) of providing links between macroscale and microscale temporal frameworks – Bailey's 'time perspectivism' (see e.g. Fletcher 1992). These discussions have tended to follow Bailey's original formulation and the original focus on developing an archaeological account of uniformitarianism:

*(a) that there are essentially only two scales of behaviour - long-term and short-term;*
*(b) that long-term processes are dominated by environmental and biological interactions, by relationships between genetics, demography, and economic exploitation of the natural environment, where as short-term processes are dominated by social and psychological processes, by social rules and relationships and individual goals and motivations;*
*(c) that behaviour at these different scales requires different sorts of*

*explanations expressing varying degrees of proximate and ultimate causation and varying emphasis on historical (in terms of the past), functional (in terms of the present), or teleological (in terms of the future) causes* (1983: 180).

Twenty years later thoroughly worked studies incorporating this approach are still few. But real questions arise about whether this focus on long and short time scales adequately captures the complex reading of temporality which has sprung from the 'science time' of radiometric dating. These questions hark back to problems of palimpsest but stem from a related concept, that of the minimum chronological unit (or minimum archaeological stratigraphic unit) (see Murray 1997; Stern 1994).

This concept arises from a consideration of the link between the resolving powers of archaeological records (i.e. the minimum analysable unit of time expressed in any record) and the constitution of observable archaeological phenomena. On the one hand it allows us to describe the structural properties of archaeological records as phenomena (which should properly become the objects of analysis), on the other it permits us to investigate the ways in which such properties constrain interpretation. In this reading the distinctiveness of archaeological records as records of human action is seen as something with which interpretation has to directly engage rather than (as is traditional) simply explain away. Again, the implications of these viewpoints for theory building and for the development of our understanding of how archaeologists might write history, have only been vaguely described. Nonetheless we should recognise that lying within these alternative readings of disciplinary ontology lie the bases of new forms of association between archaeology and other disciplines.

I have already mentioned the link between concepts of time (be they either 'science time' or 'social time') and the description of archaeological ontology. I have also sketched the links between time in ontology and time in epistemology, particularly in the sense that an understanding of the nature of archaeological phenomena should play a significant role in how we assess claims to knowledge of the past. At the same time I have been outlining a case for history and process, and identifying points of cleavage between archaeologists about the forms history-writing done by archaeologists should take. Given the wide variety of records routinely investigated by archaeologists (from the long-term of the Palaeolithic to the microscale of the nineteenth century) it is entirely proper that such points of cleavage should exist. The idea that a single overarching explanatory or interpretative scheme should operate in archaeology is as outmoded as the positivist account of science we have been struggling to overcome since the 1960s. But there are other elements which are helping to define the framework within which archaeologists might write history.

In recent years, particularly with the rising popularity of non-linear modelling and what is popularly known as 'chaos theory', archaeologists have begun to re-examine the nature of causality in ways which dramatically affect the kinds of histories we might seek to write. These are complex issues which can only be skated around in the present context (but see the papers in Van der Leeuw and McGlade 1996; McGlade 1999; Murray 1997, 1999); however, it is possible to extract from all the jargon of 'self-organised criticalities', fractals, bottlenecks, and entropic systems, a rising sense of convergence in the analysis of complex natural and cultural systems. Whereas positivist science insisted upon a model of universals as the exemplar of science (usually mathematics or physics), the science of non-linear dynamics explicitly recognises that all systems (natural and cultural) are historical, given that time is irreversible and precise reconstruction of the past impossible.

This factor of convergence has many interesting implications for history writing by archaeologists, especially in the very vexed area of causality. Classic Humean linear systems of causality, where causal pathways can be unambiguously described, have never been particularly kind to disciplines like archaeology where causation is extraordinarily complex and where very few unambiguous traces survive. This is especially true of the history of systems which evolve horizontally rather than vertically, in the sense that there is no simple linear trajectory from simple to complex (see Roth and Ryckman 1995; Shermer 1995). Just how archaeologists are to work their way towards a more diverse account of causality, and the impacts this will have on our understanding of core issues of process and identity is still a very open question, but it seems to me that it is a development we should be positive about. It is, perhaps, a sign of the times that theoretical archaeology has at long last sought to peek beneath the veil of chronological conventionalism and to actively engage with time (see e.g. McGlade 1999; Olivier 1995, 1999).

## Interpretation, Imagination and Making Choices

Although we all understand that discussions about time in any discipline are inevitably complex, recent archaeological perspectives tend to divide quite neatly in terms of the significance which is granted to the empirical structure of archaeological records as the primary means by which we assess the validity and usefulness of knowledge being claimed about the past. For time perspectivists such as Bailey, time and the issue of time-scale essentially structure the phenomena we as archaeologists observe, and in doing so, are fundamental to the formulation of archaeological questions, and to the definition of archaeological goals. The temporal structures of archaeological records thus play a significant role in describing the ontology of archaeological records. The differences between the structural properties of archaeological records and those of other records of human action (those stemming from written documents, participant observation, and statements made by informants), differences which are still being described and explored, have led to claims that the archaeological records are ontologically singular records of human action (Murray 1993, 1997).

By contrast Shanks and Tilley, and those who have followed what is loosely called postprocessual archaeology, accept the theoretical significance of time but see it as being dependent (rather than independent) of the perspectives of the people who created the material remains which survive into the present, or who had to live with monuments (such as Stonehenge) and other evidence of actions that provided structure to cultural or social landscapes (see e.g. Ashmore and Knapp 1999; Gosden and Head 1994; Tilley 1994). But can (or should) the empirical character of archaeological records (including those dimensions created by a consideration of 'science time') constrain interpretations of prehistoric social life (see e.g. Murray 2001)?

In some circles, especially in the early days of postprocessual archaeology, there was an assumption that relativism would mean the end of objective archaeological knowledge and that the only bases for choosing between competing knowledge claims about the past would be via coercion, cultural or political prejudice, trickery, or ignorance. Wylie (1992) very usefully outlined the ongoing process of convergence between opposing 'processual' and 'postprocessual' views about the nature of archaeological epistemology to a position she describes as 'mitigated objectivism'. In this account the cultural properties of science are recognised, the theory-ladenness of observation accepted, but the power of archaeological observables (i.e. empirical data) to constrain interpretation is acknowledged. In a sense there is a natural tension which exists in any science between our expectations as scientists (which clearly have a high 'cultural' component), and our ability to interrogate data and to 'hear' the answers to our questions.

It seems clear enough that postpositivist science should be built around an understanding of how this tension plays itself out, and on critical reflection about the plausibility of research programs and the answers they give us. Wylie and others (see e.g. Hodder 1991b; Renfrew 1989; Murray 2001) have argued that this notion of relativity gives no support to a notion of 'anything goes' in interpretation. Indeed, paying much closer attention to the mechanics of archaeological epistemology through the analysis of why arguments are or are not plausible makes arguments of all kinds (whatever their source) more transparent. Thus, they have to work a great deal harder to establish the clarity and force of their links to the empirical phenomena which are the subject of archaeological analysis.

However, the current state of discussion about time in archaeology has still some way to go before the union of 'science time' and 'social time' within a complex process of interpretation (which surely must be the primary consequence of constraint) can be effected. Part of this has to do with the fact that the discussions (right across the board) are still rudimentary and unsophisticated. But the most important reason stems from the cultural traditions of archaeology itself, traditions which place dramatically different constraints on archaeological knowledge than those which stem from the structural properties of archaeological records as empirical phenomena. It is clear that an integrated understanding of time in archaeology will require an intensive re-engagement with the history, philosophy and sociology of archaeology.

In recent years it has become more common for archaeologists to explore the socio-political aspects of the production and consumption of archaeological knowledge. New histories of archaeology are appearing which gain much of their focus from a concern with establishing the 'presentness' of pasts, as they have been reconstructed by archaeologists or by antiquarians. There is a great deal to be said for continuing to pursue these explorations, especially when they are undertaken by archaeologists for the purpose of enhancing our understanding of the disciplinary culture of archaeology. Such an understanding should have considerable impact on the way we form our views about the nature and purpose of our discipline and be a vital force in shaping and re-shaping the ways we respond to the challenge of making meanings about archaeological places and things.

Another reason for exploring the social and cultural contexts of archaeological knowledge is to better understand the processes whereby views of the past held by archaeologists and antiquarians have shaped broader social and political concepts and categories, and in so doing have influenced society as well as having been influenced by it. These complex interactions (which emphasise that scientific knowledge is cultural) make it essential that we identify and scrutinise the sources of authority claimed both by practitioners in their dealings with society and by members of society when they are dealing with each other.

**Concluding remarks**

There can be no doubt that the context within which archaeologists discuss temporality and chronology is far different from that which prevailed barely thirty years ago, let alone in the heyday of English antiquarianism when Ussher produced his now discredited chronology. It also seems clear enough that we are still quite a way from developing an understanding of temporality in contemporary archaeology, given the fact that discussion of time stories is still a relatively recent phenomenon in our archaeology. It takes no great leap of consciousness to appreciate that there is a great deal at stake in these discussions – both in terms of the nature of our discipline *vis a vis* other disciplines concerned with the analysis of human affairs, and in terms of the interests of the wide variety of publics who consume our product. At the very least discussions of temporality directly impact on our understanding of history and of identity, and Ussher would have had no trouble understanding the social and political implications of changing the focus of a discipline and the expectations of its public.

## Acknowledgments

Peter Hiscock, Chris Chippindale, Wil Roebroeks and Laurent Olivier offered constructive criticism of an earlier version of this paper. Nicola Stern and Josara de Lange assisted with a subsequent version. Once again I have profited from talking about archaeological time with Geoff Bailey, a conversation which has been going on since 1981. Parts of this paper were written while I was a guest of the Institut D'Art et D'Archéologie, Universite de Paris 1. I thank Alain Schnapp for arranging this visit, and Anick Coudart and Sander Van Der Leeuw for their valuable assistance and advice during my stay.

### References

ALBRITTON, C.C. Jr. 1980. *The Abyss of Time: Changing Conceptions of the Earth's Antiquity Since the Sixteenth Century*. San Francisco: Freeman and Cooper.

ASHMORE, W. and B. KNAPP (eds) 1999. *Archaeological Landscapes: Constructed, Conceptualized, Ideational*. Oxford: Blackwell

BAILEY, G. 1981. Concepts, time-scales and explanations in economic prehistory. In A. Sheridan and G. Bailey (eds) *Economic Archaeology: Towards an Integration of Ecological and Social Approaches,* pp. 97-117. Oxford: BAR International Series, 96.

—1983. Concepts of time in quaternary prehistory. *Annual Reviews of Anthropology* 12: 165-192

—1987. Breaking the time barrier. *Archaeological Review from Cambridge* 6: 5-21.

BAILEY, G. (ed) 1997. *Klithi: Palaeolithic Settlement and Quaternary Landscapes in Northwest Greece*, vols 1 & 2. Cambridge: McDonald Institute for Archaeological Research.

BARNES, B. and S. SHAPIN (eds) 1979. *Natural Order: Historical Studies of Scientific Culture.* London: Sage Publications.

BARRETT, J.C. 1994. *Fragments from Antiquity*. Oxford: Blackwell.

BEHRENSMEYER, A.K. and D. SCHINDEL 1983. Resolving time in paleobiology. *Paleobiology* 9:1-8.

BERRY, W.B.N. 1987. *The Growth of a Prehistoric Timescale: Based on Organic Evolution.* 2nd edition. Oxford: Blackwell.

BINFORD, L.R. 1981. Behavioral Archaeology and the 'Pompeii Premise'. *Journal of Anthropological Research* 37: 195-208.

BOWLER, P.J. 1990. *The Invention of Progress: The Victorians and the Past.* Oxford: Blackwell.

BURCHFIELD, J.D. 1990. *Lord Kelvin and the Age of the Earth.* 2nd edition. Chicago: University of Chicago Press.

BRICE, W.R. 1982. Bishop Ussher, John Lightfoot and the Age of Creation. *Journal of Geological Education* 30: 18-24.

BURNET, T. 1684. *The Sacred Theory of the Earth: containing· an account of the original of the earth, and of all the general changes which it hath already undergone, or is to undergo, till the consumation of all things. The first two books concerning the Deluge and concerning Paradise.* London.

DICTIONARY OF NATIONAL BIOGRAPHY, 1965. James Ussher 1581-1656, pp. 64-72. Oxford: Oxford University Press.

DYMOND, D.P. 1974. *Archaeology and History: A Plea for Reconciliation.* London: Thames and Hudson.

EBERT, J.I. 1992. *Distributional Archaeology.* Albuquerque: University of New Mexico Press.

ELDREDGE, N. and S.J. GOULD 1972. Punctuated equilibria: an alternative to phyletic gradualism. In T.J. Schopf (ed) *Models in Paleobiology,* pp. 156-167. San Francisco: Freeman.

ELRINGTON, C.R. 1848. *The Life of the Most Rev. James Ussher, D.D., Lord Archbishop of Armagh, and Primate of all Ireland. With an account of his writings.* Dublin: Hodges and Smith

FLETCHER, R.J. 1992. Time Perspectivism, Annales and the Potential of Archaeology. In B. Knapp (ed) *Archaeology, Annales, and Ethnohistory*, pp 35-49. Cambridge University Press: Cambridge.

GINGERICH, P. 1982. Time resolution in mammalian evolution: sampling, lineages and faunal turnover. *Proceedings of the 3rd North American Paleontological Convention,* Vol. 1: 205-221.

GOSDEN, C. 1994. *Social Being and Time.* Oxford: Blackwell.

GOSDEN, C. and L. HEAD 1994. Landscape - a usefully ambiguous concept. *Archaeology in Oceania* 29: 113-116.

GOULD, S.J. 1988. *Time's Arrow, Time's Cycle.* Harmondsworth.

GRÄSLUND, Bo. 1987. *The Birth of Prehistoric Chronology: Dating Methods and Dating Systems in Nineteenth-century Scandinavian Archaeology.* Cambridge: Cambridge University Press.

GRAYSON, D. 1983. *The Establishment of Human Antiquity.* New York: Academic Press.

HODDER, I. 1991a. *Reading the Past.* 2nd edn. Cambridge: Cambridge University Press.

—1991b. Interpretive archaeology and its role. *American Antiquity* 56 (1): 7-18.

HODDER, I. (ed) 1987. *Archaeology as Long-Term History.* Cambridge: Cambridge University Press.

JORDANOVA, L. and R. PORTER (eds) 1979. *Images of the Earth.* Chalfont St Giles: British Society for the History of Science:

KNAPP, B. (ed) 1992. *Archaeology, Annales, and Ethnohistory.* Cambridge: Cambridge University Press.

LEVINE, P. 1986. *The Amateur and the Professional: Antiquarians, Historians and*

171

*Archaeologists in Victorian England, 1838-1886.* Cambridge: Cambridge University Press.

LINDBERG, D.C. and R.L. NUMBERS 1986. *God and Nature: Historical Essays on the Encounter between Christianity and Science.* Berkeley, Ca: University of California Press.

MCGLADE, J. 1999. The Times of History. In T. Murray (ed) *Time and Archaeology*, pp. 139-163. London: Routledge.

MIZOGUCHI, K. 1993. Time in the reproduction of mortuary practices. *World Archaeology* 25 (2): 223-235.

MURRAY, T. 1987. Remembrances of Things Present: Appeals to Authority in the History and Philosophy of Archaeology. Unpublished PhD Dissertation, Department of Anthropology, University of Sydney.

—1993. Archaeology and the threat of the past: Sir Henry Rider Haggard and the acquisition of time. *World Archaeology* 25 (2): 175-186.

—1995. Gordon Childe, archaeological records, and rethinking the archaeologist's project. In P. Gathercole, T. Irving and G. Melleuish (eds) *Childe and Australia*. St. Lucia, Qld: University of Queensland Press.

—1997. Dynamic modelling and new social theory of the mid-to-long term. In S. Van Der Leeuw and J. McGlade (eds) *Time, Process, and Structural Transformation*, pp. 117-132. London: Routledge.

—1999. A return to the 'Pompeii premise'. In T. Murray (ed) *Time and Archaeology*. London: Routledge.

—2001. On 'normalizing' the Palaeolithic: An orthodoxy questioned. In R. Corbey and W. Roebroeks (eds) *Studying Human Origins. Disciplinary History and Epistemology*. Amsterdam: Amsterdam University Press.

OLIVIER, L. 1995. The Shapes of Time: an Archaeology of Funerary Assemblages in the West Hallstatt Province. Unpublished PhD dissertation, University of Cambridge.

—1999. The Hochdorf 'Princely' Grave and the question of the nature of archaeological funerary assemblages. In T. Murray (ed) *Time and Archaeology*, pp. 109-138. London: Routledge.

—2001. The archaeology of the contemporary past. In V. Buchli and G. Lucas (eds) *Archaeologies of the Contemporary Past,* pp. 174-188. London: Routledge.

PARRY, G. 1995. *The Trophies of Time: English Antiquarians of the Seventeenth Century.* Oxford: Oxford University Press.

PIGGOTT, S. 1976. *Ruins in a Landscape: Essays in Antiquarianism.* Edinburgh: Edinburgh University Press.

RENFREW, C. 1973. *Before Civilization. The Radiocarbon Revolution and Prehistoric Europe.* Harmondsworth: Penguin.

—1989. Comments on 'Archaeology into the 1990s'. *Norwegian Archaeological Review* 22 (1): 33-41.

RICOEUR, P. 1984. *Time and Narrative.* Chicago: University of Chicago Press.

ROSSIGNOL, J. and L. WANDSNIDER (eds) 1992. *Space, Time, and Archaeological Landscapes.* New York: Plenum Press.

ROTH, P. A. and T.A. RYCKMAN 1995. Chaos, Klio and scientistic illusions of understanding. *History and Theory* 34: 30-44.

SCHIFFER, M.B. 1985. Is there a 'Pompeii Premise' in archaeology? *Journal of Anthropological Research* 41: 18-41.

—1987. *Formation Processes of the Archaeological Record.* New York: Academic Press.

SHANKS, M. and C. TILLEY 1987. *Social Theory and Archaeology.* Cambridge: Polity Press.

SHERMER, M. 1995. Exorcising Laplace's demon: chaos and antichaos, history and metahistory. *History and Theory* 34: 59-81.

STERN, N. 1993. The Structure of the Lower Pleistocene Archaeological Record. *Current Anthropology* 34 (3): 201-225.

—1994. The implications of time-averaging for reconstructing the land-use patterns of early tool-using hominids. *Journal of Human Evolution* 27: 89-105.

SPRIGGS, M. and A. ANDERSON 1993. Late Colonisation of East Polynesia. *Antiquity* 67: 200-217.

SQUAIR, R. 1994. Time and the privilege of retrospect. In I.M. Mackenzie (ed) *Archaeological Theory: Progress or Posture?* pp. 92-113. Avebury: Aldershot.

THOMAS, J. 1996a. *Time, Culture and Identity.* London: Routledge.

—1996b. A precis of Time, Culture and Identity. *Archaeological Dialogues* 3 (1): 6-21.

TILLEY, C. 1994. *A Phenomenology of Landscape: Places, Paths and Monuments.* Oxford: Berg.

TRIGGER, B.G. 1989. *A History of Archaeological Thought.* Cambridge: Cambridge University Press.

USSHER, J. 1658. *The Annals of the World. Deduced from the origin of time, and continued to the beginning of the Emperor Vespasian's reign, and the to tall destruction and abolition of the temple and common-wealth of the Jews.* London.

VAN DER LEEUW, S. and J. MCGLADE (eds) 1996. *Time, Process, and Structural Transformation.* London: Routledge.

VAN RIPER, A. B. 1993. *Men Among the Mammoths.* Chicago: University of Chicago Press.

WYLIE, A. 1992. On 'Heavily Decomposing Red Herrings': scientific method in archaeology and the ladening of evidence with theory. In L. Embree (ed) *Metaarchaeology. Reflections by Archaeologists and Philosophers*, pp. 269-288. Dordrecht: Kluwer.

# Chapter 11

# The historiography of archaeology and Canon Greenwell

In this paper I will focus the bulk of my remarks on setting studies of Canon Greenwell in two broader contexts. The first of these comprises the general issues raised by research into the historiography of archaeology, which I will exemplify through reference to research and writing I have been doing on a yet unfinished book, A History of Prehistoric Archaeology in England, and a new single-volume history of archaeology *Milestones in Archaeology,* which is due to be completed this year. The second, somewhat narrower context, has to do with situating Greenwell within the discourse of mid-to-late nineteenth-century race theory, an aspect of the history of archaeology that has yet to attract the attention it deserves from archaeologists and historians of anthropology (but see e.g. Morse 2005). Discussing both of these broader contexts will, I hope, help us address and answer questions about the value of the history of archaeology (and of research into the histories of archaeologists), and the links between these histories and a broader project, of understanding the changing relationships between archaeology and its cognate disciplines such as anthropology and history.

My comments about the historiography of archaeology are, in part, a reaction to developments that have occurred over the last decade within archaeology, but in larger part, are the consequences of my own interest in the field. Of course the history of archaeology is not the sole preserve of archaeologists, and it is one of the most encouraging signs that historians of science, and especially historians writing essentially popular works (usually biographies), have paid growing attention to archaeology and its practitioners.

I will begin by presenting a brief overview of historiographic analysis in archaeology. I will then very briefly discuss some of the themes that have arisen from my own research in the histories of anthropology and archaeology, and outline the new book on the history of prehistoric archaeology in England where I have attempted to ground those themes in a specific longitudinal study. I will follow this with a brief discussion of *British Barrows* (1877) that focuses on the use by Greenwell, Rolleston, Davis and Thurnam and John Beddoe of crania and other human physical attributes, to both write a racial history of England and contribute to contemporary debate about the importance of race in human affairs.

There are two reasons for wanting to spend only a very short space to historiography *per se*. First, because (to put it bluntly) many of the methodological issues raised by exploring a history of archaeology are not unique to that discipline. Anthropology, geology and of course, biology and physics, have a far longer (and stronger) tradition in this area. Indeed such disciplines or fields have been significant contributors (either by way of methodology or examples) to the development of the history, philosophy and sociology of science, the perspectives of which will necessarily play an important role in the immediate future of the history of archaeology.

The second reason for moving discussion away from methodological considerations is that it provides an opportunity to consider some of the consequences that an upsurge in research into the history of archaeology might have for our cognate disciplines of anthropology and history. Both disciplines have strong historiographic traditions, but I think that it is a fair generalisation that the historians of neither discipline have paid much specific attention to archaeology. Of course George Stocking and many others have written about Sir John Lubbock when considering the genesis of an evolutionary anthropology (see e.g. Stocking 1968, 1987), some have further considered the work of Gordon Childe within the general context of discussions of the concept of culture, but apart from these, and a North American focus on the anthropology of Franz Boas and the work of theorists such as Julian Steward and Leslie White, interest has been generally slight.

So it might be interesting to consider how (if at all) recent explorations into the genesis of archaeology in Europe (for example) might affect the current story of the genesis of anthropology and history, primarily in the nineteenth century. This has been the focus of much of my own research in the history of archaeology and, as I have acknowledged many times elsewhere, this is not an innocent task. Although I am perfectly happy to accept (as many others have done) that writing the history of archaeology requires no other justification than inherent interest, my goals have more to do with diagnosing the condition of contemporary archaeology, and understanding the nature of its relationships with contemporary anthropology and history. But more of all of this after the very brief and partial historiographical survey.

**Surveying the historiography of archaeology**

These days almost everyone has remarked on the sheer amount of history of archaeology being written. At a recent Cambridge conference Bruce Trigger was moved to remark that the task of revising his influential *History of*

*Archaeological Thought* had become very much more difficult in recent years. But Trigger was reflecting about the quantity of published work he had to synthesise rather than any inherent difficulty in the content of what was being written. This is because much of this history writing has been devoted to theories, methods, discoveries, and to the lives of 'great' archaeologists. While such studies are obviously important in establishing some of the aspects of archaeological practice, they alone do not produce satisfying accounts of the process of archaeological knowledge production.

Although historians of archaeology have become much more sensitive to the demands of context, there remain few analyses of the institutional structures of the discipline, of the wider intellectual context of archaeology, or of other sociological aspects of archaeological knowledge production (though the latter are increasing). The result of these shortcomings has been rightly criticized by some archaeologists, and by historians of the human sciences that have taken an interest in archaeology. Much of what has been produced is teleological, with the nature of archaeological knowledge transcending social and historical context. Until recent years analysis of the taken-for-granted of the history of archaeological practice such as institutional structures, relations with governments and the general public, organizing concepts and categories, and archaeology's relationships with its cognate disciplines, have been few and of variable quality.

After the late 1980s things began to change with the publication of two books. First, Bruce Trigger's *History of Archaeological Thought,* which notwithstanding some significant shortcomings, represented a quantum leap from what was then available in English. Second, Alain Schnapp's *Conquest of the Past,* which has done so much to remind prehistoric archaeologists of the riches of 'The Great Tradition' as well as the great virtues of antiquarianism as a system of study. Around the same time archaeologists more versed in the history and philosophy of science such as Wiktor Stoczkowski and myself began deploying perspectives from that field, and serious discussion about the historiography of archaeology began to occur in mainstream contexts such as the Society for American Archaeology. Andrew

Christenson's *Tracing Archaeology's Past* (1989) was the first collection of essays in English from researchers strongly committed to writing the history of archaeology in North America. It is significant that at that early stage many of the issues raised by such history writing (for example its justifications, the respective pluses and minuses of internalist and externalist perspectives, the perils of presentism, and that old favourite, whether the history of archaeology is better written by historians of science rather than by archaeologists) were all given a thorough airing. Subsequent discussion, for example, Bruce Trigger's entry on historiography in the *Encyclopedia of the History of Archaeology* (2001), tended to reinforce these trends, which were also the subject of a really intense debate published by Raymond Corbey and Wil Roebroeks as *Studying Human Origins: Disciplinary History and Epistemology* (2001).

Both Trigger and Corbey and Roebroeks sought to classify academic production either through a pretty straightforward division between popular, intellectual and social histories (Trigger) or through an application of Ernst Mayr's taxonomy – lexicographic, chronological, biographical, cultural and sociological, and problematic histories (Corbey and Roebroeks). But the editors of *Studying Human Origins* were after more than classification. Their goal was to seriously explore the *why, what, how* and indeed *whether* of such histories. Difficult questions such as why historians seemed to be ignoring the history of archaeology were asked, and the manifest shortcomings of archaeologists as historians of their own discipline were given thorough discussion. This is a common theme, sometimes taking on the characteristics of a turf war.

The sometimes casual disparagement of histories being written outside (or indeed sometimes in ignorance of) the canons of the history of science might be taken as clear testimony that we have a long way to go before the history of archaeology becomes a respectable pursuit. I do not think so. In fact I think that the contrary is the case, as archaeologists have become more skilled at articulating archives, oral histories and other testimonies in their analysis (Marc-Antoine Kaeser's book on Edouard Desor (2004) and the *Ancestral Archives* issue of *Antiquity* edited by Nathan Schlanger are excellent examples). Historians of science have also become somewhat more understanding of the wide range of motivations archaeologists are responding to when they work in this area.

## Archaeology and anthropology

Archaeology, through its close connections to anthropology and history has inherited long-standing epistemological and ontological antinomies, which have at various times in the history of the discipline sanctioned historicist or universalist, materialist or idealist, empiricist or rationalist emphases within the practice of archaeology – precisely as they have done in our cognate disciplines.

In this view, by the end of the nineteenth century, the connections and distinctions between archaeology and anthropology and archaeology and history had essentially been established. Archaeology, its conceptual field defined and secure within various traditions of anthropological and historical research, and its methodology developed to a stage where the discussion of temporal and cultural classifications could appeal to a widening store of empirical phenomena, was free to pursue problems of largely internal moment. Although in the United States the predominance of cultural rather than social anthropology, meant that the boundaries between archaeology and 'historical' anthropology were somewhat blurred, the same emphasis on the writing of prehistory, and on technical matters of classification and data retrieval was still present.

While it is the case that changes in fashion and orientation in anthropology and history directly affected the interests and approaches of archaeologists working under the aegis of either anthropological tradition, practitioners could keep pace with such changes in meaning by changing the terms of their translations of material phenomena into first, archaeological and subsequently anthropological, data. These changes were readily accomplished for four reasons.

First, archaeological data were considered to be impoverished testaments of human action in comparison with the richer data derived from socio-cultural anthropology. Meaning and the power to convince thus lay with the disciplines which 'managed' that latter data set.

Second, archaeological methodologies of description and classification were substantially relative rather than absolute. Given the anthropological and historical construction of archaeological data, there were few empirical grounds upon which those data, of themselves, could seriously disturb the intentions of their interpreters.

Third, despite the overt theorizing of practitioners such as Steward and Childe, the bulk of archaeologists were largely implicit consumers of theory, devoting their energies to methodological and technical issues of data collection and classification.

Fourth, given the essentially empiricist orientation of archaeologists in the years before the 1960s theoretical disputes were either settled on the authority of the archaeologists involved, rarely explicitly discussed because they were considered to be speculative and lacking the possibility of an archaeological contribution to their solution, or were simply set aside for some future time when the data were in. Thus, again with the exception of practitioners such as Childe, Steward and Clark, few archaeologists recognized that extant conceptual and epistemological relativisms within the source areas of archaeological theory could act as spurs to the development of such theory.

I have described the long and intense association between archaeology and anthropology, and between archaeology and history as being one of enrolment and symbiosis, beginning in the nineteenth century when all three disciplines began to take on their modern forms, and concluding around the end of that century (Murray 1987). This association, although differing in particulars over the course of the twentieth century, continues to provide substantial aspects of the archaeological agenda and by far the most important body of theory used by archaeologists in their day-to-day practice.

But it is also the case that the process of translating archaeological data into anthropological or historical information (or indeed of applying the perspectives of those disciplines to archaeological data) did not (and does not) always go smoothly, and archaeologists might have had to take seriously the idea that such simple translations can be problematic. But has this really affected the way archaeologists seek to make the past meaningful – are practitioners able to abandon science in favour of intelligibility in conventional human science terms? I have sought to understand whether the plausibility of archaeological knowledge claims has been gauged primarily in terms of determinate rules of scientific method, or whether the real determinants of plausibility were 'cognitive' or 'cultural'. It was something of a surprise to find that even at the high point of empiricism in the mid-nineteenth century where the methodological rhetoric held that archaeology contributed to the development of an approach to understanding human prehistory that explicitly shunned myth and the *a priori* in favour of the objectivity of science, that the performance of practitioners fell way short of the mark. This difference between rhetoric and performance (especially as it applies to claims for the scientific status of archaeology) continues to this day, mostly unremarked.

## A history of prehistoric archaeology in England

I have sought to further explore these general themes in a longitudinal study of prehistoric archaeology in England. The scope of this as yet unpublished book is sufficiently broad (some 800 years) to allow me to demonstrate the genesis and development of the perspectives of prehistoric archaeology in that country, but my focus on the period between 1800 and 1980 will also help me to examine that history in light of the histories of anthropology and history over the same period.

Producing a comprehensive narrative history of English prehistoric archaeology is something of a challenge requiring those foolish enough to attempt it to take account of the fact that English prehistoric archaeology is a large and complex entity made up of a web of producers and consumers of archaeological knowledge who intersect with the fabric of the discipline through a wide range of institutional, social, political and cultural contexts. The difficulty of the task is increased by two related factors. First, the practice of English prehistoric archaeology has had global implications especially from the moment when Lubbock published *Prehistoric Times* in 1865. Much of the methodological and theoretical landscape of prehistoric archaeology (especially in the Anglo-Saxon world) has been strongly influenced by people based in England or working on English materials. By the same token the interpretation of English prehistory has relied on inferences drawn from all over the world. Second, each temporal division (Palaeolithic, Neolithic, Bronze Age and Iron Age) has its traditions and its rhythms, and it is uncommon for archaeologists to have an understanding and appreciation of these matters in all prehistoric periods.

Given the scale of the task my coverage is synoptic and selective. What I have been able to do is to provide a brief and very general narrative of evolution and to isolate several historically significant themes. I mentioned earlier that one of the consequences of the history of archaeology not being a mainstream area of archaeological research was the perpetuation of questionable perspectives or the burying of historical context that might be 'distasteful', 'dehumanizing' or 'unscientific'. In the book 'A History of Prehistoric Archaeology in England' this will be exemplified in several case studies – one of which explores the clear links between archaeology and racial Anglo Saxonism. I have already explored some of the broader issues in papers on the *Ancient Monuments Protection Act,* the conflict between anthropology and ethnology at the British Association for the Advancement of Science, and the work of Robert Knox, but in this context I want to very briefly discuss some of the context of *British Barrows,* Greenwell's great work of 1877, and to take things a little further.

### The context of *British Barrows*

Historians of archaeology and of antiquarianism in late eighteenth and nineteenth century England have rightly focused on the evolution of landscape and topographical studies as a major driving force in the development of method (see e.g. Sweet 2004). Exemplified in the work of Richard Gough (particularly the *Anecdotes of British Topography,* in an expanded edition of Camden's *Britannia* (1789) and in *Sepulchral Monuments of Great Britain* (1799)), landscape and topographical studies taking place across the counties of England reached a large and expanding audience. Links between such studies, the writing of county histories and of course folkloric studies became more common fostered by, among others, Charles Roach Smith whose 'Antiquarian Notes' in *The Gentleman's Magazine* and *Retrospections Social and Archaeological* (1883) are rich sources of perspective, as are the editorials of the relevant archaeological and antiquarian societies that grew up at the time. Here the *British Archaeological Association,* founded by Charles Roach Smith and the truly indefatigable Thomas Wright, is an excellent example. Major works on Romano-British sites and antiquities (by such as Wright) were matched by those produced by such as John Evans on the antiquities of earlier periods, but it was antiquaries such as Greenwell who greatly expanded the sheer mass of information on the sites and landscapes of pre-Roman times. These involved the acts of excavation, classification and comparison, the last of which was almost wholly dependent on timely and accurate publication and the sharing of information at meetings and conferences meant that all concerned were now much more aware of what others were doing. In this sense the institutional structures of archaeological antiquarianism acted precisely as they should and the English scene expanded to the local to encompass regional, national and international scales of comparison. Greenwell had a strong sense of the importance of what he was doing. In the preface to *British Barrows* he spoke of the various causes for the destruction of barrows observing:

> *still more have been destroyed under the influence of a curiosity almost as idle, by persons indeed of better education, but who thought that enough was gained if they found an urn to occupy a vacant place in the entrance hall, or a jet necklace or a flint arrow-point for the lady of the house to show, with other trifles, to her guests requiring amusement* (Preface b).

Clearly the responsible antiquary should publish, but they should also have a proper appreciation of the history of their calling. The Preface to *British Barrows* has a comprehensive and generous appreciation of the work of predecessors – particularly Colt Hoare (Wiltshire), Bateman (Derbyshire), Carrington (Staffs) and Ruddock (North Riding of Yorkshire), but published works such as Warnes' *Celtic Tumuli of Dorset,* Borlase's *Nenia Cornubiae,* and more famously, Douglas' great *Nenia Britannica* and the Reverend Bryan Fausett's *Inventorium Sepulchrale,* were also acknowledged. These works covered much of England and allowed Greenwell (among others) to detect regional differences and similarities in site types and their contents (both skeletal and cultural material). However, it is the discussion of the crania (and the historical speculations of Greenwell and Rolleston about them) that most concern me.

Rolleston's discussion of the cranial series in *British Barrows* emulated Greenwell's preface in that included a long discussion of the history of cranial analysis in Britain, focusing on data that had been retrieved from excavated tombs, as well as more modern observations taken in Europe and elsewhere. Rolleston's survey dwelt on the work of Wilde in Ireland, and of Daniel Wilson in Scotland, and of course Sven Nilsson in Scandinavia, to make the point that crania were important historical data. Indeed Davis and Thurnam's

*Crania Britannica* (1865) was able to consider the issue of the Aboriginal races of the British Isles because of the crania excavated by Bateman and others. Moreover in Davis' subsequent *Thesaurus Craniorum* (1867) his sample of Aboriginal crania had increased to 36, all sourced to barrows dug by Bateman, Ackerman, Mayer and others. Thus there was already a clear tradition of making history from what was then called 'ethnological' or 'anthropological' analysis.

For Rolleston (as for Greenwell) there was no doubt about the cranial series could be classified in traditional terms:

> *A craniographer with Canon Greenwell's series before his eyes... would be impressed with the fact that out of the series, two sets, the one with its length typically illustrative of the dolichocephalic, the other by its breadth as typically illustrative of the brachycephalic form of skull, could at once be selected, even by a person devoid of any special anatomical knowledge. An antiquary similarly inspecting this series with a knowledge of archaeological history would, if he separated it into two groups, the one containing all the skulls of stone and bronze age, the other containing all the skulls of the bronze period, perceive that while the latter group comprised both dolichocephalic and brachycephalic crania and in very nearly equal proportions, none but the dolichocephalic skulls were to be found in any set of skulls from the barrows of the pre-metallic period* (Greenwell 1877: 627).

But what did this mean? Both Greenwell (and especially Rolleston) understood that the cranial series they were working provided an exception to Thurnam's old rule that long heads went with long barrows (and were older) and broad heads went with round barrows (and were more recent). Yet neither the antiquarian nor the anatomist were prepare to argue as Davis was to do in his *Thesaurus Craniorum* that the skulls should be classified in one of the standard racial divisions (such as Gaelic) or one of the tribal divisions noted by the Romans (such as the Brigantes). The absence of secure absolute dates was obviously a problem here – both at the level of determining synchronicity or succession, as well as determining duration. But Greenwell had to account for the anomalous pattern, especially after he had accepted that Thurnam's rule generally held for the vast bulk of the data to hand and was strongly supported by the evidence drawn from material culture. It is worth quoting Greenwell's solution at length because of its focus on producing a racial history of subjection and eventual intermixture, one that seemed entirely reasonable having regard to history and contemporary circumstances:

*This condition may have been brought about, and probably was, by the fact that the intruding round-headed people, smaller as they may have been in number, were gradually absorbed by the earlier and more numerous race whom, by force of one advantage or another, they had overcome. This subdued long-headed people may very possibly, in the earlier times of the conquest, have been kept in a servile condition, and therefore were not interred in the barrows, the place of sepulture reserved for the ruling race by whom they were held in subjection, and hence the numerical superiority of brachycephalic heads in the barrows. But as time went on and intermixture between the two peoples became common, a change would have gradually taken place in the racial characteristics, until at length the features of the more numerous body, that is to say the dolichocephalic, would become the predominant type of the united people* (Greenwell 1877: 129).

So much for the past, but what about the present and the future? Much has been written by Stocking, Burrow (1966) and others about the history of nineteenth century anthropology and race theory, and space precludes a lengthy recapitulation here. Significantly both Rolleston and Greenwell were well aware of this larger dimension to their work, and Greenwell was absolutely right in his general methodological conclusion to *British Barrows.* By the end of the nineteenth century it was to become apparent that what English prehistoric archaeologists urgently needed to do was to write history, to make the classifications arrived at in England and on the continent relate in real historical terms to the patterns being noted in the field.

But prehistoric archaeology (as a part of anthropology) was far from alone in this concern with history and historicism. Although from the 1880s perceptions of human diversity made a forceful return to the ranks of anthropology, this diversity was clearly to be located in ethnic and cultural, rather than purely physical differences. Explanation for diversity and similarity was increasingly to be sought in cultural historical factors, rather than by appealing to the doctrine of independent inventions and the psychic unity of mankind. Real historical forces acting on real (different) groups of people, past and present, could explain the peculiar differences between human beings far more convincingly than generalised uniformitarian forces. Anthropology and prehistoric archaeology, previously focused on providing evidences of the evolution of human beings and their societies and cultures, now became more firmly linked to a less encompassing task – writing the ethnic histories of European nations. Greenwell's grappling with the patterns established in *British Barrows* is an excellent exemplar of what was to be transformed into culture historical archaeology.

But there was always more to doing this than making claims for the reality of strict inductions and a freedom from the *a priori* (methodological strictures that were honoured far more in the breach than in the observance). Here I want to briefly touch on two works by the eminent nineteenth century anthropologist John Beddoe. The first is *The Races of Britain* (1885) which presented the fruits of many years data collection on (among many variables) height, the colour of skin, hair and eyes, and location from a broad sample of the British population. Here was contemporary race science in action, propounding the lessons of the past to chart the course of the present and future. I confess to a fascination with dismantling Beddoe's logic and method, teasing out the normative judgments and prejudices from his 'science' and laying bare the mechanics of racial Anglo-Saxonism, particularly its hatred of the Irish and its love for the active principle of race war (which was not just a favourite of Beddoe's but to be found in the work of mainstream scientists such as Boyd Dawkins). In *The Races of Britain* Beddoe does many memorable things – deriving the Irish from the Cro-Magnons and creating his startling 'Index of Nigrescence' are just two that are worth a little comment to reveal something of his approach.

Referring to the descendants of the 'palaeolithic race' still resident in the British Isles Beddoe observed:

*There is an Irish type... which I am disposed to derive from the race of Cro-Magnon, and that none the less because, like so many other Irish types, it is evidently common in Spain, and furnishes, as Maclean remarks, the ideal portrait of Sancho Panza. It is said to be pretty common in the Hebrides, but rare in the Highlands. In the West of Ireland I have frequently seen it; but it is curious, psychologically, that the most exquisite examples of it would never submit to measurement. Though the head is large, the intelligence is low, and there is a great deal of cunning and suspicion* (Beddoe 1885: 10).

Small wonder! But if this element of method is questionable, consider how he arrived at his index of nigrescence, which can be expressed as D+2N-R-F. Beddoe wanted a scientific basis for comparing the colours of two peoples or localities so that he could link past, present and future.

*The gross index is gotten by subtracting the number of red and fair-headed persons from that of the dark haired, together with twice the black haired. I double the black, in order to give its proper value to the greater tendency to melanosity shown thereby; while brown (chestnut) hair is regarded as neutral ...* (Beddoe 1885: 5).

Beddoe took his observations from walking in the street not by carting willing or unwilling subjects off to his anthropometrical lair. Fieldwork (and his involved a lot of walking) posed some interesting problems.

*When engaged in this work I set down in his proper place on my card of observation every person I meet, or who passes me within a short distance, say from one to three yards. As a rule, I take no note of persons who apparently belong to the upper classes, as these are more migratory and often mixed in blood... Considerable difficulties are created by the freaks of fashion. I once visited Freisland, in order to study the physical type of that region. Conceive my disappointment when I found myself surrounded by comely damsels and buxom matrons, none of whom suffered a single yellow hair to stray beyond her lace cap or silver-gilt head-plate* (Beddoe 1885: 5).

Beddoe was not so deluded as to think that his index was unimpeachable race science. Far better was to measure heads and to be entirely systematic. Here archaeology was particularly useful, and Greenwell among others got a big vote of thanks, but better still was for the state to be directly involved in data gathering, because the information was considered to be vital to the interests of the state. Here the development of modern armies in the USA and in Europe was to provide a first class source of data and the opportunity to tweak the various indeces still further. We should not make the mistake of thinking that this was anything other than mainstream science, and Beddoe was absolutely convinced that further work would bear him out. His conclusion is clear enough:

*But a truce with speculation! It has been the writer's aim rather to lay a sure foundation... If these remaining questions are worthy and capable of solution, this can be solved only by much patient labour, and by the cooperation of anthropologists with antiquarians and philologists; so that so much of the blurred and defaced prehistoric inscription as is left in shadow by one light may be brought into prominence and illumination by another* (Beddoe 1885: 271).

In the second of Beddoe's works, *The Anthropological History of Europe,* which was the Rhind Lecture for 1891, and updated in 1912, he revisited his earlier work and extended the coverage to Europe in six lectures. The first: 'The Aryan Question and that of variation of type'; the second: 'Variation – Primeval man – succession of races'; which was then followed by another three lectures giving a synoptic coverage of Europe leaving the last lecture for those closest to home: 'Scotland'. In all of these Beddoe rehearsed the usual data – crania, indeces of 'nigrescence', language and folklore, common understandings of racial temperament and the like – to arrive at prognostications about the future. For Beddoe (as with others of his time and disposition) race and racial conflict was not just a formative principle in human history – it was the formative principle of the future as well. As with much of Beddoe's reasoning, the tendency to elide from straightforward prejudice to normative judgment is quick and easy. Consider these insights into the war between the dolichos and brachykephals (as Beddoe liked to call them). First, the Jews:

*But, of the increase of the Jews, at least there can be no doubt whatever. There are no data to show us whether of the two curiously discriminated Jewish types is gaining on the other; but I strongly suspect that it is the brachykephalic. However that may be, the Jews grow not only in number, living longer and dying less readily than the Gentiles among whom they dwell, but they are gradually attracting to themselves the whole moveable wealth of the earth; and wealth is power, and the world must move or halt as wealth bids it. It would be strange if, in spite of the community of religion and traditions and usages, there were not some moral or intellectual difference connected with the physical one between these two sections of the Hebrews. And I believe there is. The Shepardim, who have usually the rather small oval true semitic type of head, are said to be somewhat looked up to by the Ashekenazim, who are mostly of the broad-headed type. And whatever may be the case in the present time, in past times it has been individuals from the Shepardim who have distinguished themselves from the common heard of their fellow-believers, and that in ways more noble than money-making* (Beddoe 1891: 183-184).

Next from somewhere closer to home, Cambridge:

*Dr Venn has shown, that at Cambridge the first class men have proportionally longer as well as more capacious heads than the rest of the students. In our own islands where the breadth of head varies locally but little, and its general form more decidedly, while the complexion varies very considerably, it is safe to say that men of distinction are in large proportion natives of the more blond areas* (Beddoe 1891: 185).

Last, a more general, perhaps more direct statement:

*On the other hand, we are told that in common schools in France, the long-headed children surpass the broad-headed ones; that the world owes far more to the Englishman, the Scotchman and the Norman, than to the Kelt, the Rhaetian, the Rouman or the Slav; and that it would simply stagnate and putrefy were the northern long-headed race to be nipped and checked in its development, for the source of originality, of genius, of inventiveness, of the spirit of travel and adventure, would be cut off. 'Better fifty years of Europe' they say in effect, 'than a cycle of Cathay'* (Beddoe 1891: 187-188).

Although Beddoe would conclude the lectures with an attempt at racial inclusiveness (stating that both long heads and broad heads have much to offer humanity and that diversity is a good thing) it sits oddly with the whole tenor of what he had been saying, and with the kind of racial Anglo-Saxonism that underpinned the widespread acceptance of the very close evolutionary relationship between the Irish and gorillas. The simple point to be made here is that this was preminently popular science (although its scientific credentials even then were highly dubious), and that it was to provide a clear and direct framework within which archaeological and antiquarian studies were to gain great meaning and value well into the next century.

## Concluding remarks

Part of my goal in this all-too-brief discussion of just one aspect of the history of English prehistoric archaeology has been to support the case that the history of archaeology matters. Many histories of English archaeology have tended to gloss over aspects of past context that are either repugnant or seem to have been such obvious wrong-turnings on the path to truth. Detailed research into broader social and cultural contexts has the capacity to reveal a complex and frequently counter-intuitive history. Given the fact that English prehistoric archaeologists have long had considerable impact on the practice of prehistoric archaeology outside of Britain (particularly in the Anglo-Saxon world), a deeper understanding of its social and cultural history is as important for all archaeologists, not just those from Britain.

But having said this, I believe that while histories of archaeology should be sensitive to histories of other disciplines such as anthropology and history, historians of those disciplines should also not ignore what is happening in archaeology. Many prehistoric archaeologists in the English-speaking world still adhere to the tenets of anthropological archaeology and the proposition that archaeology is a subset of anthropology, particularly in terms of the theories it deploys. Yet in recent times the naturalness of this relationship has been questioned as practitioners begin to comprehend that the archaeological record poses significant problems and issues that have never been considered part of anthropology or historiography. Thus archaeologists might yet face the prospect that other archaeologies are possible and possibly desirable, and new histories that might conceivably reassess the history of relations with anthropology and history will need to be written.

**References**

BEDDOE, T. 1885. *The Races of Britain: A Contribution to the Anthropology of Western Europe*. Bristol and London: 1885

—1891. *The Anthropological History of Europe*. Oxford: Clarendon.

BURROW, J. 1966. *Evolution and Society: A Study in Victorian Social Theory*. Cambridge: Cambridge University Press.

GREENWELL, W. 1877. *British Barrows, a record of the examination of sepulchral mounds in various parts of England*. Oxford: Clarendon. Together with description of figures of skulls, general remarks on prehistoric crania, and an appendix by George Rolleston.

KAESER, M-A. 2004. *L'univers du Préhistorien. Science, Foi, et Politique dans l'œuvre et la vie D'Edouard Desor (1811-1882)*. Paris: L'Harmattan.

MORSE, Michael A. 2005. *How the Celts Came to Britain*. Tempus: Stroud.

MURRAY, T. 1987. Remembrances of Things Present: Appeals to Authority in the History and Philosophy of Archaeology. Unpublished PhD dissertation, Department of Anthropology, University of Sydney.

STOCKING, G. W. Jr. 1968. *Race, Culture and Evolution. Essays in the History of Anthropology*. New York: The Free Press.

—1984. Introduction. In G. W. Stocking Jr. (ed.) *Functionalism Historicized: Essays on British Social Anthropology*. Madison: University of Wisconsin Press.

—1987. *Victorian Anthropology*. London: Collier Macmillan.

SWEET, R. 2004. *Antiquaries: The Discovery of the Past in Eighteenth-Century Britain*. London: Hambledon & London.

## Chapter 12

# Rethinking antiquarianism

This paper provides the opportunity to discuss the rationale for a new collaborative research project directed at creating a global history of antiquarianism. Conventional histories of archaeology, particularly those by Daniel (e.g. 1976) and to a certain extent by Trigger (1987, 2006), stress that antiquarians were in essence amateurs and dilettantes, perfect figures of their age, exemplified by the brilliantly scatty John Aubrey, or by Walter Scott's grotesque pastiche Jonathan Oldbuck. However, following ground-breaking work by Arnoldo Momigliano (see e.g. 1966, 1990), and later by Alain Schnapp (e.g. 1996) for some time it had become clear that this was an inaccurate rendering – one designed to stress the scientific credentials of the disciplines that grew out and away from antiquarianism: the modern cultural sciences of history, sociology, anthropology, art history, archaeology, and history of religion. For Schnapp, especially in his *The Discovery of the Past*, the division between amateur and professional (a distinction also explored with profit by Phillipa Levine (1986)) was not the cause of the triumph of archaeology (or any one of the other disciplines) over antiquarianism, and it is ill informed to interpret antiquarianism as a wrong-turning on the pathway to archaeological enlightenment. In this view antiquarianism was, and perhaps still is, a full-fledged and (more important) continuing body of thought and practice.

This notion of continuity, including the probability that it has the potential to morph into a kind of neo-antiquarianism, is worthy of much further discussion, but at this point I just want to indicate that disciplinary history (with the exception of Schnapp (1993) and Rosemary Sweet (2004)) generally, has not been kind to antiquarians or antiquarianism. Part of my object in this paper is to argue that by exploring the social and cultural worlds of antiquarianism (both past and present) we might be able to redress that imbalance.

I will exemplify these explorations through a very brief discussion of the construction of remote British history in the sixteenth and seventeenth centuries, where the foundations of what I have called the interactionist methodology of antiquarianism were laid.

My approach here is based on the idea that, up until the middle of the nineteenth century, the antiquarian was a key link between the past and the present. Following Schnapp I assume that, as opposed to the historian whose task was to comment on texts, the antiquary was responsible for the management of material remains of the past – be they objects or monuments.

## Constructing remote British history

In this paper I will focus discussion on William Camden's demolition of Geoffrey of Monmouth's *History of the Kings of Britain*, and his replacement of it by an account broadly indicative of sixteenth and seventeenth century English antiquarian practice. I do this to illustrate the means by which material things could acquire significance as historical documents within a broader socio-political and historiographic context. The focus on Geoffrey also illustrates how the inductive philosophy of science of the period could readily articulate with socio-political context to dispatch his account as being essentially mythopoeic. There is a neat contrast here between the fate of Geoffrey's *History*, and that of Hesiod's *Works and Days*, or Lucretius' *On the Nature of the Universe*, two mythopoeic discourses that fared rather better when the Three Age System was formulated by Thomsen in the early nineteenth century.

I will outline the rise of, and the causes of changes to, a new antiquarian methodology and then go on to discuss some of the links between it and the wider social context of antiquarian knowledge during the sixteenth and seventeenth centuries. This new methodology, which I have called 'interactionist', allowed antiquaries to plausibly relate new sources of information (the 'ethnographic other', field monuments, coins and inscriptions) with old sources of evidence and interpretation, such as the Bible and the Classical ethnographies such as the *Britannia* and *Germania* of Tacitus. This interactionist methodology became the hallmark of English antiquarian practice during the sixteenth and seventeenth centuries. In discussing the causes of changes to this new methodology I shall emphasize three important shifts in the context of antiquarian practice.

First, the increasing historical importance of the material phenomena remains of the prehistoric British past, and of material culture associated with the 'ethnographic other'.

Second, connected with the first, the increasingly complex picture of the pre-Roman British past where the historical relationships of items of material culture could not be plausibly established through the interactionist methodology alone.

Third, the shift from empiricist to rationalist (romantic) frameworks of interpretation and justification during the eighteenth century – typified by the later work of Stukeley.

Notwithstanding what have come to be considered as the 'excesses' of practitioners such as Stukeley, and the confusion of others such as Colt-Hoare, that led many observers to doubt whether the 'true' history of the remote British past could ever be established, the rude stone monuments, barrows, and other items of material culture remaining from pre-Claudian times, were still recognized as the products of historical human action, although precisely whose action remained a matter for conjecture and debate.

I think that the forces which led to the recognition of the historical and 'ethnological' importance of material things also conditioned the methodological status of material things as supplements to other more culturally familiar data sets, perspectives, methodologies and problems. The interactionist methodology of English antiquarianism had to allow practitioners to do two things. First, to marshal all available ethnographic, material cultural, and textual evidence to counteract what were considered to be irrational or mythological histories, and second, to grade (implicitly or explicitly) the historical reliability of all the sources of evidence as testaments to the human past.

Significantly the history which antiquarians either sought to write, or to contribute to, was the history of Britain in its mental, moral and political particulars. Ethnographic generalization was, therefore, practically mediated by textual and material cultural analysis. New socio-political contexts and new relationships to the past demanded new histories. Monmouth's *History*, written around 1136, had served old contexts and was one of the first major victims of the new methodology. The standard discussions of the *History of the Kings of Britain* debated many issues concerning the sources of the work and its reception by scholars even in Geoffrey's own time. Its influence, however, is unquestioned. Sir Thomas Kendrick's superb study (1950) is a chronicle of that influence, charting the objections to the work from antiquarians such as Polydore Vergil, Leland, William Camden and John Speed. It is the antiquarian objections to the work that most concern me here, because the sixteenth and seventeenth century antiquaries marshalled the product of a different historical methodology against it. Principal among these antiquaries was William Camden, who became the archetypical English antiquary as much because of his education and political connections, as well as because of the enormous influence of his great work *Britannia* (1586).

A concern with the past thus had direct political, social and economic consequences for many who were in the Tudor (and later Stuart and Georgian) power structures, or who sought entry to them. The best example of the usefulness of the past, apart from Parliament's obsession with precedent and the functioning of common law, was provided by Henry VIII when he sought justification for the split with Rome and the foundation of a

Church of England. The appointment of John Leland as the first King's Antiquary was significant testimony to seriousness of Henry's appeal to the traditions of British history.

The task of reconciling the ancient descriptions of Europe with the political geography of the sixteenth century implied that collection and analysis would also include the need to provide the fullest possible description of the entire basis of ancient social and cultural life. Such detailed descriptions subsequently provided clear evidence of differences and similarities in customs and laws – both within Britain, and between Britain and Europe as a whole, that could broaden the understanding of history itself. The development of county histories such as Lambarde's *Perambulation of Kent* (1576) and John Stow's *Survey of London* (1598) are cases in point. Significantly, the actual visitation of places mentioned in the histories was not regarded as being essential, given that the authority of previous authors was accepted.

But William Camden adopted a different course, and in doing so raised the possibility that the analysis of material remains could play a greater role in sifting 'objective' histories from mythopoeic historical 'recreations'. So what caused the change in methodology to include an accent on actual observation and an increased emphasis on the incorporation of material objects as authorities potentially on a par with the written documents? And also what changed antiquarian studies from being set apart from the concerns of the age to a source of national interest?

Clearly the spirit of Baconian empiricism had much to do with the scepticism of other than direct observation or eyewitness accounts. Yet this scepticism most certainly was not applied to the Bible, or to the more general and derivative Classical ethnographies. In fact these, and the new ethnographies from the Americas were to become the standards, the givens, the bedrock assumptions of English antiquarianism of the sixteenth, seventeenth and eighteenth centuries. Clearly the prescription that evidence of the senses was more powerful than the authority of ancient authors had a role to play in the new emphasis on visiting the sites and cataloguing coins and inscriptions. But equally clearly, there were practical difficulties encountered by an empiricist epistemology when it came to 'filling the gaps' in the material cultural record. It transpired that material culture, after it had been subjected to proper scrutiny and classification, would be used along with the ethnographic data to flesh out the historical record.

What was rational, what was plausible, would be determined by the degree of fit between the Classical and Biblical authorities on the one hand and the material culture and ethnographies on the other. Yet this interactionist methodology was closely constrained by 'cultural' and political determinants of what was plausible to believe about the past. In the event, the weight of plausibility was to rest with literary sources.

The discussion of British origins was central to the intellectual and political background of *Britannia*. Geoffrey's story of Brutus and family had held sway, despite continuous criticism, since the twelfth century. The first major attack on it, during the sixteenth century, most closely associated with Polydore Vergil, Robert Fabyan and John Rastell, was based on an argument that Geoffrey's *History* completely lacked verification from any ancient source. Kendrick has shown that Tudor nationalists did not react favourably to the attack, or to Polydore's attempts to justify it. In the debate that followed, the traditional basis for understanding the earliest periods of British history was questioned and the construction of British history itself became problematic. The issue became one of methodology and epistemology: how were accounts of the remote past to be justified? Any solution would have political ramifications.

Ortelius may have encouraged Camden to 'acquaint the world with Britain', but Camden's real goal was to 'restore Britain to its antiquities and its antiquities to Britain', but the glory of Britain would be best served by the establishment of a clear and rationally defensible history that linked it to Rome. It would also be effectively served by a justification of the Anglo-Saxon dominance of British (read English) power structures. Camden's attack on Geoffrey's British history was as much an attack on its racial elements as it was on its fabulous nature. There was a great deal at stake.

Camden dismissed the Brutus story as a myth, one of those myths that have nationalist justification by disguising 'the truth with a mixture of fable and bring in the gods themselves to act a part... thereby to render the beginnings either of a city or of a nation, more noble and majestical'. However, Camden did not mention another vital aspect of such myths, the explanation of a past that was beyond direct observation or written documents, although he does hint at the importance of such explanations given the investment of national or ethnic pride in their particular constitution.

By Camden's time Classical, particularly Roman, accounts had become the foundation of an understanding of the pre-Roman British past. However, Camden added an extra dimension through his discussion of monuments and artefacts (particularly coins), as well as the customs and languages of France and Britain. Clearly, if any new account was to convince the lawyers and the English educated public of the sixteenth and seventeenth centuries, it had to be broadly based and admit rational assessment by the lights of Baconian empiricism.

The supply of written documents (including the depth of their textual exegesis), of Roman and post-Roman inscriptions, and of descriptions of field monuments had greatly increased since the Middle Ages, providing a broad base from which to begin writing the history of a past that had left no contemporary written documents. The analysis of material remains thus became a way of establishing the reliability of claims made on the basis of written documents that sometimes gave divergent testimony. An important issue here is that Geoffrey's history assumed a kind of authority itself, based in part on the fact that it was an agreeable reconstruction to many people, but also because it was *written*. An attack on Geoffrey's work implied an equally critical attitude to the Bible and the Classical authorities. In practice, these core areas of antiquarian 'culture' were not examined with anything approaching the vigour that was reserved for Geoffrey and other 'fabulists'.

What Geoffrey had constructed out of chronicles, king lists, folk tales, and his own imagination, Camden made from the Biblical and Classical sources and the surviving monuments and artefacts. A final issue remains here, and concerns whether the goals of Geoffrey's history matched those of Camden's. Both had national and political goals, both sought to glorify the nation through its past, and both had racial interests. Geoffrey sought to attain his goals by way of myth couched in terms of a Biblical and folkloric background to give it a measure of plausibility. Camden stressed the fact that he had chosen another path. His stated authorities were his senses and the exercise of logic, but in practice these were constrained by the *a priori* of the Bible and the Classical authorities. Thus, for Camden it was not just a matter that these authorities impregnated his supposedly hypothesis-free observation statements, far more than this. Camden's *Britannia* above all represents an extension of the Roman histories by means of enrolling the monuments, coins and inscriptions as supplements to Classical documentary sources.

By virtue of the success of *Britannia* and through his contacts with other antiquaries and historians such as Sir Robert Bruce Cotton and John Speed, Camden influenced much of the style of sixteenth and seventeenth century English antiquarian debate. Indeed, successive editions of *Britannia* (especially the 1695 and 1722 editions), acted as a kind of barometer of antiquarian methodology, or at least a point of departure for other antiquaries, through to the end of the eighteenth century. In sum, Camden's methodology, based as it was on the squaring of Classical and Biblical authorities and the material cultural evidence, became the cornerstone of the interactionist methodology to be developed and used by generations of English antiquaries who were to follow him.

Although Camden focused the bulk of his attention on coins, seals and other items of material culture bearing inscriptions, the methodology of comparison, rational reconstruction, and close observation of the empirical phenomena (be they field monuments or Church brasses) was matched by those antiquaries who concentrated on thunderstones, or *ceraunia*, i.e. what we now know to be prehistoric stone implements. Lhwyd and Plot, to name only two antiquaries more inclined to natural history, without qualm linked empirical observation of these fossils and their modern representatives with close textual and folkloric studies, in a way which anticipated important elements of the new interactionist methodology that was to become associated with the Three Age System.

Significantly, Camden and other antiquaries, having located a source for the British, and therefore a description of them drawn from the Classical and Biblical sources, paid scant attention to the need to ascertain whether those earliest Britons had changed before the time of the Romans. For them, it was enough to connect Japhet and Caesar without employing what they considered to be the kind of myth that caused the downfall of Geoffrey's *History*. Here the perceptions of 'everyday savage life' drawn primarily from the Amerindian ethnographies added colour and texture to an account which rated literary sources as far more authoritative than either ethnography or material culture.

However, by the mid-to-late seventeenth century such an implicit account was not enough. The cause of this appears to be the slow recognition (drawn largely from studies by topographers, antiquaries and others) that there was considerable variability in pre-Roman 'British' material culture (and in the societies and cultures of the 'ethnographic other') – a variability about which the Classical authors had been silent. Here the interactionist methodology began to change in the terms of the relative utility of its authorities, its object now was no more aligned towards the classification of material culture, and the establishment of meaning through comparison with the material culture of the 'ethnographic other', before the application of Classical and Biblical texts. An excellent and under-appreciated example of this attempt to reveal a reality of the past, not confined by the tastes and interests of the present, is supplied by the remarkable character of John Aubrey. Although Lhwyd and Dugdale both emphasized the importance of empiricism to antiquarian studies, Aubrey's own statement in the only recently published *Monumenta Britannica* (1981) enhances the liberating effect of the revised interactionist methodology for the seventeenth and early eighteenth antiquaries:

*I do here endeavour (for want of written record) to work out and restore after a kind of algebraical method, by comparing them that I have seen with one another and reducing them to a kind of equation: to (being but an ill orator myself) make the stones give evidence for themselves.*

This was easier said than done. For although Aubrey could query the utility of the Classical accounts, and perhaps even be wary of the application of ethnographic generalizations, nevertheless without them his 'algebraical method' could rarely achieve more than description and classification. The historical meanings of the various classes of field monuments and portable artefacts still had to be established. However, change in the interactionist methodology did not stop there. Additional tensions arose which were to occasion further doubts about the ability of antiquarian studies to banish the *a priori*.

Both Hunter (e.g. 1975) and Piggott (e.g. 1976) have effectively demonstrated that antiquarian methodology, so much a part of Baconian empiricism was, in the course of the eighteenth century, to become increasingly difficult to adhere to, as a result of the upswing in Romantic historicism and rationalism that had struck the sciences generally. Nonetheless critical elements of the interactionist methodology remained in the form of the authorities appealed to by Stukeley for what are now taken to be his wilder excesses of interpretation. In an important sense there were trends to a return of the primacy of the written text over the 'ethnographic other' and the empirical character of the material phenomena.

This is not to say that Stukeley was a Camden with a rather credulous attitude to Classical ethnography, oak groves and standing stones. Instead he, like Colt-Hoare, was responding to a different set of socio-political forces. He was also responding to an increasing need to establish the historical meaning of the, by then, confused state of inquiries into pre-Roman British antiquities. In such circumstances the Classical and Biblical authorities that had formed the essentially literary cornerstone of the interactionist methodology could only be used at the price of reduced empirical assessment. Although there were many who found Stukeley's accounts of 'barbarous Druidic rituals' among the henge monuments to be plausible, the fact remained that there were equally many who were far from convinced as they contemplated the wide variability which now seemed to characterize pre-Roman British antiquities. Whereas Camden and others could readily establish the historical value of the coins, seals, and inscriptions they used (precisely because of the presence of writing on them), the task of later antiquaries such as Aubrey and Stukeley was made the more difficult when writing no longer came to the rescue.

Consequently, the traditional reading (based on the greater authority of literary sources ably supplemented by lashings of the 'ethnographic other' and material culture) of the interactionist methodology began to break down. How could such authorities assist in the understanding of events to which they may well have not been witness? In the absence of a reliable ordering of pre-Roman antiquities, the interactionist method as practiced by Stukeley could only produce a frozen history. Meaning and, more importantly the basis of conviction, could no longer be considered to flow unproblematically from reason and the senses. The nature of British prehistory once again became shrouded in conjecture, and the two goals of the interactionist methodology – an attack on mythopoeic histories, and the grading of the reliability of sources of historical evidence – could not be convincingly attained.

What was urgently required was a means of sorting out the nightmare of pre-Roman British antiquities, so that the interactionist methodology could function once again. In the event the 'northern antiquaries' were to come to the rescue, but in so doing the new emphasis on material culture, established by the Three Age System, was to effectively realign the authorities that had been the backbone of interactionism. No longer were Caesar, Strabo (or for that matter the Bible) to hold pride of place over the empirical character of the archaeological record, and the 'ethnographic other', as the framework in terms of which the meaning of the material phenomena of the prehistoric British past was to be made manifest. This at least was the methodological rhetoric used by its promoters. What really happened is, of course, another story.

**New perspectives: a global approach**

I now outline the scope and rationale of a new research project in the history of antiquarianism that is being conducted by Alain Schnapp, Lothar von Falkenhausen, Irene Aghion and myself. The title of the project –*Traces, Collections, Ruins: Towards a Comparative History of Antiquarianism –* reflects the broad interests of the project team. Our project links historians, with art historians, philologists, archaeologists and anthropologists, and will undertake a comparative study of the practice, the epistemology and the history of antiquarians and antiquarianism on a global scale.

Our first aim is to define what is understood as antiquarian practice so that we might gain a clearer picture of what antiquarianism has been, is, and might yet become. There are numerous points of difference, as well as similarities between antiquarian traditions, and part of our goal is to establish whether there is an irreducible 'conceptual core' to antiquarianism, or whether it has a complex evolutionary history within and between different traditions.

One of my roles is to explore the complex relationships between antiquarianism and the writing of prehistory. The search for an understanding of pre-literate human societies is one of the most challenging of all investigations. Over the last five hundred years, the focus has sometimes been on the early history of Europe (for example, the history of Britain prior to the Claudian invasion), while at other times the primary concern has shifted towards an exploration of the nature of 'savage' societies found by Europeans as the boundaries of Europe expanded to encompass the world. Of course, much of the history of European antiquarianism right up to the end of the nineteenth century is a tale of how pre-literate societies encountered by Europeans came to play a vital role in humanizing the world of preliterate Europe. This long-standing form of reasoning, which is described as analogical inference or ethnographic analogy, lies at the core of much contemporary archaeological theory.

Thus the first goal is to develop a detailed history of this field, so as to elucidate an overall comparative history of antiquarian practice. This might be best described as the antiquarianism of preliterate societies, where such societies are mined for clues about the early histories of literate societies. The resulting histories or analyses have almost exclusively been the product of Europeans, or of the descendants of European settlers and colonists around the globe. However there is more to the issue than this. It has long been understood that histories resulting from the practice of the antiquarianism of preliterate societies have tended to make the past of such societies effectively ahistorical. Time for such societies is, to all intents and purposes, frozen, and the focus of analysis considers essence and stasis (something real, analyzable and stable as a form of analogy) instead of properly historical matters such as change, transformation and dynamism. Much has been written about the consequences of a lack of history and a great deal of work has been done to chart alternative paths.

The second goal is potentially more controversial and certainly much more difficult to reach. This is to extend this work (and its rationale) to a consideration of antiquarianism in pre-literate societies. By this I mean that by changing the focus of history-making to a concern with how contemporary indigenous societies (themselves now literate societies but directly descended from pre-literate societies observed at the time of contact) make history, create memorials, create heritage (both tangible and intangible) and create and mobilize memories, so we can gain a stronger sense of these societies as historical entities, in the present as well as the past.

Already this approach has had significant impact in fostering a clearer understanding of heritage in non-western settings, as well as in postcolonial societies. Significantly, it links closely to the work of material culture analysts such as Susanne Kuchler (2002) where anthropologists engage with issues of temporality and memory and their place in social ritual, and pose the important question: 'is this antiquarianism in a different vein?' The question has also been posed with respect to song, language and story as the living 'immaterial' heritage of indigenous peoples (although this clearly also applies to literate as well as pre-literate societies). Finally, an inquiry into antiquarianism in pre-literate societies also supports a stream of archaeological inquiry, begun by Richard Bradley (see e.g. 2002), into the place of the past (monuments, memories, landscapes, rock art) in prehistoric societies. I think that it is fair to say that this is all pretty rudimentary stuff at present, but there are interesting points of tension and intersection that indicate that it might be worth pursuing. It is also worth asking whether one can really speak of antiquarianism in preliterate societies without making the definition so elastic as to be uselessly ambiguous.

But the contemporary contexts of antiquarianism give us other things to consider. Chief among these is the importance of the antiquarian in local communities. Historians of archaeology (myself among them) have tended to concentrate analysis on demonstrating the complicity of our discipline in the foundation of nineteenth century nation states and empires. But what of the broader social roles of antiquarians? Of course authors such as Walter Scott delighted in making some pretty heavy-handed jokes at their expense, and the members of the British House of Commons were fond of raising the spectre of the woolly-headed antiquarian during debates linked to the passage of the first *Ancient Monuments Protection Act* (see e.g. Murray 1990). But there is no doubt about at least two things since the sixteenth century. First, antiquaries were the repositories of knowledge about local and regional histories. Second, this knowledge spanned landscapes, material culture and written documents. For these reasons alone antiquaries provided information and experiences that helped people shape identities and to understand the places they were living in.

In our new project we will search out this finer scale and explore, the role of antiquarians and archaeologists in the creation of narratives about local landscapes, monuments, material culture, histories and memories. Although we accept that these narratives need not necessarily be different to or isolated from more general national or continental narratives, there is no warrant to assume that either outcome is inevitable.

## Some interim observations

This very small example of new perspectives on antiquarianism is hardly substantial enough to allow me to draw firm conclusions about the role of antiquarianism in contemporary society. Nonetheless it does provide another kind of example of a process of which we are very aware: the changing contexts of practice in archaeology. Here the link between places, objects, identities and histories that has become such a social and cultural force under the general rubric of heritage has the potential to gain great power.

New histories of antiquarianism and archaeology are being written in an attempt to make sense of these matters, and it is fascinating to contemplate the implications of developments such as a renewed interest in what were once deemed the 'unscientific' and 'irrelevant' perspectives of antiquarianism. Archaeology had its roots in antiquarianism, history, philology, ethnology, geology, and 'natural history' generally.* From this grew the trunk that eventually branched out into various sub-disciplines (e.g. Biblical, Roman, Medieval, Scientific and 'New' Archaeology). The great meta-narratives of the history of archaeology have followed this approach, with 'archaeological thought' or 'archaeological ideas' having a common inheritance or ancestry in nineteenth century positivist European science. From this main 'root-stock', it eventually branched into sub-divisions and out into the world at large, fostering off-spring archaeologies differentiated by geography, tradition, sub-field or time period.

One of the roles of the history of archaeology is to challenge this meta-narrative and to demonstrate that there has been a great deal more variability of thought and practice in the field than has been acknowledged. Antiquarianism did not conveniently die-out with the advent of archaeology as a discipline, and its history and development has always involved multiple strands – in essence the existence of other possibilities and practices. Histories of archaeology and of antiquarianism should stimulate the explorations of these other possible archaeologies, past, present and future, and they should help us acknowledge the creation of world archaeologies, and the multiplication of interests and objectives among both producers and consumers of archaeological knowledge, will drive the creation of still further variability. However, part of any acknowledgement of alternatives and differences is the recognition of similarities that derive from a common inheritance. A significant issue in contemporary archaeological practice is the question of whether there is an irreducible disciplinary core, if archaeology as a discipline exists, and whether archaeologists working in different fields, or from different perspectives, have enough in common to engage in meaningful disciplinary conversation. I strongly believe that the history of archaeology has a vital role to play in ensuring that such conversations occur, and that they do so in an informed manner.

**Acknowledgments:**

This paper derives from a presentation at the symposium 'Locality and Place in the History of Archaeology', held at the Institute of Archaeology, University College London, March 2007. I thank my co-organizer Dr Ulrike

---

* This discussion is drawn from the introduction, written by Chis Evans and I, in our *Reader in the History of Archaeology*, published in 2008 by OUP.

Sommer and Professor Stephen Shennan, Director of the Institute, for his support of this symposium, and for my stay at the institute during the first three months of 2007. Parts of the paper also derive from the 2007 Mulvaney Lecture 'Reconsidering Antiquarianism in the History of Australian Archaeology', given at the Australian National University in May 2007. I thank Professor Matthew Spriggs for his invitation to deliver the lecture.

**References**

AUBREY, J. 1981. *Monumenta Britannica or a Miscellany of British Antiquities*. J. Fowles (ed). Sherborne, Dorset: Dorset publishing Co.

BRADLEY, R. 2002. *The Past in Prehistoric Societies*. London: Routledge.

DANIEL, G. E. 1976. *A Hundred and Fifty Years of Archaeology*. London: Duckworth.

HUNTER, M. 1975. *John Aubrey and the Realm of Learning*. New York: Science History Publications.

KENDRICK, T. 1950. *British Antiquity*. London: Methuen.

KUCHLER, S. 2002. *Malanggan: Art, Memory and Sacrifice*. Oxford: Berg.

LEVINE, P. 1986. *The Amateur and the Professional: Antiquarians, Historians and Archaeologists in Victorian England, 1836-1886*. Cambridge: Cambridge University Press.

MOMIGLIANO, A. 1966. *Studies in Historiography*. London: Weidenfeld and Nicholson.

—1990. *The Classical Foundations of Modern Historiography*. Berkeley, CA: University of California Press.

MURRAY, T. 1990. The History, Philosophy and Sociology of Archaeology: the Case of the *Ancient Monuments Protection Act* (1882). In V. Pinsky and A. Wylie (eds) *Critical Directions in Contemporary Archaeology*, pp. 55-67. Cambridge: Cambridge University Press.

MURRAY, T. and C. EVANS. 2008a. *Histories of Archaeology*. Oxford: Oxford University Press.

PIGGOTT, S. 1976. *Ruins in a Landscape*. Edinburgh: Edinburgh University Press.

SCHNAPP, A. 1997. *The Discovery of the Past*. London: British Museum Press.

SWEET, R. 2004. *Antiquaries: the Discovery of the Past in Eighteenth Century Britain*. London: Hambledon and London.

# Chapter 13

# Prehistoric archaeology in the 'Parliament of Science' 1845–1884

In this chapter, which is part of a much larger work on the history of prehistoric archaeology in England, I will very briefly exemplify the complex interplay between ethnology and the emergent disciplines of anthropology and prehistoric archaeology, through the medium of The British Association for the Advancement of Science (BAAS). Although my primary purpose is to understand the history of prehistoric archaeology in England, we will see that it is impossible to abstract debates in England from those happening elsewhere in Britain, particularly in Scotland. Indeed, while the two rival societies where much of these debates unfolded – the Anthropological Society and the Ethnological Society – were London-based, the fact that they both chose the British Association as one of their prime battlegrounds demonstrates that prehistoric archaeology in England was not only of national significance, but also considerably open to wider influences.

In any case, there are three reasons why the British Association provides the ideal forum through which to pursue this analysis. To begin with, the conflicts between ethnology and anthropology were played out on the national stage within the British Association, as well as in direct conflict primarily occurring in London (see Burrow 1966; Hodgen 1973; Stocking 1968, 1987; Weber 1974). As well, the British Association became a regular contributor to the costs of archaeological excavations (notably at Kent's Cavern), it acted as a clearing-house for archaeological information and promoted the popularity of interdisciplinary excavation teams, and aided the development of anthropological methodology through its series of questionnaires – *Notes and Queries* (see Fowler 1975; Stocking 1983; Urry 1972). Lastly, as the 'Parliament of British Science', the British Association provides a focal point for a continued discussion of the ramifications of the differences between methodological rhetoric and performance in prehistoric archaeology. Historians of science (see e.g. MacLeod 1981a, 1981b; Morrell and Thackray 1981; Orange 1972, 1981; Yeo 1979, 1981) have indicated that inductivism formed the central plank of the scientific method accepted by its proponents, and that the scientific method was absolutely crucial to the aims and objectives of the Association (see also McGee 1897; von Gizycki 1979).

I will take the response of the British Association to the debates raging between anthropology and ethnology, and about the interpretation of archaeological data, as critical support for another argument, made by me in connection with the passage of the first *Ancient Monuments Protection Act* in England (Murray 1989), that the discrepancies between methodological rhetoric and practical performance in English prehistoric archaeology were ignored both by the disputants and by the general public. My previous arguments have stressed the fact that the meanings and values of anthropological, ethnological and archaeological interpretation and explanation justified, and were in turn justified by, common-sense understandings abroad in England during the nineteenth century.

The uncertain positions of both anthropology and ethnology on the cognitive map of nineteenth century British science is demonstrated by their slow acceptance into the British Association, and for several decades their virtually constant movement through its committees and sections, as the managers of the Association struggled to deal with unceasing conflict between the adherents of either discipline. There were three crucial reasons for this state of affairs: first, as Morrell and Thackray have observed: 'the career of ethnology shows another science being excluded from the British Association so long as it appeared to be a political, social and religious tinderbox, and then being reluctantly incorporated when it had been stripped of dangerous features' (1981: 283-84). Second, the Association had little experience with generalizing sciences that spanned many pre-existing disciplines. Third, the heated debates between ethnology and anthropology as to which science was the most general necessitated numerous attempts at finding a formula of relationship that would suit the parties.

Briefly, there were four phases of movement for the sciences of man within the committee and sectional structure of the Association during the nineteenth century, and I outline them here.

Phase 1, spanning the period from the foundation of the Association (in 1831) to 1846, when James Cowles Prichard found formal recognition for the science of ethnology as a sub-section of section D – Zoology, Botany, Physiology and Anatomy. Prior to this, papers of relevance to ethnology had appeared in other sections such as geology and in section D itself. Indeed, although there was only one ethnological paper published in the first and second reports of 1831 and 1832 (bound as one volume), by 1838 when Prichard's highly influential 'On the Extinction of the Human Races' had stung the Association into contributing £15 towards the cost of producing an ethnological questionnaire (Fowler 1975; Urry 1972), the number of ethnological papers submitted to the Annual Meetings of the Association began to skyrocket. Consequently the failures of this arrangement had become embarrassing as a number of ludicrous juxtapositions between zoological and ethnological papers occurred, reinforcing the claim that ethnology was best located somewhere else. Prichard (1847: 230) outlined the history of ethnology's lack of independence within the BAAS structure and discussed the pitfalls of its formal association with physiology and anatomy, even though the majority of early papers had been read to the zoology section:

> *It may be remembered that in the series of reports on the progress of science in its different departments, comprised in the first volume of the Transactions of the British Association, there was one memoir on the contributions afforded by physical and philological researches to ethnology and the history of the human species. The admission of that paper by the editors of the Transactions, gave those persons who had made ethnology their favorite pursuit some ground for hope, that this would for the future be among the recognized branches of knowledge, for the cultivation of which provision would be made at the meetings of the Association. It is almost needless to say that this hope was disappointed, and that no arrangements having been adopted for the discussion of ethnological questions, some very elaborate memoirs having been sent to the meetings of the Association, by distinguished scholars, were returned without having obtained a hearing. It was not until after several meetings having taken place, that it was determined to afford an opportunity for the pursuit of ethnological inquiries by making for that purpose a subdivision of one of the sections devoted to natural history or physiology.*

Though he was President of the new sub-section, Prichard was not entirely happy with the arrangement, recognizing that the new science was of a different order to the sciences already admitted to the Association and that the ruling parties of the Association would therefore have trouble classifying it. The struggle to establish the particularly broad nature of such a generalizing science could only be won by indicating that whatever decisions were made as to its location within the sectional structure of the Association, the sum of ethnology was greater than its parts, even though important elements of its database might be scientifically dubious by the standards of the times. Referring to the new arrangement Prichard (1847: 230- 31) remarked:

*There seemed to be an obvious propriety of systematic arrangement in contemplating the natural history of man as forming but a part of the study of living nature in general ... If, therefore, the real scope of ethnology was merely an inquiry into the physical constitution of human tribes in comparison with each other, as it appears to have been supposed, there would be an obvious propriety in making this study a subdivision of physiology or of the science of human nature. But those who have devoted their attention to that pursuit are well-aware that the objects of ethnology are very distinct from the study of organic nature or physiology. Ethnology is, in fact, more nearly allied to history than to natural science.*

Given Prichard's conceptualization of the composition of ethnology, it is hardly surprising that he could defend ethnology as a science on two grounds. First, its clear links with established inductive sciences such as geology and anatomy. Second, the use of the scientific method in ethnography, philology, and archaeology. Despite the power of Prichard's advocacy, the controllers of the British Association – ever careful to avoid public controversy that would lead to a loss of public confidence in the objectivity of science, were equally impressed by the contentious nature of ethnological researches (Yeo 1981). True, the geologists flouted the Bible, but the facts were on their side, however uncomfortable they might be. Further, who knew where ethnology would lead? In time the new generalizing science of anthropology would become the locus of conflict, and the Councillors and committees of the Association would offer much stiffer opposition to a science that seemed to be 'about everything and about nothing'.

Phase 2 spans the period between 1847 and the admission of Ethnology into the newly created Section D (Geography and Ethnology) in 1852. During this time aspects of what was later to become prehistoric archaeology were more frequently found in the geological section than in Section D. The tradition of viewing human antiquity as being primarily a geological problem was to continue through to the end of the century, although after 1865 relevant papers were also presented to anthropology and ethnology.

Phase 3 (1852-1869) is in many respects the crucial period for ethnology and anthropology in the British Association. It was during this time that ethnology obtained its divorce from section D, was incorporated with geography (itself divorced from geology and physical geography) in section E, and was later returned as a department of section D (newly renovated as Biology).

Phase 4 (1870-1884) refers to the development of the constituent disciplines of anthropology, and its final divorce from section D by being established as a separate section (H) of the Association. The formal links between anthropology and biology were never to be restored.

## The peregrinations of the 'Sciences of Man'

The hard-fought debates between ethnology and anthropology that took place within the rival societies of the Anthropological Society of London (ASL) and the Ethnological Society of London (ESL) have been extensively discussed (Burrow 1966; Harris 1968; Stocking 1971, 1987; Urry 1972; Weber 1974). Stocking and others have stressed that since the late eighteenth century discussions in England about the natural history of human beings (especially those focusing on race, language, culture and physical form) have been very closely linked to Continental perspectives. The debates between ethnology and anthropology in London were no exception being very strongly influenced by researchers such as Paul Broca and Carl Vogt. Indeed, one of James Hunt's great innovations was to organize translations of some of the more significant Continental texts (see e.g. Poucher 1864; Vogt 1864; Waitz 1863). However they were not the only external influences, with both sides paying particular attention to the work of American race theorists such as Nott and Gliddon (1854), which had gained special relevance as a result of the American Civil War.

On the surface the difference between the two disciplines – ethnography and anthropology can be readily established. The concerns of ethnology were largely confined to documenting and understanding the causes of cultural, social, linguistic and physical differences between human beings, and to charting the relationships between different human groups. Anthropology, on the other hand, was conceived of as being a broader discipline incorporating the concerns of ethnology, but doing so within a framework that included all aspects of humanity past and present. Yet there was more to the conflict than the simple issue of which discipline effectively incorporated the other. Historians of anthropology have stressed that the acrimonious debates were in fact based as much on contemporary political and social issues as on the litigious personalities of the disputants. On this basis we already have grounds for creating a fairly clear division between the supporters of ethnology (such as Lyell, Lubbock, Huxley), and the supporters of anthropology (Hunt, Beddoe, Broca, Quatrefages, Poucher and Vogt), on the basis of their religious affiliation and their stance on such matters as equality between the sexes, slavery, imperialism and above all, whether they were monogenists or polygenists – that is, whether they believed in a single or a multiple origin for humanity. Inevitably, there were people who managed to belong to both societies and to hold what appear to be conflicting opinions.

In the hail of invective that characterized relationships between the two

London Societies, the disputants regularly accused each other of being unscientific, because they sought motivation from subjective and implicit political or religious agendas. One major area of conflict was the rights and wrongs of the Darwinian hypothesis, another was the admission of anthropology to the British Association. Like it or not, the British Association had to find a way of dealing with anthropology, and as its most prominent members were implacably opposed to the implicit (sometimes explicit) polygenism of the 'anthropologicals', the battle was to be to the death. In the process, the name anthropology survived, but much of its programme as defined by Paul Broca (and his disciple the ASL president James Hunt) did not.

My analysis is based on a close reading of all British Association records, particularly the *Proceedings and Transactions of the Annual Meetings*, and of course the records and publications of the two London societies. Together they comprise a very large storehouse of examples of scientific politics, exhibiting all the nuances of political chicanery and bad behaviour that occurred over 40 years of conflict. Excerpts from a few of the more celebrated confrontations exemplify the nature and tone of the confrontation.

The 1863 meetings of the BAAS mark the opening round of a conflict which was to prove both acrimonious and publicly damaging. It is no coincidence that these were the first meetings attended by James Hunt in his guise as an activist for anthropology (having previously been an active member of the Ethnological Society of London). He and the other 'anthropologicals' demanded a hearing, but the problem for the British Association stemmed, in part, from the breadth of anthropological researches. Papers considered to be of vital importance to anthropologists, especially those dealing with physical anthropology and the evidences of high human antiquity, were being rejected by section E as being more appropriate for zoology or geology. The other significant problem was that one generalizing science of man already held the field, and its supporters were extremely reluctant to relinquish the spoils of their hard-won battle with the central committee of the Association that had occurred some years before.

The opening shot was fired in the *Anthropological Review* (a publication of the ASL), and from the start the language used had that peculiarly intemperate flavour so beloved by James Hunt (its founder and President). Hunt's rhetorical tactics were clear enough; an attempted acquisition of ethnology by anthropology, the use of non-British authorities to support his argument, and the reported resistance of the ethnologists to plain reason:

*Anthropology in name is not yet recognized in theory; but it is to some extent in practice. It is not a little remarkable, that some of those who are most opposed to the recognition of Anthropology as a recognized branch of science into the Association, are the very men who, in practice at least, admit the claims of Anthropology, and who read papers which are entirely anthropological. For instance, Mr Crawfurd, one of England's most consistent and venerable ethnographers, lost no opportunity of protesting against the introduction of anthropological papers into Section E; and yet, with that inconsistency for which he is occasionally distinguished, was one of the very first men in the section to read a paper on a purely anthropological subject. Mr Crawfurd's paper, entitled 'Notes on Sir Charles Lyell's Antiquity of Man', was from the beginning to the end a paper on Man or Mankind, as distinguished from Ethnology, or the science of the Races of Man. No writer of any authority, either English, American, or continental, will now call the question of the antiquity of man an ethnological question. It is pure and simple an anthropological question. Other papers bearing on the same subject, we understand, were rejected by the Committee of Section E, because they were anthropological! and could not be read because Anthropology was not recognized by Section E, which was entirely confined to Geography and Ethnology* (Anon., probably James Hunt, 1863: 379).

This article established a pattern of reporting which was to continue through to the time when the Anthropological and Ethnological Societies amalgamated. Its salient features, apart from combative tone, were the classification of all papers (regardless of who presented them, or of their allegiances) into anthropological or ethnological (prehistoric archaeology of all kinds being firmly anthropological), an enumeration of the anthropological and ethnological papers (usually a strict correspondence between the paper and the speaker's institutional loyalties), and the indication of which papers were entirely new, or had been presented elsewhere. These were all aspects of the tactics of the inter-society disputes that formed the backdrop to the events at the British Association, the objects being to exclude certain data sets from inclusion into ethnology (prehistoric archaeological data in particular), to demonstrate which society was the most active, and which construal of the proper study of man the most fruitful for research. In Hunt's view there could never be any doubt that the points would go to anthropology, if only because ethnology was manifestly a branch of anthropology. Again, the rhetoric is clear. Anthropology is the coming wave of human science, ordained by the nature of the subject matter itself. For example:

*We feel sure, therefore, that it only requires a little more time to remove any jealousy that may exist in the breasts of some ethnologists, respecting the success attending the labours of anthropologists. Let them learn not to quarrel with the decrees of Nature. Astronomy was not arrested in her progress by the clamours of the astrologers; nor will anthropologists cease to develop the extent, magnitude, and importance of their science by the invectives of ethnologists. Rather let them develop their own subject, and look with rejoicing on the beneficient wave which will ere long raise them from their present state of isolation, and raise them to their place as one of the branches of light which will illuminate the great system of organic light* (Anon., probably James Hunt, 1863: 381).

The battle lines were drawn, and a conflict that had hitherto been confined to London, was now poised to ride into the provinces on the back of the British Association. By the end of the 1870s one would probably have had to be living in the Outer Hebrides to have avoided hearing the case of both or either of the parties. Significantly, the battle was to be engaged within the sectional structure of the Association. The editor of the *Anthropological Review* intoned:

*Everything bids fair to make the next meeting in Bath successful. We trust that during the time that will elapse before the meeting, Anthropologists will bestir themselves to bring all their forces together, and thus help to secure the formal recognition of Anthropological science by the Association. We understand that notice has been given by Dr Hunt, that Section E shall for the future be devoted to 'Geography, Ethnology, and Anthropology'. A general rumour prevailed that there was to be a sub-section especially devoted to Anthropology. We think, however, that an increase in the number of sections is objectionable, and we see no necessity for such a division. As an independent journal, devoted to Anthropological science, we shall feel it our duty to advocate a union of Anthropology with the present Geographical and Ethnological section* (Anon., probably James Hunt, 1863: 464).

Therefore anthropology was not to be made marginal by its inclusion in a special 'quarantine' section, but on whose terms was it to be incorporated into Section E? There could only be one satisfactory solution, the eclipse of ethnology, and Hunt gathered his forces to achieve this. Things did not go as planned.

The discomfiture of anthropology at Bath gives some idea of the forces ranged against the 'lunatic polygenists and free-thinkers' from the Anthropological Society. Perhaps this explains why Sir Roderick Murchison, who seemed to have a virtual mortgage on the Presidency of Section E during this period could constantly serve up a listing of annual 'triumphs of exploration' masquerading as a presidential address, rather than pursuing a defence of the idea of ethnology against the attacks of the anthropologists (see for example Murchison 1864).

The report of the state of anthropology at the British Association published in the *Anthropological Review* of 1864 is a tale of lost battles and fighting spirit. The anthropologists had begun with high hopes and a sense of wounded dignity. In 1863 the Section E committee had allowed anthropological papers to be read only on sufferance, and, in response, Carter Blake moved a motion before the General Committee of the Association should recognize anthropology and allow the presentation of papers written under its aegis. Blake also offered the threat that if such recognition was not granted then the papers submitted to the Association in the name of the Anthropological Society of London would be withdrawn from the meeting. Blake spoke as the representative of the Anthropological Society, and claimed a fair hearing on the basis of the Society's strength and popularity:

*I may state, sir, that this Society now numbers more than 430 members, exclusive of more than 100 honorary and corresponding members. I feel convinced that the good sense of the Committee will not allow them to refuse the claims of such a Society, which is founded, like the British Association itself, for the advancement of truth. I have been informed that there are some here, who, for reasons best known to themselves, will oppose such a resolution; but I beg the Committee to pause before they commit themselves by a step which would thus estrange a large scientific society from this Association* (Blake 1864: 294).

Murchison rose to give the first line of defence against the claims of the anthropologists. Section E was already overburdened with work, and nobody really had much of an idea of, or sympathy for, the anthropological programme:

*He told them [Dr Hunt and Mr Carter Blake] then that their science was one-half - or to a great extent - ethnological, and to a great extent anatomical. Anthropology, in the sense in which it was treated by those gentlemen, or one-half of it, was a science of which he was profoundly*

210

*ignorant. Almost all the gentlemen associated with him - his vice-presidents, his secretary, and his friends right and left of him, thirty or forty in all - were unacquainted with anthropology, with the exception of Mr Blake* (Blake 1864: 295).

The simple solution to the problem was to place the 'ethnological' papers with Section E, and the other works with physiology or geology. This view was generally supported, especially by Crawfurd a former President of Section E and of the Ethnological Society of London. Sir John Lubbock, this time in his role as President of the ESL, also rejected Blake's motion, making plain his view that ethnology and anthropology were one and the same: 'he looked upon anthropology as an ugly name for ethnology' (Lubbock quoted in Blake 1864: 296). Accordingly, if the anthropologists didn't like it in Section E, then the best solution was to transfer them to Section D. Needless to say, Blake's motion lost by a large majority, and the anthropological papers were withdrawn. The *Anthropological Review* of 1864 counted the cost:

*The scientific congress of England has thus passed away, and with it the hopes which many confidently entertained of the recognition of anthropological science at the British Association in the year of 1864* (Blake 1864: 297).

Carter Blake advanced a number of reasons for the failure of the motion, among the most significant was the fact that the ASL had no official representation on the Committee for Section E. However, Hunt and his associates were still capable of a point-by-point refutation of the arguments that had been used against them at Bath. On Murchison's characterization of anthropology as being one-half ethnological and to a great extent anatomical (Blake 1864: 297):

*... [he] fails to see that although anthropology is certainly ethnological to a great extent, yet it is a science which comprises ethnology, ethnography, archaeology, philology, but only trespasses on anatomical grounds so far as anthropotomy (the science of human anatomy alone) is legitimately included in it* [original emphasis].

However, it was Lubbock's assertion that anthropology was an ugly name for ethnology that really stirred an outraged response:

*That a serious scientific assembly, like the General Committee of the British Association, should consider which two names were the 'prettier' can hardly be imagined. We doubt if anthropology is really an ugly word; we think it glides as musically over the tongue as 'kjokkenmodding,' and that, although neither word may be very euphonious, each is an exponent of a scientific fact, and must therefore be necessarily maintained in the British language* (Lubbock quoted in Blake 1864: 298).

It was to go on like this for years, rising to fever pitch at the Annual Meeting for 1868 in Dundee. In the previous Annual Meeting at Nottingham in 1867 the Anthropologists felt that they had begun to dominate their rival Ethnologists in the Association. Time was allowed for the reading of Anthropological papers (whereas previously this had been very difficult to organize), and many of the papers were read in the same section (therefore to the same audience) and not spread around through Geology, Anatomy, Ethnology and Geography, as had previously been the case. These tactics, of restricting 'air space', and of diluting the impact of anthropology by rejecting any notion of disciplinary integrity, had been very successfully used by the managers of the Association before Nottingham.

There were early indications of trouble, always anathema to the Council of the British Association, and the *Anthropological Review* was not slow to heed the signs:

*BRITISH ASSOCIATION, DUNDEE - The Dundee Advertiser of August 24th, says: 'A considerable degree of alarm has been, and is still, prevalent about the Anthropological section of the British Association, and what may be said and done there ... Some jokes, too, good, or bad, have been cracked on the subject. Some have called the British the 'Brutish' Association. One lady is said to have remarked, that she could not believe that apes had been turned into men; but she would not have wondered though some men, for their sins should be turned into apes! Under all this outside cachinnation there runs on, however, a deeper current of vague fear, which we must, if possible, try to modify, if not 'to check'* (Anthropological Review 1867: 376).

It did not work. At Dundee, things returned to pre-Nottingham days. Anthropology completely disappeared from Section D, but Ethnology remained. The ethnologists paid a high price for their association with the Geographers. Sir Samuel Baker, Nile explorer, gave an extraordinarily tedious resume of the latest adventures in heathen lands, and prematurely consigned Livingstone to his grave into the bargain! Throughout what must have seemed an interminable ramble the delegates were warned to keep watch on Russian movements near the Afghan border (!), and to uphold the Christian and Anglo-Saxon values in their dealings with the natives. Given the fuss and furore that was breaking over the conference due to the exclusion of anthropology, even the ethnologists must have thought Baker's address to be at least peripheral.

What had gone wrong? James Hunt and Carter Blake were, for once, at a loss for words. C.W Devis from the Anthropological Society of Manchester wrote the report for the *Journal of the Anthropological Society of London:*

> *It had been apprehended that the British Association would not on this occasion renew the welcome which it had extended to anthropology as a specific science at its previous meeting. The expectation was unfortunately realized ...* (1868: iv).

It was clear to the anthropologists that once again their science had been the subject of humiliation. At Dundee, Hunt declined to accept an arrangement that separated the papers submitted as Anthropological, from those marked as Ethnological, and he accordingly withdrew the papers brought up under the auspices of the Anthropological Society. Victory for the forces of opposition seemed complete with the 'anthropologicals' being cast as being uncompromising. Indeed the Local Committee for the reception of the anthropologists reacted with indignation, but Hunt quickly showed his political mettle by turning the resulting public and professional disapproval of anthropology back onto the British Association.

> *At a general meeting of anthropologists, subsequently held, there was entire unanimity in the opinion that they would be wanting, both to themselves and to the common interests of science, if they allowed the non-appointment of their department to pass without an earnest protest* (Devis 1868: iv).

However, the protests were not directed against the Association itself, but at those opponents of anthropology who had misused their political power within it. Hunt was also alive to the need for a public reading of anthropological papers, and, as a result, an alternative Anthropological Congress was held while the Annual Meeting went on. There was a public outcry that anthropology had been unfairly treated and the British Association, ever on guard against adverse publicity, which could lead to questioning about the objectivity of science, renounced the tactics of previous years and promised that justice would be done. That signal victory achieved, Hunt wound up the proceedings of the Congress.

Part of the settlement reached between the anthropologists and the Association was that anthropological papers would be read in Section E (where the Ethnologists were) for the remainder of the Dundee meeting. However, only one paper was ever read under these conditions. This was the result of an oversubscription to Section E, and this turn of events added further weight to the demand that Geography and Ethnology be separated at future meetings:

> *Anthropology must either be conducted apart from Geography or ignored altogether; which of these issues is to become final now rests with its students; if they be true to themselves, they will in future be received into the Association in a respectful, if not a cordial, spirit; other wise, a renewed display of the inveterate hostility banded against them will be encouraged, almost justified* (Devis 1868: vi-vii).

A further demonstration of the damaging classification of anthropological papers within the Association was provided by the fact that Pengelly's report on excavations in Kent's Cavern (undertaken for the Association) was read to the geological section, and Lubbock's paper on 'The Early Condition of Man' was read to Section E.

But what caused the British Association to court the charge of unfairly restricting scientific discussion? It appeared to the anthropologists at Dundee that the Association had attempted to please what it took to be Scots' public opinion by excluding anthropology from the meeting. It sadly backfired. The Scots rejected outright that they were too benighted to cope with the revelations of the new science, and the Dundee Press had such a field day whipping up the wounded feelings of the inhabitants that the Council of the Anthropological Society later passed a vote of thanks to the press and people of Dundee (*Journal of the Anthropological Society* 1868: lxxv). Thus what looked to be a major defeat for anthropology resulted in a signal victory. The difficulties of anthropology at the British Association had been well and truly publicly aired, and for all the distaste held by the Scots for anthropology, it was widely perceived by them that the Association had acted against the interests of science generally, rather than for its advancement. The alarms and disturbances of Dundee marked a turning point for anthropology.

In the following year at Norwich, all was comparatively quiet, and prehistoric archaeology provided ample reason: at the late meeting of the British Association at Norwich, the science of Anthropology was almost wholly unrepresented. This was due not to the falling off in the general interest of the science, but to two causes that presented themselves, one depending upon the other. The chief of these was the annual meeting of the

Congress of Archaic Anthropology, the name of which was there changed to that of Prehistoric Archaeology. Mainly because this meeting occurred at the same time and place as that of the British Association, no Anthropological department was nominated in Section D, and papers that would have been brought before the latter, were read before the Congress (Gibb 1869: xxiv). The change of name from Archaic Anthropology to Prehistoric Archaeology, in the light of the preceding contests between ethnology and anthropology over its control, and given that the Presidency of the Congress was held by Lubbock, raises the possibility of further political chicanery – this time in an international scientific body. Strangely, the Anthropological Society made no protest, perhaps believing that whatever it was called, it was still a constituent discipline of anthropology. Yet the name change appeared to signify the development of specialism inimical to the overall programme of anthropology. Be that as it may, prehistoric archaeology it was, and prehistoric archaeology it was to remain.

By 1870 much had changed, possibly due in part to the death of that most prominent of the 'anthropologicals', James Hunt. The events at the Liverpool meeting in 1870 confirmed the feelings of mutual goodwill between anthropologist and ethnologist. From this point of accommodation, the object of agitation since 1863, the triumph of anthropology was shortly to become complete. In 1871, at the Edinburgh meeting of the British Association, anthropology at last stood alone as a department within Section D. Ethnology had been absorbed. Professor Turner's Presidential Address of 1871 made it clear that in those years since Prichard had gained entry for ethnology into the British Association, the real reason for trouble and strife had been the fact that ethnology had been excised from Section D. It was a strange, yet comfortable reading of events:

*Again, if a separate Ethnological Department or subsection were formed, as has been suggested, or even if ethnological papers were read, as was for so many years the case in the Geographical Section, not only would all these communications on the characteristics of the different varieties of man, or of their distribution over the globe, but even papers on comparative philology, and on questions appertaining to the early history of man, and to his primitive culture, in all probability be subtracted from our proceeding. Without doubt, all ethnic questions form an integral part of anthropological study, for ethnology is one of those subjects which form the groundwork for our science; and it is an axiom that the whole is greater than and includes the part, all these questions naturally fall to be discussed in this department, and should not be divorced from their natural allies. The decision of the General Committee that the ethnological papers should be transmitted to this department was but to restore them to the place they originally occupied in the proceedings of the Association, for in its early years ethnology was a subdivision of Section D. The brief history of this department teaches us that its struggle for existence has been a severe one* (Turner 1871: 147).

Anthropology only stayed in its temporary haven until 1884, when the final phase of the programme instituted by Hunt over thirty years before was complete. Even though the Anthropological Institute of Great Britain and Ireland continued the publication of reports of the British Association meetings, they became very much an extension of new sources of strife that arose within the Institute itself. These sources, although to a limited degree cast in the terms of the great contests of the past, found their cause in the relations between the constituent disciplines of anthropology itself. Such conflicts, in the light of the clash between anthropology and ethnology for control over archaeology, physical anthropology and philology, were inevitable.

Even in the first number of the Institute's Journal, a clear division can be found between General Anthropology (read physical anthropology), Ethnology, and Prehistoric Archaeology. The specialisms of anthropology continued to lie together under a general integrative rubric, but this remained a potential, a possibility, rather than an actuality. As the specialisms developed from the 1870s onwards, the departments of anthropology, particularly ethnology, found less and less in common. A succession of presidents of the Anthropological Department at the British Association, indeed, of the Institute itself, found it increasingly difficult to emulate Lubbock's achievement of spanning all the fields of anthropology. In recognition of this state of affairs, succeeding presidents delivered annual addresses from their pet perspective, admitting their limited range but uttering the increasingly ritual integrative incantations. The prospects of a general anthropology (as envisaged by Hunt and by Broca) receded further from view.

It is indeed an irony that Lubbock, the most bitter opponent of anthropology, was, with the possible exception of Tylor, the quintessential British anthropologist (in the most general sense of the term) of the nineteenth century. Yet, much in anthropology had been beyond even him. Hunt, ever true to the breadth of the Continental construal of anthropology – especially its wariness of Darwinian theory, and the loudly-proclaimed intention to subject all aspects of society, mental, moral and political, to questioning – would no doubt have chosen such as Broca, Quatrefages, Topinard or Waitz as his candidate.

## Conclusions

Readers of this brief history of invective and internecine strife could be forgiven for thinking that the anthropology of James Hunt and Paul Broca had triumphed over the restricted reading given of it by the ethnologists in Britain. It did, but only partially. As the promoters of the new science were fond of reminding just about anyone who would listen, the fate of anthropology in Britain was very different from that experienced by the new, vital, discipline on the Continent. What Hunt failed to mention was, that in comparison to the political restriction in France, anthropology in Britain was largely free from direct government interference.

But interference there was, and in the British tradition, the checks and balances were provided by the Parliament of Science rather than by the Mother of Parliaments. Clearly, the Councillors of the British Association had been seriously alarmed by the freethinking attitudes of the anthropologists, their willingness to discuss issues of morals and politics that most members of the physical, earth and life sciences studiously (but not always successfully) managed to avoid. True, there were contentious figures such as Huxley and Spencer, but the ideal for science was a kind of timeless objectivity separated from the subjective concerns of the everyday. Anthropology offended against these principles (so, incidentally did ethnology), it was therefore to be reined-in before it called into question the value and pristine methodology of science.

The Anthropology that survived to full-blown recognition in 1871 had, possibly because of the death of Hunt, gradually been stripped of its power to disturb the British political balance. Certain of its hobbyhorses such as its anti-Irish leanings, and its advocacy of the manifest political destiny of the Anglo-Saxon, were widely held outside the discipline itself. They occasioned no general revulsion. On the other hand, its barely concealed polygenist tendencies, with their implied support for a non-relativist interpretation of physical and moral differences between the Anglo-Saxon and the 'ethnographic other', found little support.

Although from the 1880s perceptions of human diversity made a forceful return to the ranks of anthropology, this diversity was clearly to be located in ethnic and cultural, rather than purely physical differences. Explanation for diversity and similarity was increasingly to be sought in cultural historical factors, rather than by appealing to the doctrine of independent inventions and the psychic unity of mankind. Clearly the universalist programme which was supposedly at the heart of two competing forms of anthropology – that of Tylor, Lubbock and Morgan, and that of Quatrefages, Waitz and Topinard – was replaced by historicism. Real historical forces acting on real (different) groups of people, past and present, could explain the peculiar differences between human beings far more convincingly than generalized uniformitarian forces. The revolutionary science of anthropology became the tool of imperialists and nationalists, the universal programme was at an end.

In discussing these events at the British Association, one of my goals has been to establish the manner in which anthropology fought ethnology to enrol archaeology into its programme during the nineteenth century. Briefly put, there were both liberating and constraining effects of this enrolment. On the one hand archaeological data expanded in significance, and this was to further increase during the period to the end of the Second World War. On the other, the terms of archaeology's contribution to anthropology were frozen by contemporary views of what it was meaningful and valuable to know about human beings. Archaeology was very slow to free itself from the agenda given it by both Hunt and Lubbock (as well as by the Continental anthropologists). Alone among the constituent disciplines of anthropology so defined, archaeology went on holding to an empty shell – mistaking what are effectively institutional structures and integrative rubrics for theoretical substance.

**References**

ANONYMOUS (probably James Hunt). 1863. Anthropology at the British Association, *Anthropological Review* 1: 379-464.

ANTHROPOLOGICAL REVIEW. 1867. Anthropological News. *Anthropological Review* 5: 369- 76.

ANTHROPOLOGICAL SOCIETY OF LONDON. 1868. Annual Meeting of January 14, 1868. *Journal of the Anthropological Society of London* VI: lxv-lxxvi.

BLAKE, C. 1864. Anthropology at the British Association. *Anthropological Review* 2: 294-335.

BURROW, J.W 1966. *Evolution and Society*. Cambridge: Cambridge University Press.

DEVIS, C.W 1868. Report on Anthropology at the British Association, 1868. *Journal of the Anthropological Society of London* VI: iii- xiii.

FOWLER, D. 1975. Notes on Inquiries in Anthropology: A Bibliographic Essay. In T.H.H. Thoresen (ed.), *Toward a Science of Man: Essays in the History of Anthropology*, pp. 15-32. The Hague: Mouton.

GIBB, D. 1869. Report on the State of Anthropology at the Meeting of the BAAS at Norwich. *Journal of the Anthropological Society of London* VII: xxiii- xxvi.

HARRIS, M. 1968. *The Rise of Anthropological Theory*. New York: Crowell.

HODGEN, M. 1973. Anthropology in the BAAS, its inception. *Scientia: Rivista di Scienza* cviii: 803-11.

KUKLICK, H. 1991. *The Savage Within: The Social History of British Anthropology, 1885-1945*. Cambridge: Cambridge University Press.

MACLEOD, R. 1981a. Retrospect: The British Association and Its Historians. In R. MacLeod and P. Collins (eds), *The Parliament of Science*, pp. 1- 16. Northwood, Middx.: Science Reviews Limited.

—1981b. Introduction: On the Advancement of Science. In R. MacLeod and P. Collins (eds), *The Parliament of Science,* pp. 17-42. Northwood, Middx.: Science Reviews Limited.

MACLEOD, R. and P. COLLINS (eds) 1981. *The Parliament of Science*. Northwood, Middx.: Science Reviews Limited.

MCGEE, A. 1897. Anthropology at the American Association for the Advancement of Science. *Science* 6: 508- 513.

MORRELL, J. and A. THACKRAY. 1981. *Gentlemen of Science: Early Years of the British Association for the Advancement of Science*. Oxford: Clarendon Press.

MURCHISON, R. 1864. Section E Address. *British Association Reports* 33: 130-35.

MURRAY, T. 1989. The History, Philosophy and Sociology of Archaeology: The Case of the *Ancient Monuments Protection Act* (1882). In V. Pinsky and A. Wylie (eds), *Critical Directions in Contemporary Archaeology*, pp. 55-67. Cambridge: Cambridge University Press.

NOTT, J.C. and G.R. GLIDDON. 1854. *Types of Mankind or, Ethnological Researches: based on the ancient monuments, paintings, sculptures, and crania of races, and upon their natural geographical, philological and biblical history, illustrated by selections from the inedited papers of Samuel George Morton and by additional contributions from L. Agassiz; W. Usher; and HS. Patterson*. Philadelphia: Lippincott, Grambo.

ORANGE, A.D. 1972. The Origins of the British Association for the Advancement of Science. *British Journal for the History of Science* 6: 152- 76.

—1981. The Beginnings of the British Association, 1831- 1851. In R. MacLeod and P. Collins (eds), *The Parliament of Science*. Northwood, pp. 43-64. Middx.: Science Reviews Limited.

POUCHER, G. 1864. *Plurality of the Human Race*. H.J.C. Beavan, trans. London: Longman, Green, Longman and Roberts for the Anthropological Society of London.

PRICHARD, J.C. 1847. On the Various Methods of Research Which Contribute to the Advancement of Ethnology and the Relations of that Science to Other Branches of Knowledge. *British Association Reports* 16: 230- 53.

RAPPORT, N. (ed.) 2002. *British Subjects: An Anthropology of Britain*. Oxford: Berg.

STEPAN, N. 1982. *The Idea of Race in Science: Great Britain, 1800-1960*. Hamden, Conn.: Archon Books.

STOCKING, G.W. Jr. 1968. *Race, Culture, and Evolution*. New York: The Free Press.

—1971. What's in a Name? The Origins of the Royal Anthropological Institute (1837-71). *Man* (ns) 6: 369- 90.

—1983. The Ethnographer's Magic. Fieldwork in British Anthropology from Tylor to Malinowski. In G.W. Stocking Jr. (ed), *Observers Observed. Essays on Ethnographic Fieldwork*, pp. 70- 120. Madison: University of Wisconsin Press.

—1987. *Victorian Anthropology*. London: Collier Macmillan.

TURNER, G. 1871. Professor Turner's Address to the Department of Anthropology. *British Association Reports* 50: 144-47.

URRY, J. 1972. Notes and Queries on Anthropology and the development of field methods in British anthropology, 1870-1920. *Proceedings of the Royal Anthropological Institute* 45-57.

—1984. Englishmen, Celts and Iberians: The Ethnographic Survey of the United Kingdom 1892-1899. In G.W. Stocking Jr. (ed.), *Functionalism Historicized*, pp. 83-105. Madison: University of Wisconsin Press.

—1993. *Before Social Anthropology: Essays in the History of British Anthropology*. Philadelphia: Harwood Academic Publishers.

VOGT, K. 1864. *Lectures on Man: His Place in Creation and the History of the Earth*. J. Hunt, trans. London: Longman, Green, Longman and Roberts for the Anthropological Society of London.

VON GIZYCKI, R. 1979. Lectures on Man: His Place in Creation, and in the History of the Earth The Associations for the Advancement of Science: An International Comparative Study. *Zeitschrift fur Sociologie* viii: 28-49.

WAITZ, T. 1863. *Introduction to Anthropology*. J.F. Collingwood, trans. London: Longman, Green, Longman and Roberts for the Anthropological Society of London.

WEBER, G. 1974. Science and Society in Nineteenth Century Anthropology. *History of Science* XV: 260-83.

YEO, R. 1979. William Whewell, Natural Theology and the Philosophy of Science in Mid Nineteenth Century Britain. *Annals of Science* 36: 493-516.

—1981. Scientific Method and the Image of Science 1831-1891. In R. MacLeod and P. Collins (eds), *The Parliament of Science,* pp. 65-88. Northwood, Middx.: Science Reviews Limited.

## Chapter 14

# Illustrating 'savagery':
# Sir John Lubbock and Ernest Griset

*'Utopia, which we have long looked upon as synonymous with an evident impossibility, which we have ungratefully regarded as 'too good to be true; turns out on the contrary to be the necessary consequence of natural laws, and once more we find that the simple truth exceeds the most brilliant flights of the imagination'* (Lubbock 1865: 492).

*'Reading Malthus, he* [Wallace] *grasped that living nature was in effect the workhouse world writ large. Ruthless struggle was everywhere the law, not just among London's starving poor. Adaptation comes through competition.*
*Progress costs lives'* (Moore 1997: 293).

### Introduction

Much has been written about the extraordinary impact of Darwinism during the mid- to late nineteenth century, expressed in the scholarship of 'reception studies' (see for example Ellegard 1958; Glick 1988; Numbers and Stenhouse 1999). A significant focus has been on developing an understanding of the impact of Darwinian thinking on just about every aspect of Victorian society, particularly on literature, science, politics and social relations (see for example Beer 1983; Frayter 1997; Lorimer 1997; Moore 1997; Paradis 1997; Browne 2001). A great deal of attention has also been paid (by historians and philosophers of science) into the specifics of how the Darwinian message was disseminated so quickly and so broadly. Here the interest lies in the links between the rhetoric of scientific naturalism and the politics of the day, be it Whig-Liberal or Tory (see for example Clark 1997; Barton 1998, 2004; Clifford *et al.* 2006). A consequent interest lies in the ways in which science was popularised in Victorian Britain (see especially Lightman 1997, 2007).

Historians of archaeology have generally been slow to incorporate the tenor of this research into their accounts of the rise of prehistoric archaeology during this period, though there are notable exceptions (see for example Stocking 1987; Owen 2000 Patton 2007). Taking into account this recent work, and the solid contribution of older accounts (see for example Hutchinson 1914; Duff 1924; Pumphrey 1958; Murray 1990), I attempt here to delve deeper into these complexities, by publishing and analysing a suite of pictures commissioned by the pre-eminent prehistorian Sir John Lubbock (1834-1913), populariser of Darwinism, tireless advocate for the importance of science in society and Liberal social activist. The analysis will not be straightforward, if only because of the sheer breadth of Lubbock's interests *within* science, not to mention *outside* it. Clark (1997) among others (such as Stocking 1987), has noted the great ambiguities that lie within him, and the probability that Lubbock's polymathy will resist simplistic rendering.

Nevertheless the use of the pictures is revealing. The visualisation of human ancestors has been a particular focus of past and present research, if only because it is abundantly clear that 'ways of seeing' our ancestors are very much a product of the ways we see ourselves (see for example, Moser 1998; Milner 2007). At the same time archaeologists have also begun to explore the histories of collections that lie at the heart of museums great and small all over the world, and to work out what these histories might contribute to the history of archaeology itself (see for example Owen 2006; MacGregor 2007, 2008).

The pictures to be considered in this essay come from a suite of 20 created for Lubbock by the Victorian illustrator Ernest Griset (1844-1907). Nineteen are currently housed in the Museum of the London Borough of Bromley at Orpington (some are on display in its Avebury Room). The remaining picture is in private hands in Sydney, Australia, gifted by Lubbock's granddaughter to a friend. Only two are dated, *Griset 18* painted in 1869, and *Griset 20* painted in 1871. We know from oral histories and the observations of visitors to Lubbock's house at 'High Elms' in Kent that the paintings were originally associated with Lubbock's museum there, and were subsequently distributed throughout the house. *Griset 20* was painted as a gift from Lubbock to Charles Darwin, though never presented to him, and it seems it was not displayed with the other 19 paintings. In a historiographical note at the end of this article, I determine the provenance of the pictures and try to solve the mystery of how images of this age, quality, subject matter and association with one of the founders of prehistoric archaeology can have been hidden from the history of archaeology for so long.

Griset's images are the visual equivalents of information created directly through archaeological and natural historical research, and its interpretation through inferences drawn from ethnographic analogies. Lubbock's own very forthright statements in *Pre-historic Times* (1865) make this clear enough:

> *'Deprived then, as regards the Stone Age, of any assistance from history, but relieved at the same time from the embarrassing*

*interference of tradition, the archaeologist can only follow the methods which have been so successfully pursued in geology - the rude bone and stone-implements of bygone ages being to the one, what the remains of extinct animals are to the other… and in the same manner if we wish clearly to understand the antiquities of Europe, we must compare them with the rude implements and weapons still, or until lately, used by savage races in other parts of the world. In fact, the Van Diemaner and South American are to the antiquary, what the opossum and the sloth are to the geologist'* (1865: 336).

Lubbock's Grisets prompt other objectives too: an exploration of the social and political context of Lubbock's advocacy of natural law in human history, and of Griset's other works illustrating 'savage life' that were executed before and after he was commissioned by Lubbock. Here the social consequences of Darwinism and scientific naturalism, of Lubbock's adherence to Whig-Liberal politics, and of the reception of the 'savage other' in a society where the struggle for existence and the struggle between the races was becoming more symmetrical, provide a richer context within which historians of archaeology during the mid- to late nineteenth century can begin to produce accounts that are more sensitive to the complexities of the social and political roles of their discipline. Last, but by no means least, we also have the chance to look a bit more closely at the relationships between archaeology and anthropology during this formative period, especially the construction of the category of 'savagery' within a broader inquiry into the history of hunter-gatherer studies (see for example; Schrire 1984; Barnard 2004; Yengoyan 2004).

**The Lubbock commission**

The images that comprise the Lubbock commission can be found in low-resolution format online at: (http://www.latrobe.edu.au/archaeology/Staff_directory/lubbock.htm).

Three images from this group are reproduced with this essay and are broadly representative of the group in both theme and treatment (Figures 1, 2 & 3). Griset's subject matter ranges from portrayals of the struggle between humans and animals in prehistoric times, to animals (without people) in typical environments, images of site types, humans making tools and boats, and people fishing and hunting. Figure 1 *(Griset 9),* a cave, and Figure 2 *(Griset 14),* a highly detailed close-up of a Lake Village, represent archaeological contexts that had been visited by Lubbock and which were extensively discussed in *Pre-historic Times* (1865). It is also worth noting that the Griset images differ substantially in treatment from two paintings by

*Figure 2. (Griset 9) 'Prehistoric group around fire in cave'. Bromley Museum Accession number 74.83.5 Courtesy Bromley Museum Services.*

August Bachelin commissioned by the Swiss Confederation in 1867: *Village lacustre de l'âge du bronze* (used to represent Switzerland at the Paris Exposition Universelle in 1867), and *Village lacustre de l'âge de la pierre* (in the Schweizerisches Landesmuseum).

Figure 3 (*Griset 1*), a dramatic re-imagination of a clash between mammoth and humans, is indicative of other clashes with bears, bison and stags portrayed by Griset. All but two of the images showing people have more than one person in view. In the two with people acting alone, one (*Griset 2*) has an individual pursued by a pack of wolves and possibly only minutes away from death, the other (*Griset 11*) a lone hunter sneaking up on some seals. Several images represent social action outside of the business of slaughtering wild beasts (either in self-defence or as food). *Griset 4* represents burials inside a megalithic tomb; *Griset 8* and *Griset 18* are family groups on the seashore; *Griset 9* (reproduced here as Figure 1) portrays dinner time conversation in a cave; *Griset 10* is a family group with a man hollowing-out a log to make a boat and a woman about to light a fire near the family home; *Griset 12* is a hunter returning to an earth house from the hunt with dogs, and an infant playing with a puppy in view; while *Griset 13* shows a group making spears outside the family tent with a woman and a child actively involved in the process.

These straightforward observations support other generalisations. First, the commission can be clearly divided between images that are clearly archaeological in inspiration, and those that have a much more ethnographic flavour. For example, *Griset 1* (the mammoth hunt), *Griset 4* (the megalithic tomb), *Griset 9* (the cave scene), *Griset 14* and *Griset 17* (the lake villages), and *Griset 15* and *Griset 16* (extinct fauna) differ from scenes around the camp or the chase that were commonly observed and reported by travellers in the American West or in Australia.

Second, Griset has obviously seen prehistoric material culture such as spears, axes and domestic ceramics at first hand – quite possibly from Lubbock's own extensive collection. Third, gender-based divisions of labour

*Figure 3. (Griset 14) 'Lake village'. Bromley Museum Accession number 74.83.10. Courtesy Bromley Museum Services.*

(outside of the chase) are by no means rigid. While it is true that a woman is tending the fire in *Griset 10,* and carrying a basket laden with food in *Griset 14,* in *Griset 11* she is involved in making spears. Last, these prehistoric peoples, although for the most part clad in skins and sporting long, unkempt hair, look very like contemporary images of indigenes of the American West. Significantly, they are not portrayed as being either stupid or cruel (there are no instances of conflict between people, and they are not satirised in any way). Rather, Griset's people (in this commission at least) are resourceful, personally brave, capable of group interaction beyond the immediate family, respectful of their dead, and doing their best to cope with the trials of life. Griset (doubtless at Lubbock's insistence) has produced something far more than caricature.

### The commission in context: Lubbock, Darwin, contemporary 'savages' and Liberal science

Lubbock's great contribution to prehistoric archaeology, *Pre-historic Times,* went to seven editions – the last being completed just prior to his death in 1913. All editions were lavishly illustrated (indeed the first edition had 156 figures), but none presented reconstructions of life in prehistoric times. Rather the focus is on material culture (both ancient and modern), with a smaller number of images showing views and sections of sites, such as St Acheul, and skulls (the Engis and Neanderthal skulls in particular). Many of the artefacts illustrated there came from Lubbock's private collection, the collections of friends, or from museums across Europe that were visited by Lubbock during his extensive travels. Clearly the Griset commission was not be used for that purpose.

Janet Owen (1999, 2006, 2008) has produced the most comprehensive analysis of Lubbock as a collector of archaeological and ethnographic artefacts, and has convincingly demonstrated that the bulk of his collection was acquired between 1863 and 1880. Much of her analysis centres on the uses to which the collection was put, which were primarily didactic. Lubbock's collection became a tool for demonstrating the reality of human social and cultural evolution, and the displays mounted at his home, 'High Elms', for the edification of visitors were, like Lubbock's frequent public lectures on prehistoric times, regarded as a vehicle for spreading the message of Darwinism and its consequences for an understanding of human society past, present and future. Lubbock's Grisets were perfectly suited to that context.

Lubbock's Grisets and his artefact collection (and the public and private displays of both) give us, as Owen (2000) has demonstrated, a window onto so many other aspects of the life of a Whig Liberal intellectual in Victorian

*Figure 4. (Griset 1) 'The mammoth hunters'. Bromley Museum Accession number 71.1.7. Courtesy Bromley Museum Services.*

Britain. We see his links to other collectors, who were often his friends, his belief that his collections could provide a concrete instantiation of the lessons of science and of history for contemporary society, and his adoption of new technologies of persuasion to disseminate Darwinian science. We can also see that Lubbock's interests in prehistoric archaeology were driven by much more than a fascination with the past, and this broader reading of Lubbock can help us make better sense of the final chapter of *Pre-historic Times* (a point I will return to at the end of this essay). But why did Lubbock choose Ernest Griset to create such evocative images of the prehistoric past?

**The commission in context: Ernest Griset and 'Legends of Savage Life'**

Much work has been done on the use of satirical illustration in Victorian Britain (and in France during the same period) and clear links demonstrated between satire and science (Paradis 1997; Browne 2001). Not very much is known about Ernest Griset, a fact that amazed his two biographers (Hubbard 1945; Lambourne 1977) given his great popularity in England in the 1860s and 1870s. Griset was born in Boulogne on 24 August 1843, but came to England when he was a child. Much of his life (save for a stint on the Continent learning his craft from the Belgian painter Louis Gallait) was spent in north London close by London Zoo – a place where he often went to sketch (see http:/ /www.zsl.org/info/library/ernestgriset-online-exhibition,27,PS. html). Lambourne and others have celebrated the great skill (and sympathy) of Griset's renderings of animals (he had a particular affinity for storks), but it was his capacities as an illustrator of books and magazines that were the basis of his fame. Many of these were satirical in content (he was to work for magazines such as *Fun* and *Punch)* and he was particularly adept at drawing anthropomorphic figures that were at some times funny and at others, grotesque. Perhaps the best example of this style was *The Purgatory of Peter the Cruel* (1868), one of several collaborations with James Greenwood. During the height of his fame Griset was particularly sought after for his illustrations of the denizens (human and otherwise) of 'savage lands', especially by Sir Richard Burton, but also by Colonel R. I. Dodge (an author of tales of the American West, as well as the person after whom Dodge City is named). Griset was skilled, experienced and fashionable.

Earlier I remarked that his renderings of 'savage life' in the Lubbock commission did not denigrate our ancestors or their modern representatives. However, this cannot be said for illustrations he produced for satirical works about modern 'savages', especially those illustrating the works of James Greenwood, notably *The Hatchet Throwers* (1866) and *Legends of Savage Life* ( 1867). Lubbock must have been well aware of this aspect of Griset's work, and Greenwood's sense of humour was described by Lambourne as *'possessing almost every mid-Victorian prejudice'* (1977: 42). Others, such as Forster have been damning. *'One whose images could evoke horror in any child was Ernest Griset... with its habitual association of blacks and animals, usually in a situation of slapstick cruelty, it must mark a low-point for racist art outside Germany'* (1989: 63). But stories of 'savage' credulity and cannibalism were particularly popular in Victorian Britain, and Griset's illustrations were widely regarded as being of the first rank.

Clearly *Legends of Savage Life* was intended to be a funny collection of stories about contemporary 'savages', and Grisets's illustrations, such as Figure 4, reinforced the comedy.

The last story, 'The Clay Head', is typical of the mix and describes the outcome of a conflict between two tribes of indigenous Australians, the Whoggles and the Whangs:

> *'That evening a great feast was made, at which there were fruits of all kinds and meats of -. Well, we will say nothing as to the meat. It is true*

*Figure 5. Griset: The Whoggles successfully invade the Whangs.* In Greenwood, J. 1867. 'Legends of Savage Life', p. 134. *Photograph Courtesy of the State Library of Victoria.*

*that there were afterwards found several heaps of bones that were not those of sheep or kangaroo, and it is likewise undeniable that a conquering army will at times be guilty of excesses it would blush to confess to afterwards; but then, on the other hand, the Whoggles were a people most simple in their diet, and had always set their faces in a most determined manner against can -. However, it is an unpleasant subject, and perhaps the least said about it the better under any circumstances'* (Greenwood 1867: 163).

And just in case there was any doubt about the fate of the Whangs, Griset follows this discussion with an image of 'savages' gnawing bones around a cooking fire titled 'The last occasion of the Whoggles picking a bone with their enemies'. All pretty predictable stuff, but worth revisiting by way of a gesture towards the reality of a broader context of racism in mid-Victorian Britain. However, there is something more here. Grisets 'savages' in *Legends* (Hottentot, Patagonian, indigenous North American, Fijian and Australian) are all distinguishable from each other but, as Figure 4 demonstrates, singularly inaccurate as representations of each of these groups. Finally, returning to my opening remark about the developing concept of 'savagery' in anthropology and archaeology during this formative period, Griset's inaccuracy might be plausibly interpreted as either a complete lack of interest in detail (one 'savage' the same as another, so to speak), or a reflection of just how little accurate information about the indigenous people of Australia was available to people in England.

## Some conclusions

Mid-Victorian discussion about race and cultural evolution were redolent with ambiguity. For Lubbock and like-minded Whig Liberals education and science were the foundation of a just and progressive society. While it was demonstrably the case that there were 'savages' living in the far-flung corners of the empire, there were also 'savages' (the criminal classes being a prime example) within. By understanding the causes of 'savagery' (usually a lack of education) society could defend itself against the danger of social and cultural regression. Here the benefits of understanding the meaning of prehistoric times, the gradual separation of human beings from the savagery of natural selection, could be made manifest to all who cared to look. Darwin's theory, in the hands of Alfred Russell Wallace, Herbert Spencer and indeed John Lubbock, was a true expression of natural law:

> *Even in our own time we may hope to see some improvement, but the unselfish mind will find its highest gratification in the belief that, whatever may be the case with ourselves, our descendants will understand many things which are hidden from us now, will better appreciate the beautiful world in which we live, avoid much of that suffering to which we are subject, enjoy many blessings of which we are not yet worthy, and escape many of those temptations which we deplore, but cannot wholly resist* (1865: 492).

For Lubbock the message of prehistoric times was not about the specificities of the deep past (or indeed the savage present), it was about the future. Science had uncovered the truth of natural law, of the reality of progress through human virtue. Lubbock's Grisets, revealing the reality of savage life in prehistoric times played their part in demonstrating the story of progress, thereby strengthening our collective resolve to improve ourselves still further. Notwithstanding all of the changes incorporated in successive editions (brought about by new discoveries and changes in interpretation) the closing passages of *Pre-historic Times* remained unchanged over the 48 years separating the first and last. Lubbock's views about the meaning of human history made manifest by archaeology and the theory of natural selection were adamantine:

> *'Thus, then, the most sanguine hopes for the future are justified by the whole experience of the past... and he must be blind indeed who imagines that our civilization is unsusceptible of improvement, or that we ourselves are in the highest stat attainable by man'* (1890: 600).

### Historiographical note: provenance of the paintings

The 'invisibility' of the Grisets can be mostly explained by the way Lubbock chose to use them (and not to use them). None was ever published, and documentation of the history of the collection (based on information supplied by Adrian Green, then curator of the Bromley Museum, and supported by Owen's research (2000)) makes it clear that after Lubbock's death in 1913 the paintings ceased to have an educative function at 'High Elms'. It appears most likely that they, along with his collection of artefacts, faded into the background of life at the house. *'During my childhood they were displayed along the first floor corridor at High Elms, but I don't remember them being discussed'* (Lord Avebury to Murray 05/06/2007).

Their journey back into the public domain was to begin after the death of Lubbock's second wife Alice Augusta Laurentia Lane Fox-Pitt Rivers. *Griset 7-10* were transferred into the care of the Orpington Historical Society in December 1947, with that part of Sir John Lubbock's artefact collection that had not been sent to the British Museum. The Lubbock/ Avebury collection was transferred to the newly opened Orpington Museum (later Bromley Museum) in 1965 on 'permanent loan'.

At the time of the death of Adelaide Lubbock in 1981 there was discussion between her solicitors and the museum about the ownership of the entire Avebury collection. The status of the collection belonging to the Orpington Historical Society was unclear as there was no written proof that the Society was given the Avebury material in 1947. In essence it still belonged to the Lubbock family – hence when the previous curator (Adrian Green) tried to resolve ownership in 2003 both the Lubbock family and the Orpington Historical Society were consulted. The collection was transferred as a gift in 2003.

Fourteen of the pictures (*Griset 1-14*) remained with the family after the transfer of the bulk of the collection in 1947. At some point they were transferred to Down House for storage. This group were loaned by Adelaide Lubbock to Bromley Museum in 1975. They were inherited by her children, Eric Lubbock (current Lord Avebury) and Olivia Keighley, when she died in 1981. Olivia Keighley decided to donate her share in 1983, but Eric Lubbock still retains ownership of his share (*Griset 8, 11, 13, 15-18*).

A letter of 10 March 1982 states that one of the pictures was in the ownership of Mrs Adelaide Lubbock at the time of her death. It has been surmised that this is the Griset now owned by the Sydney doctor Robert Gordon (*Griset 19*). In 2007 Dr Gordon lent the painting to the author so that it could be photographed, and advised the following concerning its provenance:

*I have known Olivia Keighley for many years. She is the sister of Lord Avebury. In the late 90s she became aware that these paintings were now at 'High Elms', the old family estate in England, and there was some uncertainty as to what to do with them. I was in England at the time and she asked me to visit 'High Elms' and to arrange that two of them be transferred to Sydney. This I did, and on their arrival here she gave me one of them'* (Robert Gordon to Murray 03/07/2007).

Dr Gordon's statement accords with advice the author received from Lord Avebury (that the painting was gifted to him by Olivia Keighley). However Gordon's dates do not fit with the timing of Olivia Keighley's gift of her Grisets to the Bromley Museum, nor with the fact that 'High Elms' was destroyed by fire in 1967. Further research is required to resolve these discrepancies, but they in no way disturb the authenticity of the Sydney Griset, nor the chain of provenance to Dr Gordon (http://ericavebury. blogspot.com/2007_07_0 1_archive.html). Certainly Lord Avebury has a strong recollection of *Griset 19: 'I remember that picture very well; it was one of my favourites, and always gave me a frisson when I saw it in the dark corridor leading to my grandmother's sitting room at High Elms'* (Lord Avebury to Murray 24/04/2007).

## Acknowledgements

The former curator at the Bromley Museum, Adrian Green, very kindly showed me the Grisets, provided documentation concerning their provenance and supplied the jpegs used in the online gallery. His successor, Marie-Louise Kerr, has also assisted with the images and permissions to publish. Eric Lubbock, Lord Avebury, gave me the benefit of his knowledge about the

Grisets and set me down the right path to locate Dr Robert Gordon and the 'missing' Griset. Dr Gordon made it possible for me to document his wonderful painting and trusted me to move it far from its 'home'. Earlier versions of this essay formed part of a lecture at the Institute of Archaeology, UCL and the Mulvaney Lecture at the Australian National University in 2007. I thank Professor Stephen Shennan and Professor Matthew Spriggs for their invitations to speak. Wei Ming (La Trobe University) and the State Library of Victoria prepared the illustrations.

## References

*Primary sources*

Lubbock correspondence and papers 1855-1911. British Library Add.496-49681.
Lubbock diaries, correspondence etc. 1850-1913. British Library Add. 62679-62693; 76 145-76147.

*Emails*

Lord Avebury to Murray 24/04/2007
Lord Avebury to Murray 05/06/2007
Robert Gordon to Murray 03/07/2007

*Secondary sources*

BARNARD, A. 2004. Hunting-and-gathering society: an eighteenth-century Scottish invention. In A. Barnard (ed) *Hunter-Gatherers in History, Archaeology and Anthropology*, pp. 31-43. Oxford: Berg.

BARTON, R. 1998. 'Huxley, Lubbock and half a dozen others': professionals and gentlemen in the formation of the X Club, 1851-1864. *Isis* 89: 410-44.

—2004. Lubbock, Sir John (1834-1914), Lord Avebury. In B. Lightman (ed) *The Dictionary of Nineteenth-century British Scientists*, pp. 1272-8. Bristol: Thoemmes.

BEER, G. 1983. *Darwin's Plots: Evolutionary Narrative in Darwin, George Eliot, and Nineteenth-century Fiction*. London: Routledge.

BROWNE, J. 2001. Darwin in Caricature: a study in the popularisation and dissemination of evolution. *Proceedings of the American Philosophical Society* 145: 496-509.

CLARK, J.F.M. 1997. 'The ants were duly visited': making sense of John Lubbock, scientific naturalism and the sense of social insects. *British Journal of the History of Science* 30: 151-76.

CLIFFORD, D., WADGE, E., WARWICK, A. and M. WILLIS 2006. *Repositioning Victorian Sciences: Shifting Centre in Nineteenth-century Scientific Thinking*. London: Anthem.

DUFF, U.G. (ed) 1924. *The Life-Work of Lord Avebury (Sir John Lubbock) 1834-1913*. London: Warts.

ELLEGÅRD, A. 1958. *Darwin and the General Reader: the Reception of Darwin's Theory of Evolution in the British Periodical Press, 1859-1872*. Goteborg: Almqvist & Wiksell.

FORSTER, I. 1989. Nature's Outcast Child: Black People in Children's Books. *Race & Class* 31: 59-77.

FRAYTER, P. 1997. Strange new worlds of space and time: late Victorian science and science fiction. In B. Lightman (ed) *Victorian Science in Context*, pp. 256-80. Chicago (IL): University of Chicago Press.

GLICK, T.F. (ed) 1988. *The Comparative Reception of Darwinism*. Chicago (IL): University of Chicago Press.

GREENWOOD, J. 1866. *The Hatchet Throwers*. London: John Camden Hotten.

—1867. *Legends of Savage Life*. London: John Camden Hotten.

HUBBARD, E. H. 1945. A forgotten illustrator: Ernest Griset, 1844 -1907. *The Connoisseur* 115: 30-6.

HUTCHINSON, H .G. 1914. *Life of Sir John Lubbock, Lord Avebury*. London: Macmillan.

LAMBOURNE, L. 1977. *Ernest Griset: Fantasies of a Victorian Illustrator*. London: Thames & Hudson.

LICHTMAN, B. 1997. 'The voices of Nature': popularizing Victorian science. In B. Lightman (ed) *Victorian Science in Context*, pp. 187-211. Chicago (IL): University of Chicago Press.

—2007. *Victorian Popularizers of Science: Designing Nature for New Audiences*. Chicago (IL): University of Chicago Press.

LORIMER, D.A. 1997. Science and the secularization of Victorian images of race. In B. Lightman (ed.) *Victorian Science in Context*, pp. 212-35. Chicago (IL): University of Chicago Press.

LUBBOCK, SIR JOHN. 1865. *Pre-historic Times: as Illustrated by Ancient Remains, and the Manners and Customs of Modern Savages*. London: Williams & Norgate.

—1890. *Pre-historic Times: as Illustrated by Ancient Remains, and the Manners and Customs of Modern Savages*. Fifth edition. London: Williams &Norgate.

MACGREGOR, A. 2007. *Curiosity and Enlightenment: Collectors and Collections from the Sixteenth to the Nineteenth Century*. New Haven (CT): Yale University Press.

MACGREGOR, A. (ed) 2008. *Sir John Evans 1823-1908: Antiquity, Commerce and Natural Science in the Age of Darwin*. Oxford: Ashmolean Museum.

MOORE, J. 1997. Wallace's Malthusian moment: the common context revisited. In B. Lightman (ed) *Victorian Science in Context*, pp. 290-311. Chicago (IL): University of Chicago Press.

MILNER, R. 2007. Portraits of prehistory: imagining our ancestors. In G.J. Sawyer and V. Deak (eds) *The Last Human: a Guide to Twenty-two Species of Extinct Humans*, pp. 237-50. New Haven (CT): Yale University Press.

MOSER, S. 1998. *Ancestral Images: the Iconography of Human Origins*. Ithaca (NJ): Cornell University Press.

MURRAY, T. 1990. The history, philosophy and sociology of archaeology: the case of the *Ancient Monuments Protection Act* (1882). In V. Pinsky and A. Wylie (eds) *Critical Directions in Contemporary Archaeology*, pp. 55-67. Cambridge: Cambridge University Press.

NUMBERS, R. and J. STENHOUSE (eds) 1999. *Disseminating Darwinism: the Role of Place, Race, Religion, and Gender*. Cambridge: Cambridge University Press.

OWEN, J. 1999. The collections of Sir John Lubbock, the First Lord Avebury (1834-1913): 'An open book?' *Journal of Material Culture* 4: 283-302.

—2000. The Collecting Activities of Sir John Lubbock (1834 -1913). Unpublished PhD. University of Durham.

—2006. Collecting artefacts, acquiring empire: exploring the relationship between Enlightenment and Darwinist collecting and late-nineteenth-century British imperialism. *Journal of the History of Collections* 18: 9-25.

—2008. A significant friendship: Evans, Lubbock and a Darwinian world order. In A.

MacGregor (ed) *Sir John Evans 1823-1908: Antiquity, Commerce and Natural Science in the Age of Darwin*, pp. 206-30. Oxford: Ashmolean Museum.

PARADIS, J. 1997. Satire and science in Victorian Culture. In B. Lightman (ed) *Victorian Science in Context*, pp. 143-75. Chicago (IL): University of Chicago Press.

PATTON, M. 2007. *Science, Politics and Business in the Work of Sir John Lubbock.* Aldershot: Ashgate.

PUMPHREY, R.J. 1958. The Forgotten Man: Sir John Lubbock, F.R.S. Notes and *Records of the Royal Society of London* 13(1): 49-58.

SCHRIRE, C. 1984. Wild surmises on savage thoughts. In C. Schrire (ed) *Past and Present in Hunter-Gatherer Studies*, pp. 1-25. Orlando: Academic Press.

STOCKING, G.W. Jr. 1987. *Victorian Anthropology*. New York: Free Press.

YENGOYAN, A. 2004. Anthropological history and the study of hunters and gatherers: cultural and non-cultural. In A. Barnard (ed) *Hunter-Gatherers in History, Archaeology and Anthropology*, pp. 57-66. Oxford: Berg.

# Chapter 15

# Writing histories of archaeology

## Introduction: diversity and its consequences

In the late 1970s when I began researching the history of archaeology in earnest (see e.g. Murray 1987; Lucas 2007) it was a pretty lonely business. Apart from the then doyen of the field, Glyn Daniel, and the increasingly influential figure of Bruce Trigger, there were few in the Anglo-Saxon world that seemed to take the field seriously. Of course there were exceptions in North America (see e.g. Willey and Sabloff 1974) and in Europe (see e.g., Laming-Emperaire 1964; Klindt-Jensen 1975), but even there the concept of an archaeologist specializing in the history of their discipline was alien indeed. The history of archaeology was something you did *after* you completed the more important work of excavation and analysis. Certainly there was quite a lot of history being written, but for the most part it was done by non-archaeologists celebrating 'great discoveries', 'great civilizations', or even 'great archaeologists' for a popular audience (see e.g. Bacon 1976).

Again, Brian Fagan was an exception here, but even in his publications of this time (see e.g. Fagan 1977) there was no attempt to use such histories to explore what might be considered to be broader philosophical issues in archaeology, be they about disciplinary epistemology or metaphysics, or even a consideration of where archaeological information was located on the cognitive map of the human sciences.

Perhaps more significant still was the contrast between the huge popular interest in the history of archaeology and the almost total absence of work by professional historians, particularly those who were participating so actively in the development of the history and philosophy of sciences cognate to archaeology such as geology, biology, and even anthropology (see e.g. Stocking 1968, 1984, 1987; Rudwick 1972). This absence of interest was remarkable, especially because archaeologists involved in the development of the New Archaeology were making quite explicit references to approaches developed in the philosophy of science, particularly discussions about reasoning (Hempel and Popper), and the drive to understand the nature of scientific change flowing from the work of Kuhn, Lakatos, and Feyerabend. Some New Archaeologists were also writing disciplinary histories that justified the positions they were taking about disciplinary philosophy.

Ironically, at that time these were not widely regarded by practitioners as being 'histories' *sensu stricto,* more (especially in the cases of Walter Taylor 1948 and David Clarke 1968, 1973) as a polemical staking-out of territory, though Willey and Sabloff (1974) was an exception.

The massive growth in the history and philosophy of science that took place during the last forty years of the twentieth century transformed both professional and popular understandings of science, but until the 1980s there was scant interest among philosophers in exploring archaeology as an exemplar of important aspects of scientific reasoning – particularly in terms of the importance of the social and cultural contexts of scientific knowledge (see e.g. Salmon 1982; Kelly and Hanen 1988; Pinsky and Wylie 1990; Wylie 2002). It was precisely during this period that archaeologists embarked on a decades-long exploration of core elements of disciplinary philosophy, with the development of schools of thought that were (in essence) grouped around divergent notions of knowledge and authority that have been present in the humanities since the eighteenth century. This lack of external interest was one of the chief characteristics of the time. The other was the lack of interest *by archaeologists* in applying new approaches to the history of science to archaeology (for an exception see Murray 1990; Stoczkowski 1994). Indeed, the major synthesis of the period by Trigger (1987) adopted a standard 'history of ideas' approach that had been around for decades before (Daniel 1967, 1971, 1975).

Twenty years later the field has been transformed, becoming both crowded and vibrant. New work has shattered old orthodoxies. Many of the original contexts of publication and research have continued, but new ones have been added. Popular interest in the field has grown unabated and there is a very large literature indeed that has grown up to service it. However, the strongest growth has been in histories of archaeology written by archaeologists (and others) who have a broader and deeper understanding of the history and philosophy of science (see e.g. Van Riper 1993; Murray 1999a, 2008a; Smith 2004; Morse 2005 ). There are also many more histories of archaeology that have been written to meet the needs of a much wider and more diverse audience – a sure sign that what was once considered to be a somewhat marginal and esoteric pursuit is now of greater consequence.

If the history of archaeology has become more significant both within archaeology and outside it, then it is also important for practitioners and others to explore its historiography. This essay is a very brief consideration of some of the issues raised by doing so. In the introductory essay to our reader *Histories of Archaeology* (Murray and Evans 2008a), Chris Evans and I drew a distinction that we considered crucial to the development of engaged and meaningful histories of archaeology:

*Archaeology had its roots in antiquarianism, history, philology, ethnology, geology, and from 'natural history' generally. From this grew the trunk that eventually branched out into various sub-disciplines (e.g. Biblical, Roman, Medieval, Scientific, and 'New' Archaeology). The great meta-narratives of the history of archaeology have followed this approach, with 'archaeological thought' or 'archaeological ideas' having a common inheritance or ancestry in nineteenth century positivist European science. From this main 'root-stock', it eventually branched into sub-divisions and out into the world at large, fostering offspring archaeologies differentiated by geography, tradition, sub-field, or time period (Daniel 1975; Trigger 1987). Our aim... is to challenge this meta-narrative and to demonstrate that there has been a great deal more variability of thought and practice in the field than has been acknowledged* (Murray and Evans 2008b: 1-2).

The late Bruce Trigger in a recent comprehensive survey also stressed the presence of significant variety in the historiography of archaeology:

*Historical works dealing with archaeology have been written to entertain the public, commemorate important archaeologists and research projects, instruct students in the basic concepts of the discipline, justify particular programs or ideas, disparage the work of rivals, and, most recently, try to resolve theoretical problems. These studies have taken the form of autobiographies, biographies, accounts of the development of the discipline as a whole, investigations of specific institutions or projects, and examinations of particular theories and approaches. They have used the analytical techniques of intellectual and social history and sought to treat their subject objectively, critically, hermeneutically, and polemically. Over time, historical studies have become more numerous, diversified, and sophisticated. Histories of archaeology are being written for all parts of the world, and in a growing number of countries a large amount of material is being produced at local as well as national levels* (Trigger 2002: 630).

Diversity (and its consequences), both in archaeology and its historiography, is the central theme of this essay. It is a quite straightforward matter to demonstrate that histories of archaeology reflect the times in which they were written, and the interests of those writing them. This wholly unremarkable observation makes explicit what historians of archaeology already know – that we should be wary of the perils of Whig historiography (of judging past accounts of the history of archaeology by the standards and preoccupations of the present). But the recognition of those perils does not in any way imply that we cannot subject such accounts to critique, especially as that very process can lead to a clearer documentation of the real and important differences between previous accounts and those we currently favour. But there are more significant consequences of diversity than these. At stake is our capacity to grasp and to coherently describe the discipline itself. Some histories, especially those of Daniel (1975) and Trigger (1987, 2006), created a narrative of archaeology that provides a coherent explanation of how we arrived at our current state. Other histories see the constitution of contemporary archaeology as being highly problematic, and eschew the fundamentally teleological approach of Daniel and Trigger and use the history of archaeology as a framework within which to posit the potential existence of other archaeologies. These are, of course, polemical histories of the kind routinely written to establish the bona fides of dissonant approaches to archaeology (see e.g. Miller 1985; Murray 1992a, 1992b, 1993, 1995, 1996, 2001, 2008b; Lyman and O'Brien 2006). As such they can be quite different in intent from, for example, critical re-evaluations of disciplinary history (see e.g. Patterson 1986; Kehoe 1998). In this, the clear identification of context (and the interests of authors and audiences) are both crucially important.

## Sketching the historiography of archaeology

It is significant that, notwithstanding decades of intense debate about archaeological theory and constant exhortation to be critically self-reflective about practice, there are few explicit discussions about approaches to writing histories of archaeology. I have remarked that Daniel devoted little time and space to reflection about either method or purpose, but more recent syntheses have made significant contributions to charting the historiography of archaeology (see e.g. Murray 1987, 1990, 1999b, 2002, 2005, 2007c; Trigger 1987, 2001, 2006; Pinsky 1990; Schnapp 1996; Corbey and Roebroeks 2001; Schlanger 2002; Smith 2004; Diaz-Andreu 2007; Murray and Evans 2008b; Schlanger and Nordbladh 2008).

We now have a good working knowledge of some of the core concerns of histories of archaeology – the histories of discoveries, methods, techniques, and theories, the histories of institutions and 'disciplinary infrastructure' such as legislation, sources of funding, university departments, and the history of relationships between archaeology and other disciplines since the eighteenth century. Accounts of these core concerns have changed significantly since the 1970s, especially in the choice of subject matter and in approach. Nowhere is this more apparent than in the field of biography – where historians have moved from what now read like hagiographies (see e.g.

Willey 1988) to more critical reflections about practice (see e.g. Gruber 1966; Trigger 1980; Murray 1999b) and to substantial explorations of practitioners in broader context (see e.g. Kaeser 2004). Older biographies (see e.g. Piggott 1985) and autobiographies (see e.g. Daniel and Chippindale 1989) have also come to provide a baseline for a new generation of historians to respond to and, in a sense, to react against. This is especially the case when historians seek to write the histories of marginal archaeologies or marginalized archaeologists (for example non-mainstream archaeologies and their practitioners) or, more frequently, women in archaeology (see e.g. McBryde 1993).

Of equal importance has been the growing interest in using biography as a framework within which to explore more complex issues, such as the interplay of individuals and institutions, the 'socialization' of practitioners into the discipline, and the social and cultural contexts of archaeology (see e.g. Levine 1986; Murray 1999a, 1999b; Smith 2004; Patton 2007; MacGregor 2008; Schlanger and Nordbladh 2008). Much good work has been done, but much more remains to do. But where there has been change there has also been continuity as archaeological biographies that are written for a wider audience retain the capacity to resonate strongly within the profession (see e.g. Walker 1995; Adkins 2003).

I have mentioned that histories grounded in the lives of individuals frequently allow access to complex matters of context, but there is a continuing interest in writing about such matters as ends in themselves. For example, there has been a long-standing interest in the histories of archaeological and antiquarian societies, and this has continued – albeit with different points of emphasis. Significant anniversaries for major institutions such as the Society of Antiquaries of London and the National Museum of Denmark have led to the publication of major evaluations of both places (Jakobsen 2008; Pearce 2007). Of course anniversaries of individuals, discoveries, or even books also provide a continuing spur to history-writing (see e.g. MacGregor 2008). Notwithstanding the great opportunities provided by the need to celebrate institutions as ends in themselves, one of the most significant recent developments has been a much stronger focus on writing the histories of collections and collectors. Here institutions take on a far more personal and, frequently, more politically engaged context, especially within a postcolonial discourse about the links between colonialism and collecting (see e.g. Owen 2006, 2008; Gosden et al. 2007; MacGregor 2007). These new developments make absolutely clear that the subject matter of histories of archaeology is not solely under the control of archaeologists, there being many interests that might be served by these kinds of histories.

Again this serves to highlight a fundamental conflict in the field, that of archaeology (as a discipline) and antiquarianism (seen by many to be an arid wrong turning on the road to the development of a science of archaeology). This disagreement about fundamentals is seen in sharpest relief in the different emphases of two of the most influential disciplinary histories – Bruce Trigger's *A History of Archaeological Thought* (1989) and Alain Schnapp's *Discovery of the Past* (1996). Trigger, especially in the second edition (2006), is properly respectful of significant antiquarian research that took place well into the nineteenth century. However, it is Schnapp's goal to reconstruct the world of antiquarianism in order to explain why it was absolutely vital to the development of humanism and, indeed, in later years, to the development of nationalism. For Schnapp antiquarianism was no wrong turning on the path to disciplinary truth, it was, instead, a coherent system of thought that survives well into the present. Schnapp's advocacy has been supported by much new research, such as Rosemary Sweet's excellent history of English antiquarianism in the eighteenth century (2004). It has also led historians to look more closely at the role of the antiquarian in society (especially during the seventeenth, eighteenth, and nineteenth centuries), particularly in terms of the influence of antiquarian works on community identity, through the creation of a plausible line between the material world (houses, churches, coins, and manuscripts) and human history.

One such antiquarian was John Stow (1525-1605), one of Renaissance England's most shining intellects, whose *Survey of London* (1598) is an enduring testimony of a world much of which has been erased by war and development. Stow's memorial (see Figure 6) lies in the church of St Andrew Undershaft in the City of London and, even though he died over 400 years ago, a new quill pen is set in his hand every three years.

This extraordinary act of remembrance is all the more remarkable because of the context of St Andrew, overshadowed (symbolically 'buried') by Norman Foster's iconic 30, St Mary Axe, and one of the very few pre-Great Fire churches remaining in the City (see Figure 7). In this sense the survival of the church (and of Stow's monument) throws into relief the survival of his

*Figure 6. Memorial to John Stow in the Church of St Andrew Undershaft, City of London.* (Photo Tim Murray)

241

*Figure 7. St Andrew Undershaft in its contemporary landscape. Norman Foster's 30 St Mary Axe (also known as the Gerkin) is in the rear.* (Photo Tim Murray)

marvellous book that has proved to be such a valuable guide to reconstructing the London landscape during the sixteenth and seventeenth centuries. The worth of Stow's work, like that of so many that were to come after, cannot be simply judged by its contribution to the growth of the discipline of archaeology. The fires of his curiosity still burn in people who would not see themselves as archaeologists.

Alongside these encouraging developments in the history of archaeology there has been a similar upsurge of highly detailed re-examinations of key passages in the history of archaeology. Previous accounts of the Three Age

System (see e.g. Daniel 1943; Graslund 1987) have crumbled under the scholarship of Peter Rowley-Conwy (2007) and Tove Jakobsen (2008). Core texts have been re-read, re-translated, and re-evaluated with the result that the Three Age System is both more ambiguous and more interesting than Daniel and others would have had. Similarly the great debates around the discovery of high human antiquity (see e.g. Grayson 1983) have recently been explored by O'Connor in her excellent *Finding Time in the Old Stone Age* (2007).

In the introduction to the final three volumes of the *Encyclopedia of Archaeology* (Murray 2001b) I made the point about Trigger:

*Contemplating the richness of new information about something that he felt we knew reasonably well, he was moved to remark that in recent decades the history of archaeology had really come of age. I think that he meant this in two ways. First, that archaeologists were now sufficiently confident about the value of their discipline and its perspectives to seek a deeper understanding of its history - an understanding that had the clear potential to challenge disciplinary orthodoxies. Second, that the sheer scale of archaeology practiced at a global scale gave rise to many interesting questions about the unity of the discipline* (Murray 2001b: xix).

In the early 1980s Bruce Trigger and Ian Glover pursued some of these questions in two editions of the journal *World Archaeology* that were devoted to the exploration of 'regional traditions' in archaeology. What Trigger and Glover (and the contributors to their project) were keen to establish was whether the diversity of experience among archaeologists and the societies they served had led to real differences in approach and purpose among nations or groups of nations such as 'Anglo-Saxon' or 'Francophone', 'First World', 'Second World; or 'Third World', 'Colonialist' or 'Postcolonialist'. But the experience of the *Encyclopedia* was also one of commonality in actions, methods, and interests, which at least allowed for the possibility that archaeologists could communicate *with each other,* as well as with the general public. This notion of unity in diversity can be directly contrasted to very strong forces that emphasize *disunity,* especially as the needs, interests, and social and cultural contexts of practitioners vary so widely across the globe. For these tensions are the direct outcomes of the fact that the history of archaeology (just like archaeology itself) is a global as well as local pursuit. The clear evidence for such tensions raises the very important question of whether a coherent discipline of archaeology can exist.

Conflict and diversity within the historiography thus, rightly, mirror conflict and diversity in the discipline as a whole and the wider society that sustains it. I have already stressed that no history of archaeology is innocent of perspective or purpose, and I now make my own perspectives and purposes as clear as I can.

**Writing history: the basis of a personal approach**

My goals have more to do with diagnosing the condition of contemporary archaeology and understanding the nature of its relationships with contemporary anthropology and history. Writing the history of archaeology involves exploring the interconnectedness of these disciplines, but it also allows us to see just how different they are, notwithstanding pretty constant attempts to explain this away as having no theoretical importance at all (see e.g. Murray 1993, 1995, 2008b).

I came to the history of archaeology through undergraduate research in the history of anthropology, specifically the history of nineteenth-century race theory. My first work focused on the monogenist/polygenist debate (over the issue of whether human beings were the result of one creation or origin or of many), as exemplified by the Scottish anatomist Robert Knox and his English disciple James Hunt (see e.g. Murray 1987, 1999a).

Understanding Knox's most famous work, *The Races of Men* (1850), posed significant intellectual challenges, not because so much of what he was saying I found to be morally repugnant, but because at its core it represented a coherent and marvellously rich intellectual tradition spanning anatomy, philosophy, biology, ethnology, archaeology, and of course philology that was radically at odds with my own training as an anthropologist. Knox (and many like him) had been written out of the history of anthropology because the victors write the histories and then use such narratives to socialize budding practitioners. Knox was the practitioner of an anthropology that no longer existed made for a world that no longer existed either.

I continued to explore these ideas in doctoral research focused on an enquiry into the authorities archaeologists appeal to, to justify their knowledge claims in contemporary archaeology (Murray 1987). The existence of such 'hidden histories' in anthropology indicated to me that such were likely to exist unremarked in archaeology as well, and that the idea that contemporary views of the archaeologist's project were 'natural' and not cultural was false as well, based on a failure to recognize that current orthodoxies have histories too. Writing the histories of such ahistorical theoretical and perspectival 'givens' provided a framework through which to seriously address problems within contemporary archaeological theory. Historical research has helped broaden my approach to this problem from being narrowly epistemological, to asking a more encompassing question: what makes archaeological accounts of the past plausible? A consideration of plausibility then led me to more detailed investigations of the links between archaeology and the society that sustains its practice. This, in turn, has greatly increased the significance of the history of archaeology as a primary source of information about related enquiries into disciplinary traditions and the 'culture' of archaeology. Finally, it helped to establish what is distinctive about archaeology, especially its philosophies and the social impacts of archaeological knowledge, and the importance of that distinctiveness.

Thus my account of the history of archaeology is directed towards the identification of enduring structures of archaeological knowledge – those structures that provide the criteria in terms of which knowledge claims are justified as being both rational and reliable and that also provide practitioners with the ability to distinguish meaningful knowledge and the relevance of models, theories, and approaches drawn from archaeology's cognate disciplines. Some years ago historian of anthropology George Stocking sketched out the ethos of that discipline in usefully uncompromising terms:

*Another way of looking at the matter is to suggest that the general tradition we call retrospectively 'anthropological' embodies a number of antinomies logically inherent or historically embedded in the Western intellectual tradition: an ontological opposition between materialism and idealism, an epistemological opposition between empiricism and apriorism, a substantive opposition between the biological and the cultural, a methodological opposition between the nomothetic and the idiographic, an attitudinal opposition between the racialist and the egalitarian, an evaluational opposition between the progressivist and the primitivist-among others* (Stocking 1984: 4).

Notwithstanding over forty years of theoretical disputation within archaeology, the fact remains that archaeology inherited these epistemological and ontological antinomies, which have, at various times over the past 250 years, underwritten historicist or universalist, materialist or idealist, empiricist or rationalist approaches to gaining knowledge and making meanings. Again, notwithstanding claims for paradigm shifts or revolutions in thinking – be they processual or post-processual – archaeologists have, for the most part, essentially recycled perspectives drawn from cognate disciplines, without making a significant *archaeological* contribution to such fundamental debates. Histories of archaeology can demonstrate the reality of continuity where claims for discontinuity are made. Radical histories of the kind I am interested in are but one response to the conservative orthodoxies of Daniel (1975) or Trigger (2006). Nonetheless it is worth exploring what roles the history of archaeology will play in moves to reform modern archaeology in the light of pressure for increasing diversity in approach and purpose among archaeologists, and among those members of the general public who consume our product.

## Some contemporary tensions

I earlier mentioned the rapidly rising interest in antiquarianism as a major force within contemporary historiography. Getting a clearer picture of how archaeology and antiquarianism have related to one another helps us to understand how these different approaches to material pasts might coexist now and into the future. But this is by no means the most significant tension within contemporary archaeology, where sources of conflict and divergence go to the very heart of the discipline and the nature of its place within society and culture.

The multiplication of interests and perspectives that has been so much a part of the last forty years shows little sign of slowing down. The identity of archaeology as a discipline (and the significance of archaeological knowledge) has been challenged both internally and externally. Internally there are the consequences of the steadily increasing growth of sub-disciplinary specializations, and the divergent understandings of archaeological ontology that have arisen since the 1980s. Of equal importance has been a growing focus on developing a critical understanding of the complex relationship between archaeology and society. Some of the impetus for this derives from internal pressures as archaeologists seek to explore the social impacts of their work. This has been most prominent in explorations of the relationship between archaeology and the foundation and maintenance of nation states in the nineteenth and twentieth centuries (see e.g. Dietler 1994; Kohl and Fawcett 1995; Diaz-Andreu 2007; Murray 2007a). Archaeologists are now very well aware of the important social and cultural roles played by practitioners, especially in the construction (and destruction) of identities.

There can be little doubt that many of these histories are profoundly shocking, especially those that make clear the complicity of archaeologists in processes of colonialism and imperialism. Recent histories also make clear that the past activities of archaeologists can act as a source of social conflict in contemporary society. Chief among these is the now problematic relationship between archaeologists and Indigenous peoples in the 'settler societies' of the United States, Canada, Australia, South Africa, and New

Zealand. In recent years Indigenous peoples have made it quite clear that they regard much of what archaeologists do, and the ways they set about doing it, to be deeply colonialist.

There is no doubt that there are no easy ways to resolve such tensions, but it seems obvious enough that archaeologists will have to reflect deeply about the impact their practice has on Indigenous groups and to become more firmly part of the very difficult process of reconciliation within settler societies. Part of that reflection will require us to think more clearly about the uses to which knowledge is put, but perhaps more important, the ways in which we, as practitioners, seek to justify the claims to knowledge that we make. A significant part of that matter requires a reflection about the links between knowledge and divergent interests both within and outside the discipline.

We very properly regard this communication with society about the ways in which knowledge about the past is built up, and the 'tolerance limits' which should be set on it statements of interpretation, as being of the first importance. However the history of archaeology makes it clear that this will be no easy task, because the core social assumptions and normative values of archaeologists are still largely unexplored, and the ways in which these values articulate with archaeological data to produce plausible accounts of 'the past' are the subject of intense, if not particularly well-informed, debate. This goal of critical reflection about the intellectual inheritance of contemporary archaeology is made the more difficult by the fact that links between the empirical data of archaeology and the ideas, theories, hypotheses, models, or guesses we have about them are very weak indeed. The goals of communication and persuasion pose significant challenges.

These great debates should (and I hope will) give rise to different histories of archaeology. It is easy enough to say this but there are real questions about the ways in which these divergent histories will relate to each other.

## Concluding remarks

It has been my goal to argue for both radical and conservative roles for histories of archaeology, and to stress its very great value in helping us to understand the social and cultural elements of archaeological knowledge. Histories of archaeology reveal a discipline in a ferment of change, but also in a ferment of self-discovery.

It has often been observed that during the nineteenth century archaeology became a pre-eminently popular science because of its potent cocktail of mystery, patient investigation, direct physical contact with the relics of ages past, and of course, the lure of foreign parts. Little has changed since then, as new civilizations have been unearthed, languages have been deciphered, and the antiquity of human life on earth has been extended to almost unimaginable depths. Archaeology has touched and continues to touch everybody, and although much of it has become highly technical and arcane, the central elements of our quest for an understanding of the history of human beings have remained largely intact. In the late twentieth century archaeologists might be a little more wary about claiming an ability to reconstruct the past, or indeed to be in a position to pronounce definitively on the question of when human beings became properly human, but there remains a core of belief that only archaeology can reveal the evidence of the whole human story from prehistoric to historical times (Murray1999c: xv).

Histories of archaeology have rightly focused on stories of discovery, analysis and, more recently, the means by which practitioners persuaded others that history could be wrung from sites, landscapes and material culture. Histories of archaeology in all their variety tell us about how and why we make these things meaningful. At their best they also squarely confront the fact that making meanings has consequences for the discipline, its practitioners, and for society in general. Archaeology has contributed to the creation and destruction of identities. The knowledge that it produces is embedded in the culture and society of its time and this is never value neutral. But with power of this kind comes significant responsibility.

In this brief discussion I have argued that writing histories of archaeology can have significant benefits for the discipline, and for the societies that nurture it and consume its varied products. I have been at pains to stress that the goal here should be to produce knowledgeable producers as well as consumers. Knowledge here refers specifically to the nature of claims, the strengths and weaknesses of theories, and the extent to which such things can be scrutinized and informed judgements made. Given that the history of archaeology amply demonstrates the very great significance of the social and cultural contexts of its practice (and the very real evidence of the use of archaeological information and perspectives to support nationalism, colonialism, and other ideologies), then the great challenge for us all is to find plausible ways of using a knowledge of the history of archaeology to defend society against archaeology and (just as important) *vice versa* (Murray1996: 26).

But there is another (related) agendum here too, and it has to do with issues of disciplinary identity and the ongoing development of the methods and theories that lie at the heart of our discipline. In this essay I have briefly reflected on the important role that histories of archaeology can play in helping us to evaluate the worth (or otherwise) of the instruments we use to make sense of the material past. In part I have seen this as being a developing argument about the significance of archaeological information, especially with respect to that created by historians and anthropologists. Bruce Trigger considered the same general issue at the conclusion of the introduction to the second edition of *A History of Archaeological Thought:*

> *This book goes to press at a time that should see archaeology consolidate its position as a mature social science devoted to the study of past human behaviour, culture and history by means of material culture. Much of this development will come about as a result of fractious theoretical confrontations being balanced by an emphasis on theoretical accommodation and synthesis. Archaeology will also establish its credentials as the only science with a broad enough temporal perspective that the historical significance of all the social sciences has to be established in relation to it* (Trigger 2006: xx).

Although it is easy to observe that perhaps Trigger was being a bit premature, and his argument for accommodation and synthesis somewhat naive, it is nonetheless highly desirable that archaeologists come to understand how their discipline *differs* from other human sciences. Such an understanding might have significant consequences, for example that practitioners work out that it can be perfectly legitimate for archaeologists to respond to that difference theoretically and methodologically, thereby helping society at large (and not just other social scientists) to come to value more highly the importance of the very real issues raised by doing archaeology. Here I speak of much more than the social and cultural impacts of its practice, such as those that have been so thoroughly discussed with respect to Indigenous communities in particular, and societies in general. Here puzzles and problems posed by archaeological phenomena (whatever their period) pose considerable challenges of understanding, and humanity has been (and will continue to be) greatly enriched by their consideration. In this sense too writing histories of archaeology will become central to writing philosophies of archaeology.

**References**

ADKINS, L. 2003. *Empires of the Plain: Henry Rawlinson and the Lost Languages of Babylon.* London: Harper Collins.

BACON, E. (ed) 1976. *The Great Archaeologists: The Modern World's Discovery of Ancient Civilizations as Originally Reported* in *the Pages of the Illustrated London News from 1842 to the Present Day.* London: Seeker and Warburg.

BAHN, P. (ed) 1999. *The Cambridge Illustrated History of Archaeology.* Cambridge: Cambridge University Press.

CLARKE, D. 1968. *Analytical Archaeology.* London: Methuen.

—1973. Archaeology: the loss of innocence. *Antiquity* 47: 6-18.

CORBEY, R. and W. ROEBROEKS 2001. Does Disciplinary History Matter? An Introduction. In R. Corbey and W. Roebroeks (eds) *Disciplinary History and Epistemology: Studying Human Origins,* pp. 1-7. Amsterdam: University of Amsterdam Press.

DANIEL, G. 1943. *The Three Ages: An Essay on Archaeological Method.* Cambridge: Cambridge University Press.

—1967. *The Origins and Growth of Archaeology.* Harmondsworth: Penguin.

—1971. From Worsaae to Childe: The Models of Prehistory. *Proceedings of the Prehistoric Society,* 37: 140-53.

—1975. *A Hundred and Fifty Years of Archaeology.* London: Duckworth.

DANIEL, G. and C. CHIPPINDALE (eds) 1989. *The Pastmasters: Eleven Modern Pioneers of Archaeology.* London: Thames & Hudson.

DIAZ-ANDREU, M. 2007. *A World History of Nineteenth-Century Archaeology: Nationalism, Colonialism and the Past.* Oxford: Oxford University Press.

DIETLER, M. 1994. 'Our Ancestors the Gauls': Archaeology, Ethnic Nationalism, and the Manipulation of Celtic Identity in Modern Europe. *American Anthropologist* 96 (3): 584-605.

FAGAN, B. 1977. *Elusive Treasure: The Story of Early Archaeologists in the Americas.* New York: Scribners.

GOSDEN, C., LARSON, F. and A. PETCH 2007. *Knowing Things: Exploring the Collections at the Pitt Rivers Museum, 1884- 1945.* Oxford: Oxford University Press.

GRASLUND, B. 1987. *The Birth of Prehistoric Chronology: Dating Methods and Dating Systems in Nineteenth Century Scandinavian Archaeology.* Cambridge: Cambridge University Press.

GRAYSON, D. K. 1983. *The Establishment of Human Antiquity.* New York: Academic Press.

GRUBER, J. 1966. In Search of Experience: Biography as an Instrument for the History of Anthropology. In J. Helm (ed) *Pioneers of American Anthropology: The Uses of Biography,* pp. 3-27. Seattle, WA: University of Washington Press.

JAKOBSEN, T. (ed) 2008. *Birth of a World Museum.* Acta Archaeologica Supplementa: Volume 78.

KAESER, M-A. 2004. *L'Univers du préhistorien: Science, foi et politique dans l'oeuvre et la vie d'Édouard Desor (1811 - 1882).* Paris: Harmattan.

KEHOE, A. 1998. *The Land of Prehistory: A Critical History of American Archaeology.* New York: Routledge.

KELLY, J. and M. HANEN 1988. *Archaeology and the Methodology of Science.* Albuquerque, NM: University of New Mexico Press.

KLINDT-JENSEN, O. 1975. *A History of Scandinavian Archaeology.* London: Thames and Hudson.

KOHL, P. and C. FAWCETT (eds) 1995. *Nationalism, Politics, and the Practice of Archaeology.* Cambridge: Cambridge University Press.

LAMING-EMPERAIRE, A. 1964. *Origines de l'archéologie préhistorique en France.* Paris: A. and J. Picard.

LEVINE, P. 1986. *The Amateur and the Professional: Antiquarians, Historians and Archaeologists in Victorian England, 1838-1886.* Cambridge: Cambridge University Press.

LUCAS, G. 2007. Visions of Archaeology: An Interview with Tim Murray. *Archaeological Dialogues,* 14 (2): 155- 77.

LYMAN, R. L. and M.J. O'BRIEN 2006. *Measuring Time with Artefacts: A History of Methods in American Archaeology.* Lincoln, NE: University of Nebraska Press.

MCBRYDE, I. 1993. 'In Her Right Place…'? Women in Archaeology: Past and Present. In H. Du Cros and L-J. Smith (eds) *Women in Archaeology: A Feminist Critique*, pp. xi-xv. Canberra: Department of Prehistory, Research School of Pacific Studies, Australian National University.

MACGREGOR, A. 2007. *Curiosity and Enlightenment: Collectors and Collections from the Sixteenth to the Nineteenth Century.* New Haven, CT: Yale University Press.

—(ed) 2008. *Sir John Evans 1823-1908: Antiquity, Commerce and Natural Science in the Age of Darwin.* Oxford: Ashmolean Museum.

MILLER, D. 1985. *Artefacts as Categories.* Cambridge: Cambridge University. Press.

MORSE, M. 2005. *How the Celts Came to Britain: Druids, Ancient Skulls and the Birth of Archaeology.* Stroud: Tempus.

MURRAY, T. 1987. Remembrance of Things Past? Appeals to Authority in the History and Philosophy of Archaeology. Unpublished PhD., Department of Anthropology, University of Sydney.

—1990. The History, Philosophy and Sociology of Archaeology: The Case of the *Ancient Monuments Protection Act* (1882). In V. Pinsky and A. Wylie (eds) *Critical Directions in Contemporary Archaeology,* pp. 55-67. Cambridge: Cambridge University Press.

—1992a. The Tasmanians and the Constitution of the 'Dawn of Humanity'. *Antiquity,* 66: 730- 43.

—1992b. The Discourse of Australian Prehistoric Archaeology. In B. Attwood (ed) *Power, Knowledge, and Aborigines* [special issue of the *Journal of Australian Studies*] pp. 1-19. Melbourne: La Trobe University Press.

—1993. Archaeology, Ideology and the Threat of the Past: Sir Henry Rider Haggard and the acquisition of time. *World Archaeology,* 25 (2): 175-86.

—1995. Gordon Childe, Archaeological Records, and Rethinking the Archaeologist's Project. In P. Gathercole, T. Irving, and G. Melleuish (eds) *Childe and Australia,* pp. 199-21. St Lucia: University of Queensland Press.

—1996. From Sydney to Sarajevo: A Centenary Reflection on Archaeology and European Identity' *Archaeological Dialogues,* 3: 55-69.

—1999a. Excavating the Cultural Traditions of Nineteenth Century English Archaeology: The Case of Robert Knox. In A. Gustafsson and H. Karlsson (eds) *Glyfer och Arkeologiske Rum - en Vanbok til Jarl Nordbladh,* pp. 501-15. Gothenburg: University of Gothenburg.

—1999b. The Art of Archaeological Biography. In T. Murray (ed) *Encyclopedia of Archaeology: The Great Archaeologists,* 2 vols, pp. 869-83. Santa Barbara, CA: ABC-CLIO.

—1999c. Introduction. In T. Murray (ed)*, Encyclopedia of Archaeology: The Great Archaeologists,* 2 vols, pp. xv-xviii. Santa Barbara, CA: ABC-CLIO.

—2001. On '*Normalizing'* the Palaeolithic: An Orthodoxy Questioned. In R. Corbey and W Roebroeks (eds) *Studying Human Origins: Disciplinary History and Epistemology,* pp. 29-44. Amsterdam: University of Amsterdam Press.

—2002. Epilogue: Why the History of Archaeology Matters. *Antiquity* 76: 234-8.

—2005. The Historiography of Archaeology and Canon Greenwell. *Bulletin of the History of Archaeology* 15.(2): 26-37.

—2007a. Peripheral Matters? *Cambridge Archaeology Journal* 17 (3): 358-62.

—2007b. Rethinking Antiquarianism. *Bulletin of the History of Archaeology* 17 (2): 14-22.

—2007c. *Milestones in Archaeology.* Santa Barbara, CA: ABC-Clio Press.

—2008a. Prehistoric Archaeology in the 'Parliament of Science, 1845-1884. In N.

Schlanger and J. Nordbladh (eds) *Archives, Ancestors, Practices: Archaeology in the Light of its History,* pp. 59-71. New York: Berghahn Books.

—2008b. Paradigms and Metaphysics or 'Is This the End of Archaeology as We Know It'? In S. Holdaway and L. Wansnider (eds) *Time in Archaeology: Time Perspectivism Revisited,* pp. 170- 80 Salt Lake City, UT: University of Utah Press.

MURRAY, T. ( ed) 1999c. *Encyclopedia of Archaeology: The Great Archaeologists.* 2 vols. Santa Barbara, CA: ABC-CLIO Press.

—2001b. *Encyclopedia of Archaeology: History and Discoveries.* 3 vols. Santa Barbara, CA: ABC-CLIO Press.

MURRAY, T. and C. EVANS (eds) 2008a. *Histories of Archaeology.* Oxford: Oxford University Press.

—2008b. The Historiography of Archaeology: An Editorial Introduction. In T. Murray and C. Evans (eds) *Histories of Archaeology,* pp. 1-12. Oxford: Oxford University Press.

O'CONNOR, A. 2007. *Finding Time for the Old Stone Age: A History of Palaeolithic Archaeology and Quaternary Geology in Britain, 1860-1960.* Oxford: Oxford University Press.

OWEN, J. 2006. Collecting Artefacts, Acquiring Empire: Exploring the Relationship between Enlightenment and Darwinist Collecting and Late-Nineteenth Century British Imperialism. *Journal of the History of Collections* 18: 9-25.

—2008. A Significant Friendship: Evans, Lubbock and a Darwinian World Order. In

A. MacGregor (ed) *Sir John Evans, 1823-1908: Antiquity, Commerce and Natural Science in the Age of Darwin,* pp. 206-30. Oxford: Ashmolean Museum.

PATTERSON, T. 1986. 'The Last Sixty Years: Toward a Social History of Americanist Archaeology in the United States. *American Anthropologist* 88: 7-26.

PATTON, M. 2007. *Science, Politics and Business in the Work of Sir John Lubbock.* Ashgate:Aldershot.

PEARCE, S. (ed) 2007. *Visions of Antiquity: the Societies of Antiquaries of London 1707-2007.* London: Society of Antiquaries of London.

PIGGOTT, S. 1985 [1950]. William Stukeley: An Eighteenth-Century Antiquary. 2nd rev. edn. London: Thames and Hudson.

PINKSY, V. 1990. Introduction: Historical Foundations. In V. Pinsky and A. Wylie (eds) *Critical Traditions* in *Contemporary Archaeology,* pp. 51-4. Cambridge: Cambridge University Press.

PINSKY, V. and A. WYLIE (eds) 1990. *Critical Directions* in *Contemporary Archaeology.* Cambridge: Cambridge University Press.

ROWLEY-CONWY, P. 2007. *From Genesis to Prehistory:* The *Archaeological Three-Age System and Its Contested Reception* in *Denmark, Britain and Ireland.* Oxford: Oxford University Press.

RUDWICK, M. 1972. The *Meaning of Fossils: Episodes in the History of Palaeontology.* London: MacDonald and Co.

SALMON, M. 1982. *Philosophy and Archaeology.* New York: Academic Press.

SCHLANGER, N. (ed) 2002. Ancestral Archives: Explorations in the History of Archaeology. *Antiquity* 76: 127-31.

SCHLANGER, N. and J. NORDBLADH (eds) 2008. *Archives, Ancestors, Practices: Archaeology* in *the Light of Its History.* New York: Berghahn Books. .

SCHNAPP, A. 1996. *The Discovery of the Past: The Origins of Archaeology.* London: British Museum Press.

SMITH, P. J. 2004. A Splendid Idiosyncrasy: Prehistory at Cambridge, 1915-1950. Unpublished PhD. University of Cambridge.

STOCKING, G. W. Jr. 1968. *Race, Culture and Evolution: Essays in the History of Anthropology.* New York: Free Press.

—1984. Functionalism Historicized. In G. W. Stocking Jr. (ed) *Functionalism Historicized: Essays on British Social Anthropology,* pp. 3-9. Madison, WI: University of Wisconsin Press.

—1987. *Victorian Anthropology.* London: Free Press.

STOCZKOWSKI, W. 1994. *Anthropologie naïve, anthropologie savante: De l'origine de l'homme, de l'imagination et des idées reçues.* Paris: CNRS.

SWEET, R. 2004. *Antiquaries: The Discovery of the Past in Eighteenth-Century Britain.* London: Hambledon.

TAYLOR, W. W. 1948. *A Study of Archaeology.* Washington, DC: Memoirs of the American Anthropological Association, No. 69.

TRIGGER, B. 1980. *Gordon Childe.* London: Thames and Hudson.

—1987. *A History of Archaeological Thought.* Cambridge: Cambridge University Press.

—2001. Historiography of Archaeology. In T. Murray (ed) *Encyclopedia of Archaeology: History and Discoveries,* 3 vols, pp. 630-9. Santa Barbara, CA: ABC-CLIO Press.

—2006. *A History of Archaeological Thought,* 2nd edn. Cambridge: Cambridge University Press.

VAN RIPER, A. B. 1993. *Men Among the Mammoths.* Chicago, IL: University of Chicago Press.

WALKER, A. 1995. *Aurel Stein: Pioneer of the Silk Road.* London: John Murray.

WILLEY, G. R. 1988. *Portraits in American Archaeology: Remembrances of Some Distinguished Americanists.* Albuquerque, NM: University of New Mexico Press.

WILLEY, G. R. and J.A. SABLOFF 1974. *A History of American Archaeology.* London: Thames and Hudson.

WYLIE, A. 2002. *Thinking from Things: Essays in the Philosophy of Archaeology.* Berkeley and Los Angeles, CA: University of California Press.

# Suggestions for Further Reading

The most accessible general histories of archaeology are (in order of publication): Schnapp (1996), Trigger (2006), and Murray (2007c). Murray and Evans (2008a) is a reader that provides a general introduction to many of the issues related to writing histories of archaeology. The most comprehensive source of information about the history of archaeology is the five volume *Encyclopedia of Archaeology* (Murray 1999c, 2001b), but Bahn's *Cambridge Illustrated History of Archaeology* (1999) is a very useful, and visually exciting, general introduction. The *Bulletin of the History of Archaeology* is the only journal specifically devoted to this field (see http://www.archaeologybulletin.org/), although other archaeological journals, such as *Antiquity,* regularly publish contributions to it. These also, occasionally, find their way into journals related to the history of cognate disciplines, or indeed of science generally.

# Index